Blackhouse God's House

❦

A Lewisman Recalls
the World He Left Behind

Murdina D. MacDonald

ISBN 978-1-64416-590-4 (paperback)
ISBN 978-1-64416-591-1 (digital)

Copyright © 2019 by Murdina D. MacDonald

All rights reserved. No part of this publication may be reproduced, distributed, or transmitted in any form or by any means, including photocopying, recording, or other electronic or mechanical methods without the prior written permission of the publisher. For permission requests, solicit the publisher via the address below.

Christian Faith Publishing, Inc.
832 Park Avenue
Meadville, PA 16335
www.christianfaithpublishing.com

All sketches were written by Angus Morrison MacDonald
Edited with commentary by Murdina D. MacDonald
New Bern, North Carolina
2018. Gaelic translations provided by Annie Macsween from North Dell, Ness, Isle of Lewis

Printed in the United States of America

Skigersta's skylarks.

In what appeared to be a relayed pattern from dawn to dusk, our Skigersta skylarks gracefully soared aloft in sweet strain to encircle for a spell in perfect singing form. Then, they suddenly stay put as if affixed in the firmament — still singing with abandon. In this seemingly attached posture they sang their sweetest, prior to descending in a glorious glide in the general direction of the nests — out pouring heavenly music all the way down. The shapely skylark, adorably crowned with a tiny plumage — hence the Topag, can be mistaken for the common sparrow. The skylark's contour is more delicately outlined than the sparrow, who betrays puffiness and awkwardness in flight. Our Skigersta skylarks, who never seemed to tire, praise and song provided us four "Baile shuas" youngsters: two Normans, Alick and Angus, with a musical aura of such lofty quality that only artistic geniuses like Burns and Byron could appreciate. As inseparable four out-door "Baile shuas" young cronies, we frequently stretched out on some cozy patch of green, drowsily listening to the Topag, while happily indulging in the unrealistic day-dreamings common to innocents since the world began. At that wonderful care-free uncomplicated phase of our happy young lives, the four of us felt as free and secure as the high soaring skylarks, whose limitless domain was the eternal canopy of the blue, from which they so devotedly and sweetly entertained us in Skigersta of long ago.

This book is dedicated to my father's Free Presbyterian father and mother, Norman and Christina Morrison MacDonald of Skigersta and to my mother's Free Church father and mother, Murdo and Bella Smith MacDonald of Back and to all who have ever loved or will ever love the isle of Lewis.

Contents

Acknowledgements 9
Preface 11
1. Beautiful *Baile Shuas* of Long Ago 23
2. Eighteen Ninety-Three: Sad Discord of Yesteryear 57
3. An Eerie Sabbath Whistle 74
4. Grief Unutterable 82
5. Lord Leverhulme 105
6. My Own Dark Ages: 1908–1917 131
7. Duncan Macbeth: Divine of His Day 152
8. The Ablest Man of His Generation 179
9. Working 197
10. Of Fish and Fowl: *Cudaig*, Ling, *Guga*, and Skylarks 220
11. Worthies, Wags, Wits and Oddballs 229
12. Dying 263
13. Emigration 271
14. Angus on Angus 287
15. Epilogue: Home at Last 304
Appendix 1. Residents of *Baile Shuas* 311
Appendix 2. Drownings 1862–1900 313
Appendix 3. Skigersta *Bodaich* 317
Appendix 4. Tribute to the Skigersta Bard 319
Appendix 5. Nicknames 329
Appendix 6. Labor, Slavery, and Toil 331
Appendix 7. Sermons for Himself 333
Appendix 8. History as He Saw It 343
Appendix 9. On Celebrities 357

Acknowledgements

I wish to express my gratitude to the Ness Historical Society of Lewis for its willingness to share photos of the Skigersta Bard, of Duncan MacBeth and my family members; to Annie MacSween of North Dell who did the translations of my father's older gaelic; to Anne Thomson who shared family history with me and shepherded me to Skigersta, especially to No. 7 Skigersta; to the Free Presbyterian Magazine which granted me permission to reproduce the obituary of the Skigersta Bard, Norman Morrison; to the helpful staff of the Mitchell Library, Glasgow, who guided me to birth, death and marriage certificates of family members; to Bill Lawson and his staff at the Genealogy Service, Seallam Visitors Center, Isle of Harris, for assistance in family history; to my good friend Catherine Hewlette who assisted, with her daughter Laura, in the placement, arrangement and identification of photos, to Captain Alex and mate Pam for their whisky salute to Angus off the west coast of Skye; to Dr. John I Durham of Southeastern Baptist Theological Seminary, my mentor and friend, who made it possible for me to go to Oxford and to Dr. Barrie White, my Oxford supervisor, who taught me what historical research was all about and held me to the highest standards of excellence. R.I.P.

Preface

In Search of Angus

Had you asked me any day from the day I was born to the day my sister died "Who was your father?" I would have said that I hadn't the foggiest idea. Of course, I knew that the man who lived in our house was my biological father, but I did not know him. He was a ghost who filtered through the rooms of the house, quiet and unengaged in the activities going on in those rooms—except for supper time, when he could talk enthusiastically about Mary, Queen of Scots, and John Knox or Lord Kitchener or Sir Walter Scott or David and Solomon or the Valley of the Kings. Except for those times, he essentially lived in his room.

But when my sister died, I inherited both my father's ashes and his papers. He had been dead for twenty-one years by the time my brother-in-law handed me the ashes to take home to New Bern and thence to Scotland or the Great Lakes. He and Christine had planned to send the ashes, or to bring them, to Scotland. But over the years, they had convinced themselves that my father's relatives would not approve of cremation or the scattering of ashes. Jim was fine with my dispersing the ashes on the Great Lakes where my father had worked as a seaman for seven years, but I had no interest in going to the Great Lakes, so I prepared for a trip to Scotland.

The papers, stored originally in a suitcase, came to me from Texas in two very bulging "if it fits, it ships" boxes of the largest size, stuffed to the gills with about two thousand manuscript pages. They consisted mostly of single-page vignettes, devoted to a person, a theme, a scene, an incident, the majority of which had to do with my father's life in Lewis before he emigrated to Canada in 1924 at the age of twenty-one. Of these, I made a separate notebook which forms the basis of this book.

About three hundred pages had to do with biblical themes, for which I created a second notebook and divided the rest of the material into historical themes and "other" themes. Historical figures in which Dad had some interest included Richard Baxter, Pope Boniface VIII, Vespasian, Josephus, Cranmer, Columba, Bonnie Prince Charlie, Churchill, Franklin Delano Roosevelt, Alexander the Great, and both great queens of England named Elizabeth. When it comes to "other" themes, the sky was the limit: John Barrymore, Dana Andrews, Robert Burns, Frank Lloyd Wright, Billy Graham, D. L. Moody, Stephen Foster, Margaret Mitchell and others.

The exception to his normal single-page format consisted of two narratives. One told the story of the wreck of the *Iolaire*, a ship carrying surviving veterans of WWI back home to Lewis. Two hundred five of them drowned in Stornoway harbor on January 1, 1919, within a mile of their homeland. My father translated from Gaelic to English the first published account of this tragedy, portions of which are included here. The other detailed the fortunes of Lord Leverhulme, soap magnate, who had bought the island of Lewis and Harris in 1918 and had great plans for its economic development, only to depart the scene after losing several fortunes, it is said, in the attempt. And so, according to my father, his departure set in motion the events leading to the "Second Highland Clearing" of which he was a part.

Meticulous in the extreme is how I would describe the penmanship of the papers. He had lined each page with a ruler before writing his text and corrected errors in grammar or spelling or just sloppy penmanship by either correcting with tape or rewriting the entire page. For a man who had education only up to age fourteen and claimed he learned little in the process, he wrote very well. His writing was direct, simple, detailed, and showed that he could tell a story with a humorous punch line or a poignant one. His spelling was standard British style and his grammar was excellent with the exception of a few idiosyncrasies I attribute to island ways.

The papers revealed a person I never knew, a father I never knew. Now I know where he was all those years. He was heart, mind, and soul in the land of his birth, in the world he left behind. And for however long he could continue to think about all of them, back there, remember them, write about them, he would always and forever *be* there. Home.

About Angus: What I Know

My father was born in Skigersta, Isle of Lewis, Scotland, on January 20, 1903. He was the youngest of five children born to Norman MacDonald of Skigersta and Christina Morrison of Eoropie, who had been married on February 4, 1892. The marriage certificate records both the mark of his father and his mother which would indicate that both were illiterate, a not surprising situation given the lack of compulsory education in their youth. Despite this handicap, both parents went on to distinguish themselves in different ways in their society.

In 1893, the Free Presbyterian Church of Scotland was formed, a group that came out from the Free Church of Scotland. Dad recorded that twenty-seven Skigersta families came out with the FPs, which presumably represented the majority, if not the totality, of the village. My grandmother's people in Eoropie had no further dealings with her and her growing family, which meant that my father and my father's family were forever cut off from social contact with his mother's family.

Grandfather Norman must have been something of a go-getter, an enterprising sort. He arranged to sail to Canada three times in my father's lifetime to lumberjack with a relative in Scotstown, Quebec, for two years at a time. This at a time when transatlantic journeys were not exactly a risk-free enterprise. He came home to cash-poor Lewis with hard-earned gains, no doubt, but it seems that one of the major casualties of this exchange was his son. My father was raised essentially without a father but with a devoted mother and three doting sisters, a family dynamic that would have serious life consequences for him.

Angus spent his first year at school in Skigersta where he apparently had the distinction, at age five, of being thrown out the window one day by the schoolteacher. He then went to school in Lionel and had to pass a gauntlet each day of students who lobbed stones and adults who lobbed insults at the FP children. School at Lionel meant being under the tutelage of a dreaded teacher whom my father ultimately "redeemed" at the time of his sailing in 1924.

When he was almost fourteen, the local minister made a visit to his mother with the purpose of encouraging Angus to go to the only secondary school on the island, the Nicolson Institute, in Stornoway. Presumably he said things like Angus is intelligent, he has talent and ability, and I think he would do well at the Nicolson. Perhaps he offered to write a letter of recommendation. Didn't matter. Wasn't meant to be. Dad would have none of this and only wanted to hang out with his cronies.

As a teenager, Dad worked (one year and three months) to build the Skigersta to Tolsta Road, a project of Lord Leverhulme. At seventeen he and a friend moved to Glasgow and took a job in the Glasgow Shipyard building dredges. His father had sternly advised him not to do this, saying it would be back breaking labor and would ruin his health. Nevertheless, he went. It appears that the highlight of his time there was his visit to St. Jude's to hear the "Billy Graham" of his FP denomination preach: Neil Cameron. He and his buddy Angus Thomson were awestruck.

On his return to Lewis, it appears Dad did further local road repairs "on Leverhulme's disastrous departure." His notes say, "[Seven] months at South Dell. Walk ten miles a day." He made no reference in his memoirs to his father's death on September 27, 1921—why, I do not know.

The next note in Dad's own survey of work talks about emigration on the *Marloch* in 1924. There was no work for young men in Lewis. Lord Leverhulme had failed to realize his particular vision for the island. The British government decided to provide free transportation for island men to Canada in exchange for two years of labor on Canadian farms. Leverhulme's post-WWI period had proved to be one of civil unrest, squatting and protest, not a happy mixture for a whole generation of robust young men with nothing to do.

So those robust young men, about a thousand of them 1923–1924, got on boats and sailed to Canada. My father describes a sorrowful scene at Stornoway harbor where loved ones were saying goodbye and were pretty sure they would never see their family members again. He describes his own sister and his favorite teacher in deep distress at this parting. But they parted and were gone.

In Montreal, my father and another two Anguses decided to jump ship. Rather than serve in some isolated farm for two years, they decided to grab a taxi and head out for Scotstown, Quebec. There Dad found lumberjack jobs for a year and lodging with friends.

In 1925, he boarded with Marion Nicholson in Windsor, Ontario. At some point, he lived with Norman Murray's (Whitey) sister Annie in Detroit. In 1926, he shipped out on a boat to suck gravel from the bottom of Lake Erie. He left the Lakes in the fall of 1928 and went to New York City, apparently to work for D. B. Mackay, who owned a shoe tree factory (for five years, 1928–1933).

In New York, my father met my mother, D. B.'s stepdaughter, Effie. She was working as his secretary and also his chauffeur, helping to deliver weekly salaries to workers—in cash—in highly dangerous neighborhoods. Wonder they were never mugged. There were so many Scots in New York City that different island communities had their own social associations: the Lewis Society, the Barra Society, the Harris Society, and so forth. All the societies offered an evening of dance and entertainment for a very modest fee, and my mother and father gravitated to these places.

Mom and Dad went to California around 1933. They hung out with my mother's sister and best friend, Murdina, and her husband Howard Prather. Depression era stories from my mother include days when she and Murdina, both working as secretaries, would meet for lunch, which consisted of a cup of coffee and a doughnut for five cents.

On May 9, 1936, my mother and father were married in Reno, Nevada and moved to their first apartment in Oakland, California. In 1939, my father's notes say that he went back to the Great Lakes after eleven years. Another note says that he worked on the Great Lakes for seven seasons, a season being seven months, and was idle five seasons. My reconstruction would be, Great Lakes 1926–1928, 1939–1944.

At some point, my parents moved back from California to New York City where Dad apparently worked for D. B. for another ten years. We moved into an apartment on W 17th Street. Here in New York City, my brother Norman was born in 1942, myself in 1944, and my sister Christine in 1947.

In 1950, D. B. Mackay passed away, and my parents were able, with his benefits, to purchase a home in Bayside, Long Island, in Queens. It was a lovely Dutch colonial-style home, brick façade, three stories, with a nice front and back yard and sycamore trees in front. We didn't have a picket fence, but we had a home in a beautiful neighborhood, were a family of three children, two parents and a dog – Lucky, a hunter pointer. For a working class family in America in the fifties, this was pretty much the "American dream" as people perceived it.

It was here, I believe, that once comfortably settled in a new house, my father set himself to write these sketches. The process kept him emotionally alive, kept him connected to the people he loved and admired in Lewis, a community that he knew he never would be able to replicate in the US. Once started on this project, he continued for almost forty years. So it is to that place, 42-25 206th Street Bayside, Long Island, that I say "thanks for the memories" you have brought me from my father, for I believe without the stability that this home gave him, he never would have created the sketches.

Dad's journey brought him from New York to Hawaii, where we briefly lived together in a small apartment while Norman and I attended the University of Hawaii. After Hawaii, my mother and father separated. Dad moved in with my sister Christine and Jim, while Mother found her own place in Dallas. Ultimately, Dad found his own place in Arlington, Texas, a nice duplex which we helped him furnish. And I believe he was quite comfortable there, listening to the news ten times a day as well as the local baseball, daily boiling his beloved potatoes and enjoying the local catfish. And continuing to write his sketches.

He died of natural causes on January 11, 1990.

Finding Angus

I do not presume to have "found" Angus. I think only God knows who he was. But after reflecting on memories of him and looking at what he wrote over a period of forty years, I do feel closer to the person he was.

- He truly valued religious ideals. He may not have been in his own eyes the kind of Christian he ought to have been, but he clearly revered the persons in his life who lived up to the highest standards of morality and spirituality. We have to start with his mother. Here was a woman who was so respected for her knowledge of the Bible and her spiritual insights that the local clergymen loved to spend time with her. He admired his sister Annie's spirituality, as we can see in the comments he wrote of her at communion season. His brother Donald became a lay minister, while his next-door neighbor and hero, the Bard, became a notable person in the church. Duncan Macbeth, Free Church minister, takes up a whole chapter in his memoirs.
- He valued education. Although he ran away from school as quickly as he could at age fourteen, there are explanations for that. He wrote of two cousins, peers of his, who just loved to learn. Clearly he envied them. In my college days, he praised Norman and I for our pursuit of education.
- He had genuine intellectual curiosity, eagerly reading the works of historians and theologians. I gave him the complete works of Josephus and *Haley's Bible Handbook*, both of which he read from cover to cover, not exactly light reading for the faint of heart. He read mostly nonfiction.
- He valued the ties that bound him to all his family members in Lewis. Family was not just mother and father and siblings. All the members of this close-knit village were "family." So that when I think of the wreck of the *Iolaire*, every single body on the beach would have been a member

of his family. Surely he would have grieved for all of them as his brothers.
- He grieved the loss of a beautiful natural world that was Eden to him—missed the birds and fish, the plants and flowers, streams and ocean, moors and cows, the sounds of skylarks.
- He is revealed in the memoirs to be a more sensitive person than I ever suspected or knew as a child growing up. He felt the sorrows and tragedies of the people he talked about. He was affected by the yearly separation of lambs from their mothers in Lewis and touched by their pitiful cries. And it was his unenviable task to take our beloved dog, Lucky, to the vet to be put down, a story I never knew and never would have known without his sorrowful reflections here.
- He had a healthy sense of humor and could tell a funny story and enjoy one told by another.
- He had genuine artistic talent. Completely untrained, he apparently did sketches all his life, two of which are really stunning—the portrait of my Aunt Murdina and that of Robert Burns.
- He never grew up, which he says himself. He became a handsome, physical specimen of a man, but his interior "wiring" never connected in proper ways. He left Lewis at age twenty-one unprepared to face life as an adult. He was a beloved little boy, doted on by his mother and sisters—and a fatherless child. Little did his womenfolk know that heaping all kinds of affection and attention on him without concurrently inculcating a sense of responsibility would rob him of essentials he needed for the challenges of life.

Why Angus Matters

My father was clearly an ordinary man. He left school in Lewis at age fourteen and therefore was uneducated, as we understand what "educated" means. The stories he left behind have significance, I think, beyond interest for his family members because

- He is describing a world that no longer exists, Lewis between 1903 and 1924. He was born in a blackhouse, none of which exist today except as museum pieces. However primitive they were, they were the very center of family and community life, loved and revered as just exactly that, a place full of memories of social gatherings, laughter and fun as well as just ordinary existence.
- He is describing a world full of portents, omens, and prophecies. The breaking of a carriage wheel on the way to a wedding, the predictions of a respected minister about the deaths of men who opposed him, the disappearance of the ling fish within a three-mile radius of the coast, all these pointed to something, all these were "witnesses" of things to come.
- He is describing the life of a child who is a Free Presbyterian Church of Scotland child in the early part of the twentieth century. He allows us to see what life was like for such a child in such an age. His village, Skigersta, consisted of almost all FP people. But he and his family had to deal with a larger community that essentially shunned his people—on religious grounds.
- He is describing an education system that routinely used corporal punishment, so much so that some children really couldn't concentrate on learning for fear of punishment. Our own history in the US has the same dismal story, which thankfully is behind us now, as it is for the UK.
- He is celebrating some of the giants of his time: his next-door neighbor, Norman Morrison the Bard, who is clearly a phenomenally gifted individual; Duncan Macbeth, whom he revered but never knew in the flesh, as he died in 1891; the other Skigersta bard, Alex Nicholson; and the great FP defender of the faith, Neil Cameron of St. Jude's in Glasgow.

- He provides a personal perspective on three great moments in Lewis history—WWI, the wreck of the *Iolaire* and the world of Lord Leverhulme.
- He is describing ordinary life as he remembers it on the island—catching and curing fish; tending to cows and sheep; cultivating oats, barley and potatoes; building and repairing houses; attending worship services; collecting and storing the peat; celebrating a wedding; tending to the sick and honoring the dead.
- He is describing what humor meant in a small village community before cable television and the Internet: a man shaves off a moustache he had for thirty years, a couple fight over how to build a pile of peat in front of their house, a cow learns how to love flour, and two friends stage a mock battle of fisticuffs in public.
- He is describing what it is to live surrounded by all the beauties of nature, by the flowering of plants in spring, the favorite creek, the sight of whales afar off, hills and mountains in the distance, and most hauntingly, the sound of skylarks which can no longer be heard in Lewis.
- His remembrances matter to me because they are the main way I have come to understand a little of who he was. In the telling of his story, I seek to honor his father and his mother and those of that generation who took a stand for their faith and created a new denomination. I may not be of their faith, but I honor the faith commitment that motivated them.

Nineteen Twenty-Four

It is now sixty years ago (April 1924) since we gathered on the Stornoway pier in scattered sorrowful groups of weeping women while awaiting our turn to board the barge which ferried us onto the *Marloch*—looming beyond Goat Island. As I look back on it now, I keep wondering if the heavens either frowned on the unhappy occasion, or shed a last farewell tear, as the evening suddenly darkened and light mist moistened everything from Cromwell Street to Chicken Head.

It was not by any means a happy departure, with so many crest-fallen countenances and sad faces within easy glance shattering morale—and emotions about to snap and give way. I thought that my own sister was the most downcast of the lot, but there were many others sharing her loneliness. The marvelous Mary Ann, our favorite schoolteacher, strained to hold back the tears.

I am now in my early eighties, living as a great-grandfather deep in the "heart of Texas," after residing in several states of the USA: New York, Michigan, California, Hawaii, Florida, and Texas. When I somberly think of that memorable evening on the Stornoway pier sixty years ago, that sad verse of Jeremiah 22:10 (All scriptures are taken from the King James Version of the Holy Bible. N.Y. Oxford University Press. 1945.) sorrowfully crosses my mind:

> Weep ye not for the dead,
> neither bemoan him;
> but weep sore for him that goeth away:
> for he shall return no more,
> nor see his native country.

1

Beautiful *Baile Shuas* of Long Ago

Who can forget the line from *Gone with the Wind* where Mr. O'Hara says to his daughter, "It's the land, Katie Scarlet, the land." Of course the Irish, or Irish Americans, have no monopoly on a sense of connectedness with the land, since so many other cultures share the same feeling, of which my father's was one.

For Angus, Skigersta was Shangri-la, a perfect place where no one was ever forgotten. All loved ones lived on in the memories of the living. All the bards, *bodaich*, saints, of course, but also the sinners, the flawed, the foolish—they and their stories lived too as long as there were people to remember them. And my father was a prime rememberer.

Angus had a deep sense of place, formed, I think, from a combination of elements which are in evidence in his writings: the beauty of the land, the emotional tie of family, and the customs, beliefs, traditions, and shared activities that knit a community together as one. That community shared not only a common culture and history but a common DNA. Everybody appears to have been related, just about, to everybody else.

My father was born and raised in a traditional *taigh dubh*, a blackhouse, living examples of which are no longer extant in Lewis except as museum pieces.

MURDINA D. MACDONALD

Aig an Teine (At the Fire)

The center compartment (rooms) of our *taigh dubh* of long ago—where most of my generation, born at the turn of the century, were reared—was always referred to and known as *an teine*, the *cagailte* (hearth), our living room, no less. *Suidh aig an teine* (take a seat at the fire), *seas aig an teine* (stand at the fire), *thig a steach chon teine* (come in to the fire)—a passing stranger or acquaintance was invariably invited in such manner.

This at once indicated the preeminence of the middle room, *an teine*, above the other two rooms, the *cùlaist* (sleeping quarters) and the old objectionable *todhar* (cattle beds) where in my young days three contented cows were nourished and milked from year to year in our sprawling three compartment *taigh dubh* of long

In our center rooms, the middle of the floor peat fire was more or less constantly ablaze from early morning until midnight, flamed by two grades of peat moss, the *mòine dhubh* (black peat) and *mòine bhàn* (pale peat). The black peat, as it was known, was of higher heating propensities and more durable, slightly resembling shiny chunks of coal. The light-colored type known as pale peat, on the other hand, consisted of more smoke properties—*deathach*—than its sturdy counterpart, with a bright, hasty flame of mere minutes' duration

Upon retiring, the *tasgadh* (hoarding) of the peat fire took place by bunching the remaining peat tightly against one another atop the ashes accumulated throughout the day. With some luck, the early riser could still catch a tenacious *caoran dubh* (small lump of black peat) or two in adequate fiery form to start afresh the first morning fire as the shiny, soot-covered reptilian-looking *slabhraidh* (chain) hovering above eagerly awaited action.

All the social activities of the entire *taigh dubh* household were conducted *aig an teine* (at the fire), including welcoming and comforting the stranger, a cordiality in which Skigersta folks excelled. Two doors and one window were the standard lighting and exits of the typical *teine* of our time. *Doras a' chùlaist* of course led into the bedrooms, while its opposite number, opening toward the cattle layout, was called *doras a' stil*. This busy door also led toward the only front door, most of which were so crudely constructed that one modern joiner insisted they were cut and jointed with a blunt spade.

In the idle months of winter, the family and guests huddled by the hour around the peat fire discussing every current problem bedeviling suffering humanity from sin to scarcity of *buntàta is sgadan* (potatoes and herring). The *teine* compartments of our day differed very little in design and décor; their similarity was uncanny. Usually they consisted of a large oblong room of scrubbily constructed interior wall facing, with a long wooden bench, *being*, squared alongside the inner wall, where the *bodaich a' cèilidh* (old men visiting) smoked, chewed, squatted, and argued to their hearts' content. A scattering of wooden stools, finger holed in center for moving about, were always available, along with a chair or two specifically aimed at comforting church dignitaries or important people who unexpectedly dropped in.

However, the tall four-tiered wooden *dreasair* (dresser) where all dinner plates, mostly pictured, were meticulously lined on edge, row upon row, invariably facing the fire, was by far the most decorative piece of furniture beautifying the warm *teine* of our day. Its many artistic picture plates (copies of ancient masterpieces) projected an air of class, culture, and coziness from *doras a' stil to doras a' chùlaist* in our humble hearths of long ago.

The Butt of Lewis

In the foreground of the protrusive tip of the Butt of Lewis, which, like a stubby forefinger eternally points toward the bountiful north Atlantic, is the seemingly adjoining villages of Eoropie, Fivepenny, and Knockaird. None of our age bracket, who wasted our young days enmeshed in irrelevant balderdash, ever knew the exact boundary lines between those three important villages.

In prosperous days of yore, with comely crofts in bloom stretching to the shoreline, all the way from Knockaird's southern border to Eoropie's western eminence, was as delightful looking a corner as one could see anywhere on the face of the globe. Beautifying *bailtean an taobh-thall* (villages over yonder, i.e., references to Fivepenny and Eoropie) as some *bodaich* called them was a wide flat, daisy-covered *machair* (sandy, arable land near the coast), also in foreground, reaching to Lionel's croft boundaries, and stretching to the white sands of the colorful *traigh mhòr* on the west side—a magnificent-looking *machair* of pastoral tranquility.

In our youthful years of long ago, Eoropie's delightful background, enhanced by the austere and ancient "temple" of millennial antiquity, provided the only "posh" piece of topography in our entire rural landscape. This progressive and swanky area was the modern surroundings of our solid and splendid lighthouse, standing majestically atop menacing-looking crags and cliffs, defying eighty- and ninety-mile-an-hour gales in typical "Gael" tenacity.

To us, Skigersta's so-called yokels who hadn't yet ventured as far as Cromwell Street (Stornoway), this mini-metropolis of big city-like buildings, smooth pavements, and fancy houses was something akin to stepping onto "Piccadilly." We understood that dazzling, sophisticated interiors, including cushion-like, wall-to-wall carpets, beautified the homes of those in charge of the comely and colorful Butt compound, one of the best known lighthouses on the so-called Seven Seas.

Perhaps the doleful, penetrating blast of the massive foghorn, a depressing groan during dark, precipitative skies, like a ghostly harbinger of coming calamity, was the only feature to mar its rugged beauty. Its strange, spooky, foreboding moan eerily emitted in the wee small hours was in direct contrast to the beauty of the Butt—a lovely maritime landmark of great renown.

Sgeadhirtstaigh

Our small closely knit village of Skigersta was comprised of three evenly separated streets rising from beautiful *Lathamor by the sea* to the *Baile Àrd* (High Street) with my favorite beautiful *Baile Shuas* highlighting the whole hamlet in the center. Population prior to the big migrations ranging from 1907 to 1909 was in the neighborhood of 285 souls.

The *Baile Shuas* was comprised of seventeen homes, eight of which faced the *cladach* (shore). Four faced south, three faced north, and *Taigh a' Chaoinich* directly west along with Isabel's small home at the back of Donald's house on No. 9.

When our age crop, born shortly after the turn of the century, was about nine or ten years of age, there wasn't a square yard of Skigersta's crofts left untilled nor hardly a foot of cultivable soil lying dormant—mostly tilled with the spade. In autumn, from the MacKenzie's *àird* (high place) to the Murray slope of No. 11, there was a sweeping mass of ripened commodities: barley, oats, and potatoes in beauteous bloom which, with many croft boundaries obscured by the long-stemmed barley and oat shoots, obliterating foot paths, appeared to be one vast farm—awaiting scythe and sickle. When viewed from offshore with crops in full-bloom Skigersta was the epitome of both pastoral and littoral loveliness.

So highly sprouted were our late autumn crops that even busy *Tobair a' Choilich* (the Well of the Cockerel) was dwarfed to a mere speck on the face of our favorite hillock *Cnoc a' Choilich* (the Hillock of the Cockerel). Only the heads of water carriers, trudging up and down the narrow footpath to the famous *tobair*, were visible between the high barley and oat shoots in ripened bounty, majestically sprouting on both sides of the walkway.

From our own *Baile Shuas*, ten young men and four maidens emigrated—three to the USA and one to Canada. They were Kate Morrison of No. 9, Johanna MacDonald of No. 4, and the Buchannan sisters Christine and Robina, who emigrated to the state of Michigan. Kate emigrated to Illinois.

Amid these amenities and pleasant surroundings, a daily stroll to the busy quay, where three big *sgothan, eithrichean mòra* (big boats) were on a hectic six-day schedule to *Cara Phìobaire, Grunn Mùirneag*, and elsewhere, was almost a compulsive urge with us boys at that age.

At the turn of the century, these waters which included *Cara Phìobaire, Grunn Mùirneag*, and others were renowned fishing grounds of both ling and herring. Also, in these waters, five Ness *sgothan*—one from Skigersta—perished in the Great Drowning of December 1862 in which thirty-one fishermen, including my grandfather and next-door neighbor skipper Donald Morrison, the Bard's father, were lost. Their *sgoth* was washed ashore on *Tìr Mòr* and was kept there on the beach for many years. The Rev. Alick MacLeod, Fivepenny, a Storr minister, saw it.

It was nothing uncommon for us youngsters of that era to literally wade through several species of fish on the flat, concrete L-shaped section of our quay when catches arrived. Such species ranged from massive skates to hefty halibuts, deep-sea eel and cod, with the prestigious ling strewn about in abundance.

Our compact Skigersta quay of those days was alive with excitement when the three sleek *sgothan* touched on shore: fish everywhere, the *bodaich* buoyantly mingling as swarms of seagulls shrieking overhead in colorful frenzy added to the bedlam, which we at that age so thoroughly enjoyed.

Therefore, with our sweet-singing skylarks providing music from above on sunny summer days, and all that treasure from the sea, along with barley, oats, and potatoes heading for the barn, lowly Skigersta of our young days was one of the most secure and happy hamlets on the face of the globe.

Delightful Dawns of Long Ago

One of the truly rewarding sights of early rising on the beautiful *Baile Shuas* of my boyhood years was the vague outline of the majestic Sutherlandshire mountains looming across the calm waters all the way up to Capewrath. Occasionally, long horizontal reddish streaks of first morning light halved the mountain tops from Storr to the Cape, rendering an aura of glory and awesomeness to the whole eastern skyline.

Into this gorgeous panorama fluttered countless seagulls, along with a large variety of coastal fowl, some gracefully gliding to and fro as others banked and flapped, shrieking with abandon. At closer scrutiny, the dazzling white downward streaks of the tireless gannet, diving champion of all fowl, heading straight for the brine, came into focus, as the ocean surface frothily erupted in white splashes of diving frenzy—a sight (in itself) well worth the *mocheirigh* (rising early).

Scarcely a mile out the huge herring whale—*muc an sgadain*—suddenly breaks the glistening waters, spouting profusely, as the shiny long hump again slowly and gracefully curves back into the deep.

At that enchanting post dawn glow, a couple of trawlers and a tardy drifter or two usually puffed their way toward Stornoway, underneath unperturbed morning skies, while playful seals roared and frolicked around Bragg rock, enjoying the happy dawn of another new day.

Early Rise on the *Baile Shuas* of Long Ago

My first early morning sight as a boy upon bouncing out of bed on the beautiful *Baile Shuas* was our village landmark *Taigh Oighrig* on the edge of the Gil. I spent much of my preschool days around *Taigh Oighrig*, about an eighth of a mile downhill from my door. Effie's son Angus—widely known in those days as *Aonghas-na-Gil*—was my own age and a Gil lover, and we traipsed barefooted up and down that delightful *sruthan* by the hour. Sometimes we reached as far as *Lios Dhòmhnaill Tharmoid—ceap-garadh*—a square enclosure tunneled from end to end with rabbit burrows.

On balmy mornings, I'd sneak out of bed while everybody slumbered, and the dawn breaking over the Sutherlandshire mountains across the waters in that calm enchanted stillness was a sight well worth the *mocheirigh*.

My patient mother—knowing of my burning anxiety to be off and running on calm mornings—made allowances and prepared a hasty bite; after which, I'd madly dash through *doras a'stil* and front door to race barefooted across *lot-a-Bhaird*, *lot-Iain-Bhig*, *lot-Dhomhnaill-Tharmoid*, and *lot Iain Dhoiligein*, (*lot* equates *croft*) followed by our loud barking black dog amid startled chickens scampering for their lives.

Effie, *Oighrig Aonghais Ghuinne*, an early riser and tireless, hardworking woman, invariably lit her fire before dawn, and as most village homes faced near her homestead on the Gil, everyone's first morning gaze was toward Effie's chimney, where on calm mornings languid puffs of smoke slowly ascended straight into the clouds—in dreamy, pastoral loveliness. Memories, memories.

Skigersta's Autumns of Long Ago

Some of Skigersta's more judicious crofters in our young days invariably altered their seeding patterns each season, planting the three basic commodities, barley, oats, and potatoes, in different areas of their modest plots from year to year. Others didn't. My own father, for instance, planted in the same sections of our less than four-acre croft from season to season.

In an offshore view, it was impossible to determine which of the various planted segments looked more picturesque as the seasons unfolded with each fresh autumn decorously blooming in exotic beauty. Our own *Cnoc a' Choilich* looked especially lovely viewed from offshore at that time of year.

In gentle autumnal breezes, reeling in ripened splendor, Skigersta's barley and oat fields gracefully swayed smoothly across the land, enchantingly simulating languid ripples of the sea. This particularly fascinating spectacle attracted us no end as the heavy-laden shoots barely held on. Our *Baile Shuas* crofts sloping toward the *cladach* looked like one vast prosperous farm.

Our beneficial potato patches of long ago, scrupulously planted in square segments all along each croft, highlighted Skigersta's autumn season to perfection. At that point of time, the pretty potato rose, an attractive flower of exquisite loveliness, whose multicolored presence ornamenting freshly hoed straight rows, was a most charming eyeful, invigorating sight and soul.

For a brief spell, the so-called crude potato patch conspicuously and majestically emerged as the idyllic queen of the crops, profusely arrayed in flowery finery for all to see and like a beautiful dream, suddenly disappeared.

Am Baile Àrd

Beautiful arable patches of land dotted both sides of Skigersta's High Street—*Am Baile Àrd*—throughout all of our twenty-one years at home. In the early twenties, the migration era, our picturesque *Baile Àrd* exuberantly flourished in its day-by-day chores, when we waved our final farewell from *Tarmod Pìobaire*'s intersection over half a century ago.

High Street's modest land developments were painstakingly labored out of hard-bed formation of peat moss, two and three feet thick, by the Mackenzies, Thomsons, Mackays, MacLeans, MacDonalds, and Murrays of long ago—all sturdy squatters.

Consequently, the most enterprising and attractive of our village streets mushroomed loftily above the other two as if asserting superiority. Upon settling down and moving into high gear with fishing on the decline, High Street became, as if overnight, the lively cynosure corner of town. The so-called new *Baile Àrd* was in our day where the action was to be had and the place to visit for an evening's entertainment. Boredom never entered the lively little *Baile Àrd* of a mere few paces long and tiny population of scarcely fifty souls.

Also, the High Street of our day was the village breadbasket, boasting of two grocery stores, operated by the poet Alex Nicholson and John MacIver. Curiously enough, two of the most prominent-looking homes, which still stand, were built by the dexterous and literary Alex, on High Street of long ago, and, if another curious angle is excused—neither Alex nor John was a native of Skigersta.

Alex's first home, currently owned by Donald MacLean, was next door to one of our village worthies, so endowed with wit and outgoing personality that fishing cronies whom he amused for years with hilarious satire were almost in mourning when he suddenly packed in his fish gear and took the family to Canada. He was the popular *Tòl*, Donald Mackenzie, subsequently well known in Scotstown, Quebec, Detroit, and Windsor, Ontario.

About fourteen years after their departure from the *Baile Àrd*, three Skigersta Anguses—*Marloch* migrants—enjoyed the privilege of visiting the Mackenzie family on the outside of Scotstown where they owned a farm.

It was no secret that Mrs. MacKenzie, the former Catherine Morrison of *Lathamor, Catriona-Iain Ruaidh*, a strikingly beautiful woman, never quite shook off homesickness, candidly confiding to intimates that its lingering effect marred much of her happiness from day to day. Her remark to us that night as we prepared to leave following a grand long *cèilidh* is still etched in memory. Looking us over with those big round eyes, clearly betraying a tinge of sadness, she said, "Whatever problems you boys encounter in Canada, don't let homesickness get you down, because when it didn't destroy me, you sturdy three shall most assuredly survive."

The *Sgoth Niseach*

Three discarded twenty-one-foot *sgothan* snuggled in their berths awaiting eventual extinction reminded us, prior to our migration half a century ago, of Skigersta's colorful, bygone fishing days. Upright and still beautiful, the slick receding stemmed onetime swift *sgoth Niseachs* (Ness-built boats) aged in dignity, proudly on even keel—silent but not forgotten. In winter's storms, two of their smaller three-thwarted successors of similar design were hauled astern of the big ones, comprising a nostalgic fleet of five.

Long and lingering warm memories hover around the windy berth opposite the old winch for the survivors of my age bracket, born shortly after the turn of the century. Many of our village males, of all ages, converged on this natural recess in our day to exchange the local tidbits, laugh lustily at the *bodaich's* witticisms, and *Seòras's* latest hilarious observations.

By a rare coincidence, two of the big *sgothan* as they were called were skippered by my immediate next-door neighbors: the noted bard sailed *Ladysmith*, a *sgoth* also noted for fantastic speed and sleek nautical lines; the *Try Me* was skippered by the easygoing *Iain Pìobaire*, John MacKenzie, whose quiet wit and comical clichés were always uplifting to the crew's morale. The third of the big ones was skippered by the famed salty, Malcolm Mackay, *Calum Dhòmhnaill 'ic Fhionnlaigh*, a no-nonsense bonafide "boss" once perched on the stern end.

Malcolm, on becoming a landlubber, used to stand seemingly motionless for long periods of time on the ridge above the berth, peering down on the silent *sgothan* no doubt preoccupied in fond memories of happier days on the high seas.

Our own age bracket, give or take a year or two, is the last *Niseachs* to remember when the big boats were on round-the-clock schedule to *Cara Phìobaire*, *Grunn Mùirneag*, and elsewhere, the same age category that recalls when the picturesque Skigersta harbor was a beehive of fishing activity, with coastal fowl, especially seagulls, almost canopying the bay from the *Lòn Gorm* to *Leac Cùsgair*.

Our L-shaped concrete quay, bulwarked by a sturdy parapet, where generations of Skigerstonians basked during stiff southeasterly breezes, along with a tranquil lee cove and fine slip, is a monument to both Donald Weir's faculties, a colorful mason of storybook personality—and a nostalgic reminder of Skigersta's glorious past.

Skigersta's Mariners of Long Ago

Late in the autumn of 1923, Skigersta's youngsters witnessed one of the last spectacular performances of a twenty-one-foot *sgoth*, just prior to our migration on the *Marloch* the following year. It was a precarious race against the menacing waves, which on certain stormbound days rapidly rolls into our narrow bay one behind the other in stiff easterly breezes, the dreaded, unloved *gaoth an ear* (east wind).

This daring deed demanded a fast escape during the occasional deceptive lulls between breakers, a quick getaway right into the teeth of the elements. It was the kind of maritime feat where skilled seamanship made the difference between survival and complete disaster, especially manifested on first tack, when, in the abrupt swerve to port at the southern shallows, canvas was reversed in mere moments of time to avoid smash up against the *Craigeachan*.

The *sgoth* was the noted speedster and slickly shaped *Ladysmith* skippered by my famed next-door neighbor, the Skigersta Bard. *Dànaidh* MacKay was the able *gille tòisich* (first boy). The occasion was transporting cured ling to the Stornoway market, probably the last transaction of a dying trade, in which the prestigious ling were in our grandfather's time caught in copious quantities just three miles off the Ness shoreline.

So great was the risk involved that when the perilous event was successfully accomplished and the men safe in open waters, with *Ladysmith* looking like a mammoth sailfish assailing the elements, a retired fisherman, who nervously watched from the quay, remarked as follows, "*That* was by far the most foolhardy episode that I've seen in a lifetime at sea."

In 1973, exactly half a century later, on my last trip home to Skigersta, neighbor Norman, the Bard's son, remembered the event and told me he distinctly heard my uncle Murdo make that statement standing beside him on the quay fifty years ago that autumn.

Family

My father's father was Norman MacDonald (1857–1921), who married Christina Morrison (1867–1966) in the year 1892. That he was illiterate in 1903 is evident by looking at my father's birth certificate. There an *X* marked the spot that called for my grandfather's signature. I have no reason to think that he learned to read after that date, unless special circumstances, such as employment, demanded that of him. I thought, until recently, that my grandmother was literate, as I have a picture of her as an old woman with a Bible on her chest and many stories of her knowledge of the Bible and her ability to discuss theological issues with ministers. But I understand now that this was a traditional pose, a Bible on one's chest, for people of faith and that this did not necessarily mean that they could read. Recently I saw the marriage certificate of my grandfather and grandmother, and they both signed with an *X*. This, of course, in my view, means my grandmother's achievements as a biblical scholar in her community was all the more remarkable.

Norman MacDonald

My father Norman MacDonald, *Tarmod Dhòmhnaill Bhuide*, of Skigersta's beautiful *Baile Shuas* was a robust crofter-fisherman who, according to many acquaintances, bore a striking resemblance to Lord Kitchener, a great English general of WWI who died in 1916. He was among the most admired and respected men of his age. (See *Kitchener. Architect of Victory, Artisan of Peace* by John Pollock, 2001.) Due to his lowly status, however, the great aristocratic general would probably vigorously deny the similarity.

Several years prior to the turn of the century, my hardworking parent packed in his fishing gear and took off to Scotstown, Quebec. Even as recently as the turn of the century, such a drastic move across oceans meant a journey of no return for most of the migrants. For example, only three of the fourteen, including four girls, who left the small *Baile Shuas* of seventeen homes are buried with their fathers.

My father's trips to Scotstown were of a different nature however, because the security of a job awaited him through his cousin D. L. MacRitchie, known to Lewismen as *Dòmhnall Beag Tharmoid Chailein*—with Knockaird, Habost, and Skigersta ties. D. L., a forest and timber expert, with a prestigious position as Bush ranger in staking out the exact amount of trees to be annually hewed down, arranged that my father worked steady for two years, returned home for a spell, and then repeated the procedure.

It proved to be a happy plan for my father who made three trips in all, thereby becoming a sophisticated world traveler among the *bodaich*. They looked forward to his arrival with traumatic tales of the stormy North Atlantic, which he crossed six times in a creaky cattle boat, feeding the beasts for his fare.

Without fail, he lugged home a few long handled lumberjack hatchets, some of which he gave away—a rugged instrument which in only six years of on-and-off toil in the Quebec forests he handled with uncanny skill for a fisherman. He could also handle the cant-hook-cant-dog, to Canadians, "Peavey"—a devilish poled instrument with a scythe shaped, fast movable sharp hook on its tip, to stab into the log at faster than eye speed.

When the three Skigersta Anguses landed in Scotstown in 1924, my father's tremendous popularity with the Gaelic-speaking residents, consisting of about 50 percent of the town's inhabitants, became evident. He was known to them as *Tarmod Mòr* (Big Norman), not because of his height (5'10") but because of his rugged, massive frame.

Not too far from Scotstown, a colony of my mother's people, the *Buachaillean*—Morrisons—were settled on an attractive eminence known as *Cnoc nam Buachaillean*, with beautiful homesteads, farms, and merry Morrisons all over the place. It was grand to know and feel how well liked and well known my father was in Scotstown, especially in view of the fact that in Ness and Skigersta, he was no social lion and was even shy and a very private person with only a handful of real close friends.

Christina Morrison

What I know of my grandmother Christina (1867–1966) is limited. She was from Eoropie, a neighboring village, apparently had numerous siblings, and was not only devout but a woman of considerable knowledge of the Bible and theology. My father said that she was a magnet not only for the bard next door but for the ministers, who loved discussing all things theological with her. In these discussions, she more than held her own, he said. Surely this must have been as unusual, if not more so, in Skigersta of more than a hundred years ago as it would be today.

As my grandfather was away in Canada for extended periods of time, a pattern he evidently began early in his married life, Christina had to run the household and raise the children, five in all, on her own. Apparently, she did this well. She died a few months shy of her one hundredth birthday, at which time she was scheduled to receive a congratulatory note from the queen.

Below are Angus's recollections of how two Donalds treated my grandmother, one kindly and the other with clannish hostility. She apparently took the hostility with equanimity, thanks to her faith, no doubt, as well as with the help of the "good" Donald.

Dòmhnall Ailean

Long ago in our village of Skigersta, there were more than twenty outside women married to Skigerstonians, while seven married native daughters. Only two outside males (Murdo MacDonald and Norman MacLean) married Skigersta girls and settled in the village in our young days. These women came from the various villages of the Ness district ranging from Cross to Eoropie, Lionel to Adrabrock, Fivepenny to Habost and so forth.

Our current Ness youngsters will find it hard to believe that some of these women encountered male hostility, even in pastoral, benign Skigersta of long ago. The following brief sketch is for the purpose of throwing some light on the two contrasting Donalds who lived and died in Skigersta of our day. The story concerns our family friend *Dòmhnall Ailean Bhain, Lathamor*, a rough-hewn outspoken and strapping individual who was a male servant in our house shortly after my mother settled down, amid in-law hostility, on the beautiful *Baile Shuas*. If nothing else, the sketch should serve as an interesting item for those taken up with the mysterious moods and mores of human behavior.

No sooner had my mother arrived from Eoropie than the resentment of a bachelor brother-in-law, another *Dòmhnall*, was keenly felt from the *cagailte* to the *cùlaist, doras an t-sabhail* to *doras an stil*. As the youngest of the family, the bachelor was openly annoyed at anyone possessing what to him was his mother's so-called sacred soil, a sad situation as old as Adam's fall. Besides these considerations, bachelor Donald was by nature hard to please, utterly lacking any Chesterfieldian charisma.

While Mother made very little ado about the matter, it appears that if it weren't for *Dòmhnall Ailean's* moral support and kind consideration toward her during those trying times, with my father away in Canada, she in all likelihood would have returned to *Taigh Choinnich Buachaille*—whence she came. By a sheer stroke of good fortune, the bachelor also took off for Canada, where he remained until I, youngest in the family, was a grown lad before he returned.

Now, in the eyes of the world, the drastic difference between the two Donalds was the fact, accepted by one and all, that one was a saint and the other a sinner. The bachelor was a man of prayer and a communicant of many years standing, looked up to by multitudes, whereas rugged *Dòmhnall Ailean*, though honest, fair-minded, and hardworking, was considered by the same multitudes as the most mundane of men. As humans, it appears that our sense of values are so irreparably warped that we can scarcely distinguish our right hand from the left.

One has the right to ask in this particular case who was the saint and who was the sinner? *Dòmhnall Ailean* held my mother in great esteem all of his days and never failed to ease her load under any physical or emotional stress. She on the other hand never lost an opportunity to remind us as we grew up of Donald's admirable traits and manly, unvarnished forthrightness.

Therefore, it should be a foregone conclusion that, inasmuch as dauntless *Dòmhnall Ailean* alleviated the burden of "one of these little ones" with innumerable acts of kindness, he shall, as Scripture promised, be rewarded on "that day" a hundredfold.

With respect to my father's brother Donald (1894–1961), who was nine years older than Angus, I know essentially nothing. All I know is what my father's sketches reveal of the man, with one exception. As a child in New York, I remember my parents talking about what changes Donald had brought to the old house in Skigersta. Apparently, in the early fifties, he himself had installed indoor plumbing to the house. As a child I wondered how strange it would be to not have indoor plumbing. As an adult, I celebrate Donald's talent and ability to do this work

Bashful Brother

My only brother Donald was throughout his youthful years rather shy, a disposition which nevertheless didn't impede his diversions any nor prevented him from enjoying himself—even at crowded *cèilid-*

hean. He loved to laugh, and his loud *lachan* (hearty laugh) when amused was more or less contagious in the sense that everyone within range of it also laughed.

As an older brother, I looked up to him, and his handsome pal *Iain Chròic* in genuine admiration; both of whom were my childhood heroes. Upon reaching my twenties however and while observing my reserved brother in modest gatherings, it always bothered me to see how reticent he was and reluctant in volunteering an opinion on the discussed topics of the day. It even embarrassed me a little to see him so hesitant; always the last to say his piece, and even when he did, his few words betrayed an awkward bashfulness, which I, as a precocious youngster, equated with some innate timidity—a flaw of some sort—ill suited to a normally secure family or so I haughtily concluded.

As the *sgoth's* crew member, in my father's stead (who from time to time toiled in Scotstown, Quebec), the *bodaich* loved to have my brother Donald aboard, not only because of his deep respect for his elders but also for his efficiency in any given assignment from stem to stern.

Up until the time I left home in 1924, my brother remained reserved, soft-spoken, and keeping a low profile, quite content to let others do the talking, as he quietly sat and listened, hoping that everything would somehow someway turn out all right in the end: wholeheartedly agreeing with William Shakespeare that "all is well that ends well."

Therefore, one can imagine my violent reaction upon returning home after an absence of twenty-eight years, in finding my one time painfully bashful brother in complete personality reversal to his former behavior. So drastic was the transition that when first I heard him boldly and audibly leading in prayer in a fairly crowded church I was stunned. So sudden did the matter hit me that I was bombarded with such a variety of emotions. I could neither count them nor hold them at bay. I was shocked, a mite proud, somewhat scared, and wholly flabbergasted—as I sat right beside him perspiring from head to foot with embarrassment.

What my father had not been privy to was the conversion of his brother that had made possible that moment in a crowded church. Bashful brother had been transformed.

Donald: Strange Causes of Conversion

My brother Donald in his youthful years liked a lively *cèilidh*, and his loud laughter when amused was equally amusing to those around him: they also laughed. This happy-go-lucky state prevailed until something very unusual occurred in which his whole lifestyle was completely reversed, giving way, after years of tribulation, to a somber disposition and serious behavior.

It happened in the following manner. Bosun Donald Murray, Swainbost, a mariner since his late teens, with whom my brother sailed as an able seaman, died of a waterfront accident. His wake was held in Kate Mackenzie's home of No. 20 Skigersta, because Kate and Donald had just gotten married shortly before Donald's untimely end. His sudden death deeply affected my brother, who attended his wake in sadness for his former Bosun and shipmate.

On his late walk back home to the *Baile Shuas*, he felt as if being closely hemmed in by a multitude of men, somewhat akin to our funeral processions. He was quite aware of being surrounded by something supernatural and was aghast at the rapid draining of his energy as he moved along.

When he reached our door, he was absolutely exhausted and scarcely made it to the bed. Donald stayed in that bed—more or less—for the next four years but was released from his bonds in about that time and became a "valiant for truth" for the rest of his days.

Donald: Free from Pettiness

My brother Donald was by nature free from the spites and pettiness which most mortals are prone to but was a bold "valiant for truth" since his conversion, which came late in life. I felt good in 1952, on my first trip home from America since the *Marloch*, when Norman MacKay, High Street, a former New York coworker, said to me concerning Donald that my brother was no ordinary convert. "He has less animosity toward opposing factions than most converts in these parts. Besides, to converse with the man is a refreshing change of pace."

My brother was like that—an interesting conversationalist for one of very little schooling. It was truly amazing how well informed he was. Even our Free Presbyterian clergymen, all highly educated men, were deeply impressed with his keen knowledge of scripture.

In his own quiet way, Donald could show a spark of wit and humor on occasion. One day, while meeting his warm friend and pastor, the esteemed Reverend William MacLean, M.A., formerly a Free Church adherent, Donald was somewhat startled to see the Reverend William riding with a Free Church counterpart, who happened to pick up Mr. MacLean somewhere along the way. "Ah ha," snapped Donald, good-naturedly, "*Tha an Declaratory Act annad fhathast!*" (The Declaratory Act is still within you!)

On one Sabbath morning, a pious woman he knew, obviously feeling a mite downcast, joined Donald on his way to morning service. As they walked along, she confided to Donald, "*Ah Dhòmhnaill 's e Sàtan a thug an droch àm dhomhsa tràth anns a' mhadainn.*" (Satan gave me a hard time early this morning.) "*Oh ho, thubhairt Dòmhnall, tha am fear tha siud moch-èireach.*" (Oh ho, said Donald, that fellow is an early riser.)

Sister Margaret

My father's sister Margaret (1893–1978) worked for Lord Leverhulme as long as he occupied Lews Castle. Dad describes in the following sketch the excitement on the street when one day his Lordship's private car pulled up in front of No. 7 and a chauffeur popped out to escort Margaret to the door.

Margaret and Angus were the only two of five siblings to marry and have children. Margaret gave birth to Isabel and Norman (twins), Murdo, Alex, and Dolena.

When I was young, both Murdo and Alex visited the family in New York. Both were merchant seamen, their skin a georgous copper color formed by sun and wind. Murdo gave me a small birthday book, the *Burns Birthday Book*, in which a small portion of Burns's text is set to each day of the week. I treasure it—and use it—to this day.

At one point, Murdo asked my mother for an egg. She started to make him an eggnog, which we frequently had in those days, but before she could make it, he just gulped the raw egg down with glee. Must have been a long time since he had had a fresh egg! The only other thing I remember about Murdo was the enormous respect with which he addressed my father. Here he was, to my sister Christine and I a bronze god of twenty-six years or so, bowing his head and saying to anything my father was saying, "Aye, yes," "That's so," and "Aye, yes, indeed." So respectful.

No. 7

In Skigersta of long ago, when Lord Leverhulme's slick touring car pulled up in front of No. 7 on the *Baile Shuas*, the neighbors, even prior to becoming aware of its passengers, were in a curious mood. Then, in a flash, word got out that indeed it was the bonafide article, his Lordship's private car no less, and just as quickly the onetime lively and lovely little street was inundated with myriads of speculations.

No. 7 of all places, they pondered out loud, an ancient *taigh dubh* of multiple shapes and hues, with black globs of smoke pushing through its thatchy hump, straight from the middle of the floor, hosting a millionaire *Sasannach* was as shockingly anachronistic, they thought, as Queen Victoria sipping tea in a brothel.

Mary Mackensie, *Bean Iain Phìobaire*, our good-humored neighbor was puttering outdoors when this shiny oddity suddenly swished by her and abruptly stopped at our door. Startled, Mary threw away her garden tools and excitedly raced inside to fetch John, who was already making his way to the door a mite disturbed, on being informed by his old maid sister Christine that something speedy and glistening flew by her window heading for the *cladaichean geala*.

The three of them, John, Mary, and Christine, furtively and tensely gaped from their *ursainn* (doorpost) alarmed at the sudden commotion and even more so when they saw the thing parked at our door. There is a middle-aged man in shiny (knee-high) boots and a black beaked uniform cap and navy-blue clothes briskly stepped out of the car to open the door for my sister Margaret in the gracious manner a chauffeur attends on royalty.

Now, the Mackenzies were really curious, and so were the street's population, who by now were outdoors en masse from *Cnoc a' Choilich* to the Murray's southern slope, all gazing toward No. 7, the lowly *taigh dubh* which all of a sudden became a village celebrity. It was when Margaret walked toward the door carrying a small travelling bag, followed by the chauffeur with her coat on his arm, that it suddenly dawned on many that Margaret was on Baron Leverhulme's staff in the castle—and everybody relaxed.

Mr. Leverhulme, in typical gracious gesture, instructed his chauffeur to see Margaret to her door, with an even more gracious request, not to hurry matters in allowing ample time with her parents. If the sagacious soap mogul had decided to drop in and confront our perennial welcoming committee of three drowsy cows to his left, relaxing on unsightly naked *todhair* (manure pit), a neurotic barking dog showing off in *doras a' stil*, and two skittering cats madly racing for *doras an t-sabhail*, there is no telling what his reactions might have been.

Sister Annie

My hardworking sister Annie (1897–1968) devoted most of her adult life comforting and looking after the welfare of the people of God. Furthermore, it was obvious by her attitude that with her, it was purely a labor of love. She enjoyed being near God's people, and it was quite evident in her conversation and general relationships that she felt more comfortable in their company than a constant association with wordlings.

This was clearly manifested at communion seasons when our old *taigh dubh* was full of strangers who came from all corners to celebrate the Lord's Supper for five solid days twice a year.

This was Annie's best ten days of the entire year. She went all out to make sure that everybody was happy, comfortable, and well fed. What makes this report so unique is the fact that she was the only one of the four women around me in my youthful years who did not openly confess her faith before angels and men.

The other three were pious praying people whose daily conduct gave clear evidence that they feared the Lord. However, it was left to Annie to serve like Martha of the Bethany household—but with a difference. Martha complained. Annie didn't.

In warm climate, some Tolsta people walked barefoot across the eight-mile trek of moorland dividing the two villages, and much feet washing took place on arrival. Annie warmed the water, filled the basins, supplied the towels, and even washed the elderly—just as scripture admonishes. As an expert cook, she also baked all kinds of fancy little scones for the occasion, and everybody enjoyed the five holy days of complete separation from the world, the devil, and the flesh.

Sister Millie

Oddly enough, there is no sketch in my father's memoirs of his sister Millie (1900–1981), whose formal name was Gormelia. I have no explanation for this. She lived longer than any of his siblings.

The uncle who appears to have provided the greatest merriment to his friends and neighbors was Uncle George, whose tempestuous relationship with his wife kept sparks flying and moods elevated.

Uncle George: Part 1

George, married to my father's sister Mary, lived next door to his brother Norman and sister Christine, an eccentric old maid, both of whom appeared to bring witty scathing remarks out of George from day to day. However, deep-rooted spites and pettiness had no part in George's personality. Also my aunt's (tinder) temperament contributed much to the frequent rounds of comical situations which arose out of their long and amusing married life.

By a strange trait in George's mentality, the more annoyed he got, the funnier he became. Life's anxieties and irksome drawbacks enhanced his natural wit, and when really riled, he turned into a riot of comedy. In America, his type of comedy would have made him a multimillionaire.

Like the time he and my Aunt Mary hotly disagreed on the correct size of the *cruach mhònach's* (pile of peat) foundation which was annually built in front of their home. Hilarious disagreements within the *cagailte* kept the family of three girls and Donald amused from year to year, but out in the open was public property—everybody got in on the ploy.

They both started their own dimensional idea of the *cruach's* size amid shouts, arguments, rancor, and bitter discord. Neither would give in, as peat upon peat were stashed upon the two separate foundations of a yard's differential—as neighbors held on to their sides from laughing.

Finally, the old-timer gave in and in sheer desperation fired the peat in hand violently into the pile and walked down the street, where he ran into neighbor *Dòmhnall Anna* and said, panting with emotion, "Donald, I had to turn my back to her before I'd be tempted to clobber her into kingdom come."

Uncle George: Part 2

Sister Christine, a spinster of large glaring eyes, slender features and pointed nose, developed a pesky Peeping Tom habit in her old age. When her piercing eyes furtively glanced about in the shadowy doorway, one was at a loss to see anything but her two blazing orbs.

Knowing her brother's impatience with silly games, she, with darkness descending on *Lathamor,* frequently stuck the old thin face and luminous eyes out a mite beyond the *ursainn* (doorpost) as

George ponderously approached. Her timing and range were perfect; she'd wait until positive that he spotted her, then swiftly withdrew to amuse herself listening to unsavory epithetical semantics, shocking Free Presbyterians.

Three special annual days surpassed all others in sterling importance to Uncle George. They were fank (sheep-pen) days, dip days, and, most momentous of all, that sad crucial day when the young lambs were forever severed from their mothers' milk and security. These tender, beautiful young creatures piteously moaning their loss in heartbreaking unison, droopily and sadly groaning their way through the heather in motherless quandary, was and is enough to soften the most callous of souls. On such hectic days, Uncle George was always overwrought and touchy as tinder. Neighbors literally avoided him on special days, and even Christine stayed indoors.

One late evening, while trudging along the *Lathamor* road, *Seòras* was guiding his modest flock of nervous separated lambs, when Christine, completely forgetting what day it was and alarmed at the barking dogs and general commotion, stuck her sharp thin face through the doorway; at the sight of which, every lamb bolted off in wild panic all over the landscape. Never before or after was pastoral and lovely *Lathamor by the sea* subjected to such awesome adjectives as George roared at his sister Christine that unforgettable twilight of long ago.

Uncle George: Part 3

For some reason, it was obvious to one and all that the mere sight of a *cearc* (hen) infuriated my uncle, and my Aunt Mary—noted for her tinder temper—raised a covey of the capricious critters from year to year. Allegedly his feeling of contempt for chickens arose out of their scraping and plundering the freshly thatched *mullach an taighe* (the top of the house) in the autumn *Sùcha* turnover which everybody contended with—back in those days. With his volcanic temper, this sort of mischief on the part of a creature he disdained drove him bananas—like they say in Texas.

One midautumn, on peat cutting chores, Mary Mackenzie—*Màiri Eithig*, later of Detroit—and myself awaited a passing shower as the crew sat at George's fireside. Mary enjoyed a lusty laugh in those days and considered my uncle the funniest man alive.

George paced the floor, furious at the weather, furious at the chickens, and furious at the whole world. Upon opening old *doras a' chùlaist* (scullery door) outswished a few entrapped panicky chickens against his face and frame, shrieking with abandon.

Oh mo chreach-sa mhòr, ghlaodh Seòras. (Oh my goodness! shouted George.) *Tha na cearcan tha seo anns na lùchairtean.* (These hens are in luxury.) For the rest of her life, *Màiri Eithig* was amused at *Seòras's* equating our crude *cùlaist* (utility room; scullery) of long ago with *Lùchairtean a' chaisteil* (the splendor of the castle).

Angus said that people in Skigersta generally did not have the same affection for dogs in his day that people have today. Yet in the following sketch, written 1987, it is clear his mother had tender feelings for the family dog, as did he. It seems right, then, to think of Fannie as a member of the family. She became notorious not for her sheepherding skills, her tracking and pointing skills, her vermin killing, duck fetching, nor any other worthy Hebridean dog skills, but for her prowess in reproduction, a source of embarrassment for Dad's sisters and, it would seem, a source of amusement for him.

Where Is Fannie?

When in my early teens, a family crisis regarding our female dog Fannie so gripped our fishing village of Skigersta that the gentle creature became the talk of the entire forty-seven homes within its borders. Little Fannie was scarcely eleven inches high, of regal bearing, proudly strutting about like the queen of canines, with head high and pointed ears—always in eager upswing during family conversations.

Her tiny torso was of dark-brown color, blending into light fawn underneath the belly, with a narrow white strip stretching from throat to midriff: a small white dot decorated each paw and the tip of her narrow tail—nature's express beauty marks highlighting the comely contour of a noble animal.

Household discussions so fascinated Fannie that she'd tilt her head back and fore while intently gazing into our faces as if absorbing the meaning of every spoken word uttered around our *teine meadhan an làir* of long ago. Her sharp innate perception in grasping the gist of conversations and reactions inspired the following true tale concerning a unique episode—still recalled in Skigersta.

Fannie was as productive as she was beautiful, a large litter nearly every year, and thereby hangs a true story of courage, love, perseverance, and devotion to match the ineffable heroics, sufferings, and sacrifices of mothers down through the ages.

With three growing sisters—young but shy—in the uppity Victorian climate of those days, suffering a barrage of good-natured teasing from their male admirers concerning Fannie's fertility, the poor defenseless creature found herself the object of caustic remarks from the blushing maidens of the No. 7 household. Their callous attitude greatly annoyed a compassionate mother who, for a spell, remained broodingly silent while increasing her affection toward the distressed Fannie, who understood every verbal blast hurled her way.

Then, one memorable winter, Fannie's natural cycle was again evident, and a harsh finger-pointing lecture from an elder sister so psychologically bruised the sensitive Fannie that she endured the remaining part of her pregnancy in what David Thoreau called "quiet desperation." Gone were the robust tail-waggings and affectionate little snorts by which she impartially greeted everybody that opened our door. Even her former crackling barks dwindled to pitiful whimpers in marked reversal of her natural outgoing personality.

At first, this drastic change wasn't considered a particularly significant matter in view of her condition, but a mother's keen intuition caught the scent of something sinister, not in Denmark but on our own *cagailte*, and we, as if overnight, found ourselves in the lowly *taigh dubh* of long ago on the brink of becoming a bitter "house divided."

Back in those days, dogs weren't regarded on the same level of affection as they are now, and our household's accusatory moods were of necessity kept strictly within doors in fear of a so-called solid Christian family getting overly emotional at the erratic antics of the common canine. Our clandestine mumblings were abruptly exposed to the whole world however by none other than Fannie herself who, when sensing that delivery was at hand, quietly disappeared out of sight, and "Where is Fannie?" became the prime query of neighbors and residents alike for several hectic days. After four days without a trace of Fannie, many old-timers came to the conclusion that in her awkward state, she tumbled into a deep culvert and perished.

Meanwhile, on the morning of the fifth day, my boyhood crony *Tarmod Beag* of No. 11 on the southern slope of the *Baile Shuas* was in his usual lively form, hopping all over the landscape, when he heard a familiar snort near Donald Morrison's square turf-enclosed garden—tunneled with rabbit burrows from end to end.

Filled with curiosity, Norman moved along the dyke examining every hole, when suddenly he came face-to-face with Fannie, standing and snorting in the entrance of her burrow hideout—greeting him as she always did at our own door. *Tarmod Beag*, slightly stunned at the sight of her, looked into the burrow, which to his amazement housed four wiggly puppies huddling together as lively and normal looking as if born in a swanky London kennel.

In a flash, Norman raced through the *Baile Shuas* heralding the news, and everybody was both elated and astonished. How Fannie survived her ordeal without nourishment for so many nights and days feeding her young in the bosom of the earth was still a matter of conjecture when I left on the *Marloch* sixty-three years ago.

A Sense of Community

As he left on the *Marloch*, my father said good-bye to not only a beautiful place with childhood memories in every crag in the rocks, a family he was not likely to see again for many years, if ever, but also the community that had been his psychological "overcoat," identity beyond his own skin. He was never again to know such a sense of connectedness in his life.

There was, of course, the tie of religion that held the Seceders together. Those ties would be reinforced with Sunday services, two high holy seasons each year—communion—and on any occasion that required the presence of a minister. These worthies looked in on their people not only when they were sick or grieving but in regular visitations.

Many of the activities of the villagers were done communally: fishing and fish gutting certainly were, as was gathering peat, tending sheep, building and repairing structures, and, for women, washing large linens outside. There must have been many occasions to draw people together in communal work. My father and his family's history would have been well known to everyone in Skigersta. They all would have known that his grandfather was one of those lost in the "Great Drowning" of 1862, that his father went away to Canada for two years at a time, that his sister Margaret worked for Lord Leverhulme, and that his mother was a devout woman known for her Bible knowledge. And just as they knew him, he knew all of them and *their* family histories. Anonymity was clearly nonexistent here.

The people of Skigersta shared similar values, destinies, Viking genes, hardships, and joys. They were reportedly very sociable and appear to have entertained themselves mainly by talking. Was not the hero of every gathering the one who could tell a really great story? Second only to the ministers in social prestige, and perhaps their equals, in some ways, were the bards—men who could parry words like expert swordsmen handled rapiers.

And they would not be the first people on earth who were all the more tightly bound together by that special centripetal force: the knowledge that they were scorned by others.

In the following sketches, Angus describes a wedding and a custom called *luadh*, or "waulkings," two social events, other than gatherings in private homes—*cèilidh*—and worship services that surely did their part to foster a deep sense of community.

Skigersta's Weddings of Long Ago

During my adolescent years, wedding festivals in Skigersta were the height of excitement and a conversation piece from morn till night. The noisier the nuptials, the bigger the joy as old and young warmed into a holiday mood for a couple of carefree days, a refreshing change of pace.

In order to meet the expected demands for scones and other victuals, the immediate neighbors assisted in baking enough on hot griddles to feed a multitude. Prior to the big night, it was the custom for two male couriers to formally visit those selected for the feast and cordially announce the espoused couple's special invitation in a most warm and personal face-to-face manner. Everybody seemed to like this folksy feature of our Hebridean wedding ceremonies, perhaps because it made those invited feel a mite important.

I have had the privilege of attending five wonderful weddings, two on the *Baile Shuas*, a mere two and three doors away. My first was neighbor *Anna Dhòmhnaill Tharmoid*'s wedding; groom, *Doilidh Mòr* of Eorodale. After that came *Mairead Iain*'s wedding, Annie's next door neighbor; groom *Tarmod Iain Ruaidh*, Norman Gillies of Lionel. My cousin *Mairead Sheòrais* on *Lathamor by the sea* had a big wedding, which we all attended. The groom was the *Ùigeach* of Swainbost. Witty *Seòras* was in great form that night; his mixture of witticism and sarcasm kept everybody in stitches.

Margaret's two cousins Peggie and Jessie next door had two huge weddings which we in our teens greatly enjoyed. Peggie got married to *Iain Mhurdo*, Port, hero of the *Iolaire* and Jessie to John MacDonald, four doors from ours, who perished on that ill-fated craft on New Year's morning of 1919.

Portend of Long Ago

When my *Baile Shuas* neighbor John MacDonald was home on leave, not too far from the cessation of First World War hostilities, he and Jessie Finlayson decided to give the war-weary villagers something to cheer about—a lavish wedding. John was one of about forty Skigersta men engaged in the First World War and one of the six fatalities from our village.

The traditional and romantic three-mile walk to the *Eaglais Mhòr* was ruled out when John hired a shiny horse carriage, complete with an immaculately dressed driver, befitting the happy occasion. Amid many cheering well-wishers, the gay wedding party, seated in the carriage, left the front of No. 18 *Lathamor* with the blessings of a lively, happy crowd wishing them Godspeed.

Within a mere few minutes of smooth uphill riding, when approaching *Tarmod Pìobaire*'s house, prior to making the turn onto the main road, the carriage abruptly malfunctioned, breaking in two parts—a portend indeed. The shock of such a sudden, adverse turn of events, on a wedding eve, no less, clearly affected one and all, especially John and Jessie. Both, however, bravely encouraged the wedding party to proceed on foot, which they did, though inwardly deeply perturbed.

On the way back from Cross, as man and wife, the young newlyweds encountered an even more ominous omen than the former, upon discovering, to their horror, that the broken carriage left behind was hurled by us rowdies, who rode it up and down the road in their absence into a slimy ditch near *Taigh Dhòmhnaill Mhòir*—a frightening sight to behold.

This dastardly deed, especially in view of what subsequently transpired, brings a sense of shame and guilt to my generation to this day. Within a couple of days thereafter, John was off again to meet the foe but never returned. He perished on the *Iolaire*.

In the *luadh* description, the older Angus is looking back at this custom and wondering how, in conservative Skigersta, it was considered socially acceptable. He describes the scene from the perspective of a nine-year-old.

Ludicrous *Luaidhean* of Long Ago

A half-naked *luadh* (waulking) in yesterday's Skigersta, when female legs were exposed to the crotch at a time when revealing a mere couple of inches above the knees was perennially frowned upon, was a shocking experience for us tender tykes of nine and ten.

Only one waulking was ever performed in our home on the *Baile Shuas*. Our humble home of those days, though supposedly the center and criterion of Victorian prudery of the era, was suddenly invaded and overrun in reckless abandon by white, flabby, female flesh (nine bare-legged maidens in all) prettily prancing all the way from *doras a' chùlaist* to *doras a' stìl*.

My inseparable boyhood cronies, cousin *Tarmod Geal*, Norman Murray, and his cousin *Tarmod Beag* along with *Alastair Chaluim*, were a mite older than I was at nine. All of us enjoyed the side show and were astounded to discover that female legs were virtually the same shape as our own, having never been previously permitted even a furtive gaze on pain of a whack from a heavy right hand.

Waulking preparations entailed a bit of bother. First, a smooth makeshift oblong wooden platform was installed; on the opposite sides of which were either chairs or benches to seat five on one side and four on the other. No one seemed to know why the odd seating arrangement, except that it was in perfect harmony with all its other strange aspects and weird contrasts.

Then, with the platform firmly installed, the blanket or blankets were carefully snaked in roundish fat, rope-like form all along the boards in front of the nine girls. While standing at their posts, ready for the next revealing episode, the girls almost in unison swiftly tugged their lengthy clothing up in one scoop between their legs, shoved it back of the buttocks—and sat down. The drastic transition of the sublime to the ridiculous, or vice versa, nakedly unfolded before our very eyes in split seconds of time.

Waulkings were commonplace back in those days. Every village performed several within the course of a year, but the First World War (1914) saw the end of it.

As soon as the girls were seated in their place, the singing and entertainment phase of the ancient custom began, with every toe now touching the rolled blankets all ready to push against their opposite counterparts, in rhythmic motion to the medieval tune of *Ho na filibhig*—whatever that means. All of our *luaidhean* started off to the cue medley of *Ho na filibhig*, repeated in solo two or three times by the leading voice of the group, followed by the rest with great gusto and rhythm, as every foot in paddle-like motion kept time to the tune while briskly pounding against the blankets in bare feet from both sides. And the seminude show was underway.

The weddings described above make no mention of music or dance. Clearly singing, though, was a part of social life, as the *luadh* custom makes clear, but music generally was not a part of worship life for Free Presbyterians. This absence was puzzling to Angus.

Our Esteemed FP Clergymen

It was ten years after our Skigersta parents rejected the Declaratory Act that I first saw the light of day. As I approached manhood, there were many questions racing through my mind about this and that which I stifled because of my great respect for our ministers, parents, and neighbors who, in all likelihood, were the most steadfast and courageous cluster of Christians since the days of the apostles.

Looking back on it now in my early eighties, I regret that I didn't press for more information as regards their utter rejection of music, which, as keen Bible scholars, they all knew was like second nature to all Jews since Reuben, the firstborn of the chosen, came into the world.

All Jews down through the ages loved music, talked music, played music at home and festivals and even when going into battle. The great King David himself, an inventor of musical instruments, arranged for five different musical instruments to be played when removing the sacred ark to Jerusalem. It must be remembered that this voluminous crescendo of music reaching to heaven was not the cause of the Lord's anger that day.

It is quite obvious that King David, probably the greatest monarch of all time, played music often in his spare time, as royal occupant of the magnificent House of Ceders. It would be most interesting to hear one of our many exegetical FP pastors explain minutely, step by step, how their rejection of music came about. One thing is certain—their explanations, whatever they might be, would be solidly founded on scripture.

Murdo Mackay's Jib

Fishing was serious business. The community depended on the sea for survival, as crofting in and of itself could not sustain it. So it is particularly delightful to read a lighthearted tale involving middle-aged men caught up in boyish competition on the water in their *sgothan*. Surely the incident provided merriment and extended commentary for years thereafter as it was fondly recalled from *cagailte to cagailte*.

In the olden days, a Port *sgoth* and one from Skigersta occasionally went to *Sùlaisgeir* for the precious *guga Niseach* (a bird) at the same time. One particular year, *Geadaidh's sgoth* arrived about the same time as the Bard's crew, with Murdo Mackay, himself a skipper, aboard. *Geadaidh* was a famous *sgoth* skipper and hardy mariner all of his adult life.

While in *Sùlaisgeir* gathering the guga, they all agreed to fill the two *sgothan* to capacity and divide the totals either in Port or Skigersta, depending on which of the two *sgothan* first touched on shore in a race for home. The challenge and race appealed to both crews, who weren't exactly *bodaich* at that particular point of time but able-bodied middle-aged fishermen, still full of youthful *còmhstri* (rivalry) and keen competition.

On the forty-mile stretch of open waters heading for the shoreline, the race was on in earnest, as a temperate breeze barely bulged the sails. About two miles offshore, *Geadaidh's sgoth* held a commanding lead, and the innovative *Murchadh Dhòmhnaill Ruaidh*, who never accepted defeat, rigged up a makeshift jib, first ever seen on a *sgoth*, and managed to hoist it up in addition to the sail—shocking *Geadaidh* and his crew. The Skigersta *sgoth* sailed right by them into the *Lòn Gorm* a full furlong ahead.

There are still two surviving in Skigersta who can remember this race, my next-door neighbor Norman, whose father was skipper, and *Dòmhnall Beag Mhurchaidh*. The incident occurred in the early twenties.

2

Eighteen Ninety-Three: Sad Discord of Yesteryear

In 1892, the Free Church of Scotland's Declaratory Act set ablaze a theological firestorm that would ultimately lead to schism and the formation of the Free Presbyterian Church of Scotland. What it was about was subscription to the articles of the Westminster Confession. Adopted in 1646, this confession had been the creedal norm for Presbyterians since that date and also influenced confessional statements of Calvinists of other denominations such as Baptists and Congregationalists.

Below is the Free Presbyterian Church of Scotland's explanation of these events:

> All office-bearers in the Free Church of Scotland subscribe the Westminster Confession of Faith which states: 'There is no other head of the Church, but the Lord Jesus Christ; nor can the Pope of Rome, in any sense, be head thereof; but is that Antichrist, that man of sin, and son of perdition, that exalteth himself, in the Church, against Christ and all that is called God (chapter 25, section 6).

The Free Church Declaratory Act of 1892 was a device which allowed those who did not believe all the teaching of the Westminster Confession of Faith to continue as office-bearers in the old Free Church. It allowed office-bearers to subscribe only to "the substance of the reformed faith therein set forth." This is a loose phrase, for "the substance" was not defined by the Assembly. This worked to the advantage of those who did not believe some of the teaching of the Westminster Confession of Faith.

It meant that those office-bearers who subscribed the Westminster Confession of Faith in the light of the Declaratory Act could privately resile from doctrines in the Confession, without indicating which ones they did not believe, such as the six days of creation (chapter 4, section 1), or that the pope is "that Antichrist, that man of sin, and son of perdition, that exalteth himself in the Church." This was mental reservation.

Some people protested at this changing of the old Free Church's doctrinal constitution, and when it became apparent at the General Assembly in 1893 that the Declaratory Act would not be repealed, and that it was here to stay, the Rev. Donald Macfarlane protested against this and left the Assembly. This led to the formation of the Free Presbyterian Church of Scotland in 1893. (Cited from the official Web site of the Free Presbyterian Church of Scotland)

Below are some of Angus's reflections on this schism as it affected himself, his family, and others in his world.

Robert Rainy's Declaratory Act of 1892–1893

The Declaratory Act, allegedly formed and pushed through by the scholarly Robert Rainy, was disastrous to the warm Christian relationships of about forty of my close kindred, including my aged grandparents. Within this rather wide circle of relatives were five uncles and aunts whose offsprings amounted to thirty (four of which were of my own age bracket), born about ten years after the separation. They were of course my first cousins—alienated from me forevermore.

The chilly impasse dividing our families since 1892 was never really paved back with good intentions from either side of the spectrum because at times it appeared that even natural compassion itself went completely by the board. For example, one day at a sheep fank (sheep pen) out on the moorelands, I happened to be standing right next to my Eoropie Uncle John *Iain Buachaille* an FC (Free Church) elder, so diametrically poisonous against all FPs (Free Presbyterians) that he disdained passing by their Lionel church on common errands.

He considered my mother an out-and-out heretic and never darkened our door since 1892. I was quite shy in my early teens, and I kept inching closer and closer to my uncle, eagerly wishing he'd recognize me and ask about my mother. He didn't even budge. The psychological scar that brief encounter caused—or lack of it—stayed with me for many years.

His warmhearted brother Donald, whom we saw nearly every week, made up for his brother's hatred. He was an ardent *Aonadair* (Unionist), filled with love for his fellowman. "Ye shall see the difference" etc.

Eighteen Ninety-Three to 1903

It was ten years after our Skigersta forbears, consisting of twenty seven homes, who separated themselves from the Free Church of Scotland, that I, along with four more of our village age crop, first saw the light of day. By this tumultuous separation, our Skigersta elders became, as if overnight, somewhat synonymous with the scattered Israelites of old—fables and outcasts throughout a large thickly populated district of thirteen villages—a "gazing stock" as Paul puts it.

Every Ness village stayed under the Declaratory Act except three families in Lionel, one in Habost and two in Swainbost. For example, there wasn't one Free Presbyterian family from the southern tip of Knockaird to the western periphery of Eoropie, home of my ancestors. The scholarly Robert Rainy, who went to his own reward in 1909, was the alleged archvillain of this sad separation, whose dismal aftermath and chilly relationships are keenly felt to this day.

Those Skigersta stalwarts of long ago, who equated the Act with sheer heresy, did not consider their stance of 1893 a sad one by any stretch of the imagination, however. As far as is known, none of them ever glanced back from the plough. They all passed away without any regrets whatsoever over their controversial past.

In a sense, we their offspring suffered much more than they did, through the hostility of some of our schoolteachers who considered our parents way beyond the pale of common sense—and even common salvation.

The following sketch, entitled "Irony," tells the story of a young Skigersta woman who is stricken with double pneumonia and yet ignored by the local doctor who apparently had no intention of taking care of Seceders. The date of the story is 1896. The woman is described as assertive, articulate, and outspoken about her faith, a Bible scholar and a woman who lived to within four months of her one hundredth birthday. All these things are consistent with my father's mother Christina, so it is a mystery to me why she is not named in this sketch. I think this is a story about my grandmother.

Irony

Only for the happy fact that there are still some surviving Ness folks who recall hearing about the following true tale, its terrible irony and implications, this story would be considered another old wives' tale.

About four years prior to the turn of the century, a young mother in Skigersta, just two miles from the villages of Lionel and Habost where our haughty doctor flauntingly paraded his fancy gig and shiny steed to awe the peasants, came down with double pneumonia.

For three nights, the entire village residents were hushed into prayerful silence, tensely awaiting that grim messenger who is no respecter of persons. Our district doctor of that era, residing in his white lordly manor just a few miles from South Dell, was duly summoned prior to the woman's high feverish stage. The arrogant medic ignored all pleadings while maintaining his showy trots up and down the villages, as was his wont and joy.

The people of Skigersta—"valiant few" to their friends and "seceders" to their enemies (a derogatory misnomer which spitefully cleaves onto them to this day)—waited and prayed. It so happened that the ailing mother was the leading spokesperson for the other loyal spouses who followed their husbands into the fledgling new order. None of this was lost on the doctor.

She was young, assertive, and articulate, besides being one of the most astute Bible scholars of her generation. The sturdy mother survived and lived to be one hundred years of age—save four months. How ironic that this remarkable woman outlived the doctor (who cared less whether she lived or died) by a span of over half a century.

Below is a sketch of a woman of Eoropie who married a Skigersta friend of the Bard in 1892. Once the separation took place in 1893, her relatives would have had additional reasons to disapprove of this marriage to one not only socially inferior but now a near heretic.

The people of northern Ness villages apparently looked down on the folks of Skigersta as crude and unsophisticated. This seems all the more remarkable given the fact that the distance from Skigersta to these villages was a matter of a few miles. For those who had horses, another mark against the Skigerstonians was the fact that they had none. This forced them to do farming the old-fashioned way—with bare knuckles and brawn.

The woman and man in question are clearly my grandmother Christina and grandfather Norman. All the descriptions, including the year of their marriage, 1892, point to them. He was called "Big Norman" not for his height but for his large physical frame. She lived within a few months of her one hundredth year. They settled in the middle of the *Baile Shuas*. Why my father was reticent to name these people as his own parents, I do not know. Have some theories, but think I have to leave it as a mystery.

Bizarre Misunderstanding

So far-reaching and incredible was a strange matrimonial affair, gravely affecting distant Eoropie and so-called remote Skigersta, which occurred in 1892, that Eoropie's inhabitants and Skigersta's residents were astounded at the incongruity of the whole matter, like interfering with the perfectly balanced forces of nature.

Back in those dark divisive days of acute class distinction, Eoropie's people, along with those of Fivepenny and Knockaird, in conjunction with all Northern villages, regarded themselves much more cultured, refined, and even more devout than the crusty, allegedly artless Skigersta natives holed out in the peat bogs—a bleak mile from civilization. On the other hand, fiercely independent Skigersta stalwarts considered the pompous northern *Niseachs* a breezy bunch of ridiculous airs, far too prone to peer down their noses on the so-called crude characters south of the border.

Amid this ludicrous climate, a comely young and slender, ostensibly frail, Eoropie maiden fell in love with a strapping Skigersta fisherman, whose outstanding physical appearance and that of his handsome next-door pal were favorably commented on at the colorful Stornoway "Drills" of Lewis lore. The pal was none other than the famed Skigersta Bard.

When the surprised Eoropie folks first learned that their tender creature was about to become a Skigersta sacrificial lamb, an *Oh bhrònag bhochd* (Oh, you poor soul) became a rueful household litany, mournfully whispered from *cagailte* to *cagailte*. By the same token, when the reputedly rash and rugged Skigersta gaffers woke up one morning to be informed of the coming nuptial to one so fragile looking of sensitive breeding, like *Nighean Choinnich Buachaill* (the daughter of Kenneth the Shepherd), they were aghast at Norman's naivety in even pondering such a venture.

They failed to reckon how she could possibly cope in horseless Skigersta with the raw slam-bang labor essential within the last noble corner still proudly thriving on bare-knuckle toil and brute strength. Love's normal function prevailed however, and the sacred contract was signed and sealed, followed by the happy couple settling down almost dead center of Skigersta's beautiful *Baile Shuas*, where the supposedly delicate Eoropie maiden lived out a hardworking meaningful life as mother, grandmother, and great-grandmother until reaching ninety-nine years and eight months of age.

To be the children of Seceders had consequences at school where it appears at least one teacher, John Gunn, especially enjoyed punishing them. At least this is how my father saw him.

Twilight Reflections (John Gunn)

One early morning long, long ago, four of us Skigersta boys on our way to the Lionel school were sort of mesmerized by a smooth solid stretch of ice in front of *Taigh a' Mhonaich*—an old landmark. So enticing was this shiny patch of ice, hard by the roadside, that a wild spurt of ice-sliding ensued at such an ecstatic pace that time, teachers, thrashings and tribulations went by the board.

Suddenly, amid our most joyous revelry, that awesome moment of truth dawned on someone—and the panic was on. We streaked off like four mad gazelles toward Lionel, but to no avail—too late, every single minute of a long twenty minutes too late.

To the *Giagan*, John Gunn, our current teacher, dreaded in those days as the "teacher terror," twenty minutes late was unvarnished mischief and next to a capital crime. He tensely awaited our arrival in fumed anticipation, eager to commence his daily diversion of thrashing someone, anyone, with a four-fingered cowhide strap for the dual purpose of releasing frustration and showing who was boss.

His ego was such that he loved the "teacher terror" label. Three heavy smacks apiece were violently meted out on frozen fingers in rapid succession, as his nostrils widely expanded with every blow, signifying sadistic satisfaction.

It did not help matters that our Skigersta parents, whom he hated with a passion as rebel seceders, strongly disapproved of his overbearing yen for corporal cruelty on defenseless children. This sinister syndrome is usually the true mark of cowardice in most mortals, according to experts in human behavior, but in all fairness, the *Giagan* was no coward.

When the people of Skigersta first separated from the Free Church, they were offered a place in the village school house. But they soon outlived their welcome and were forced to find another place. That turned out to be my father's house, his modest *taigh dubh* thatched cottage. I cannot but imagine that this was a special point of pride for my father as he looked back on his history fifty years after the fact. I suspect that this choice had something to do with his mother, a very significant spiritual presence in Skigersta.

Our Old *Taigh Dubh*: A House of Prayer

In Skigersta of long ago, when our village fathers and spouses abandoned the Mother Church in 1892–1893, the educational authorities provided a temporary room for weekly prayer meetings in our small school house, which still stands.

Yet another door immediately opened, in which they found themselves every Thursday worshipping in our long three compartment *taigh dubh* on the beautiful and busy *Baile Shuas* of my young days.

I was in my late teens, strong and lively, helping to gather neighborhood chairs and cozily arrange them around *Teine meadhan an làir*, with special seating places for the missionary, elders, and deacons. Merchant *Iain Chalum*, one of our best Ness precentors, was a respected elder. His Lionel neighbor, the pious Norman MacRitchie, was the church's doorman and also a devoted deacon. The Bard was famed for his poignant *Là na Ceist* (Friday) discourses, and *Oran Sheumais Anndra* was an elder, much given to prayer.

My father, Norman MacDonald, newly added to church membership, was a deacon. Esteemed missionary *Calum a' Ghobha*, Malcolm MacLeod, was the Presbytery appointed missionary of the Ness FP congregation—feared the Lord from his youth. When the meeting got under way, the singing of Gaelic psalms sweetly emanating from the old *taigh dubh* reached clear across *Cnoc a' Choilich*.

Peat Fire

When our village fathers abandoned the mother church in 1893, the authorities of the small schoolhouse improvised a temporary prayer meeting for the twenty-eight village families which separated. However, a specific hygienic understanding was agreed upon—that absolutely no expectorations were committed under pain of sure and swift eviction.

For some of the *bodaich*, two hours without a chew or smoke frustrated them to the point of wishing that the respected devout curtailed their prayers a mite, which in some cases were long and laborious. As youngsters, we frequently watched them disperse and light up the old pipes as they trudged toward the road, amid nicotine halo of pale white bogey roll puffs—matching their hoary heads.

At any rate, some of the more rugged old-timers firmly rejected the classroom restrictions of the most unsanitary of all vices, and much cheating of the so-called solemn agreement ensued, infuriating the teachers in residence. Several warnings were issued to no avail, and the inevitable result quickly followed.

This eviction was the reason for the small separated flock finding themselves worshipping on Thursdays in our old long *taigh dubh* of No. 7—a privilege enjoyed by the faithful few for many years.

However, an irritating problem immediately emerged from this unique arrangement. Should our middle-of-the-floor peat fire be freshly started and set aglow at commencing of service, risking the embarrassment of blinding everybody to tears with the dreaded *detoch* or have it blazing on early, with the prospect of a flattened-out fire sometime before the two-hour service ended. The easy alternative of ignoring it altogether was ruled out because of the cold winter months and other considerations.

We were concerned about that peat fire, frequently a smoking dervish and a pain in the neck, not to mention the eyes. To mother's credit, she decided to start a brand-new fire prior to arrivals, which she did with much care every Thursday afternoon.

Today, there is no one surviving in Skigersta who sat in on those prayer meetings except myself. However, on my first trip home in 1952, after an absence of twenty-eight years, there were several FPs around who attended those weekly meetings, who could testify to the happy fact that that peat fire behaved propitiously like a glowing saint for two solid hours throughout the years that our small Free Presbyterian faithful availed themselves of the lowly thatched house on the beautiful *Baile Shuas*.

My father's old *taigh dubh* was superseded as a place of worship in due course with the construction of a Free Presbyterian church in Lionel. He tells the tale in the following sketch.

Our Embattled Parents of Long Ago

Years ago, during the frightful factious days when black ominous clouds of rancor and discord hovered over our comely community, strange and somewhat amusing episodes cropped up all over from Swainbost to Skigersta, Knockaird to *Cnoc a' Choilich*. When Skigersta's residents, almost en masse, rejected Robert Rainy's Declaratory Act in 1893, they became, as if overnight, the so-called oddballs of the whole Ness community.

Therefore when ground was broken for erecting a snug modest Free Presbyterian church right in the center of Lionel, Skigersta's avowed adversaries, the Lionel inhabitants, like Victoria of old, weren't amused. It was irksome enough to have the pesky Seceders a bleak mile south of the border, amid boggish wastes, ditches, and drudgery, but to serve as host, for a sanctuary no less, was tantamount to becoming an accessory after the fact.

This awesome moment of truth, in rubbing elbows with rebels, augured trouble, if not disaster, for the formidable Free Church militants; puffed up with prestige, popularity, money, and manses. The embattled Free Presbyterians, barely surviving within the eye of the hurricane and stripped of everything but their bibles, took courage in a challenging situation, synonymous with the dauntless boy David moving against the gargantuan Goliath. Similar to the lowly but potent ark of the testimony heading for Gilgal as the Perizzites and Girgashites trembled in their boots.

From a purely financial standpoint, the Lionel Free Presbyterian church seemed to be utterly out of harmony with common practical procedure if not with common sense. According to reliable reports handed down to us by our elders, no one in the village of Skigersta even owned a bank account in that scanty and stormy era of time. On the contrary, there were scarcely enough commodities available to prevent that dreaded animal from roaring through the front door and onto the *cagailte*. It appears to be a case of the just shall build by faith.

Another baffling aspect of Skigersta's cause was their dismal failure in claiming any of the contributory monies, all of them willingly given out of their meager sums toward the completion of the beautiful and hallowed *Eaglais Mhòr*. So eager were they of avoiding entanglements in Robert Rainy's Declaratory Act that they unilaterally reacted like certain species who, when about to be entrapped by predatorial craftiness, promptly relinquish limbs in order to escape with their lives—truly an amazing breed.

Hardworking Skigersta *bodaich*, volunteering for laboring chores during the church's construction period, were compelled to retain, like Nehemiah's men on the wall, their wits and wisdom girded on continuously while strolling around Lionel on common errands. Their opponents were at once auspicious, articulate, and aggressive, basking in the cultural background of highly educated pastors, teachers, merchants, and money. Armed with such copious amenities, they from all corners of the country. People came from far and wide to see and hear Mr. Cameron; some just curious to see an individual who weathered such verbal virulent onslaught for twenty-seven years and still managed to minister to a large Glasgow church—a packed house every Sabbath.

Our arrival at St Jude's on the first Sabbath morning was apprehensive. The small groups gathered at the church's door instantly became aware of our presence, just what we wished to avoid. As we sat down, we took notice that nearly everybody affixed their gaze on the door to the left of the pulpit. We reckoned it had to be Mr. Cameron's entry.

Suddenly it opened and in walked the distinguished-looking gray-haired Rev. Cameron, exuding the most somber, no-nonsense expression ever to project from a human face. An arched left eyebrow and the celebrated piercing stare were the first two facial features to catch the eye. A small elderly, gentle-looking lady, dressed completely in black, followed closely behind him, obviously quite happy with her role as mother to the foremost "valiant for truth" of our generation.

In the context of the death of Neil Cameron, my father tells the story of a minister who changed sides in the great divide of 1893. He was apparently tormented by the consequences of his decision, which he could not undo, for the rest of his life. From another sketch, it appears the minister was a Reverend Mackay.

Sad Situations of Long Ago

So sad and serious were the traumatic separations of the churches in those dark and divisive days before the turn of the century, 1892–1893, that one scholarly clergyman, beloved of multitudes, who was the most vocal in supporting the original small stalwarts of unpopular Separatists, derogatorily labeled "seceders," subsequently turned tail.

This learned pastor, endowed with leadership qualities, slinked back to the so-called materialistic advantages and prestige which he so willingly abandoned and eloquently condemned but paid an awful price. It was no secret that the ambivalent minister spent the remaining part of his long life bemoaning his double-minded conduct.

According to reliable reports, it clearly showed in all of his behavior, whether preaching or mingling, studying or strolling, or even relaxing. He could no more hide his guilt syndrome than part with his shadow. Also, according to reports, he humbly asked for forgiveness and chance to return but was rejected. Anyone with an ounce of compassion must at once realize that this situation in itself was truly a sad one.

One day, as an old man, news of the death of Rev. Neil Cameron of Glasgow (a seminarian Christian crony of other days) reached him, and he was both stunned and grieved. Mr. Cameron, who stood like a rock against untold verbal abuse, insults, and harassments in defense of truth, had just entered into the "saint's everlasting rest." The aged minister was heard to say softly, "Oh no…Neil didn't die…I am the one who died".

These two worthies are now in heaven where their differences shall be remembered no more.

My father was able to see a lighter side to the sad discord, as evidenced by two sketches below. In the first, two of his uncles "duke it out" verbally, oblivious to the humorous aspects of their dueling. In the second, a man, a mare, and a miracle mile prove to be harbingers of an ultimate, if guarded, reconciliation.

Two Uncles

What happens when the supposedly meekest man since Moses argumentatively entangles with the world's quickest tempered individual over explosive church discipline, creeds, and tenets? The logical answer of course would be, fireworks. Well, to us Skigersta lads of long ago, born after the 1893 upheaval, who gleefully watched this curious imbroglio between my two zealous uncles, on the opposite sides of the denominational spectrum, it was, if nothing else, fascinating to behold.

As far back as I can recall, this strange wrangle occurred nearly every week when my soft-spoken, easygoing Uncle Donald Morrison (Eoropie) confronted his trigger-tempered counterpart, Uncle Murdo, *Murchadh Buidhe*, and clashed on *Cnoc a' Choilich*. My pious Eoropie uncle, an ardent, inflexible *Aoneadair*, perhaps established some sort of record in our corner of the world. No one, young or old, in Ness or abroad, could recall ever seeing or hearing my uncle in bad temper, even for fleeting seconds, surpassing even the great Moses in human restraint.

Uncle Murdo's volcanic temper, on the other hand, along with his booming voice, tall, straight frame, and shiny, hairless head, holding sway as king of *Cnoc a' Choilich*, was a legend of our time. As a rampaging Separatist—Seceder to his opponents—a mere negative word from the so-called misguided opposition turned my uncle on, sometimes in savage sarcasm. Adding fuel to my uncle's fury was the well-known fact that soft-spoken, calm people like my Uncle Donald drove him into panic.

He acquired this sinister syndrome as a bellowing, lifelong *Gille tòisich* (fellow at the front]) in the windy *sgothan* when mumbling crew members, especially those abaft of midships, kept him in a constant state of frenzy. My Uncle Murdo maintained that anyone exuding complacency in those dark, divisive days, with a spate of heretical theses on the loose and Robert Rainy running wild, had to be confused above the clavicle.

To bypass *Cnoc a' Choilich* was impossible for my quiet uncle in reaching our house, his weekly stopover, because the main road climbed past the big fellow's door, and thereby the famous *Cnoc* became the verbal combat zone of the most bizarre dialogue since the confusion of tongues. In mere moments, my loud uncle resorted to shouting, flailing, and gesturing with abandon, as the calm one became more exasperatingly inaudible, tenaciously sticking to his guns, driving the big fellow to madness—invariably retreating in complete emotional shambles.

God's Benevolent Wonder Mile

So isolated and far removed from the mainstream of normal functions did horseless Skigersta become during the traumatic division of the churches of long ago, that for quite a spell, it was impossible to determine which were the most conspicuous oddities in separatist Skigersta—a horse or an *Aonadair.* Moreover, so hopelessly remote was the cloistered colony at the time that the bleak, boggish mile between them and aberrant Adabrock and evasive Eorodale—Robert Rainy's followers almost to a man—was by many considered God's benevolent wonder mile in completely secluding Skigersta from civilization.

True, a misguided Skigersta *Aonadair* or two emerged out of the celebrated so-called professorial mischief, but like that petrified group who holed up underground for fear of the Jews, they prudently remained indoors. At that particular period of time, the searing insurgency of crusading Skigerstonian separatists had reached the apex of its fervor and fury, and as discretion is the kernel of the will to survive, the poor *Aonadairs* had no options but to stay out of sight purely from self-preservation.

Nevertheless, one fearless, easygoing, and respected Eoropie resident of strong contrasting views, Donald Morrison, *Dòmhnall Choinnich Buachaill,* suffered no qualms whatsoever in boldly bringing the two so-called peculiarities, himself and his equally easygoing and long-suffering brown mare, to the No. 7 doorstep on the *Baile Shuas* every week, year in and year out, during the siege.

Donald, an ardent *Aonadair,* was so unanimously loved by all villagers, along with the calm, benign mare, that both were tolerated in quiet Christian resignation. Besides, being an avid reader, well aware of current national and international events, he relayed important news bulletins from the outside world to the ostracized *bodaich* until the dust died down and the belligerent residents were again accepted back into society—with many reservations.

3

An Eerie Sabbath Whistle

My father was eleven when the Great War began. He was of a generation that was too young to serve in the First World War and too old for the second. Next to the realization that he was part of a religious and social minority, for which there were daily reminders, I suspect that his next significant childhood awareness was that of a world at war, the long hand of which reached down and touched his own small village, where forty served and six never came home. The six were Angus Morrison, John MacDonald, Alex Murray, John Morrison, Murdo Mackay, and Angus Finlayson.

It is said that every other man from Lewis joined up, either in the Army, Royal Navy, or Mercantile Marine. Lewis apparently suffered losses that were proportionately higher than any other district in Scotland. My father shared the view that kilted regiments were often maneuvered into the most dangerous hotspots on the battlefield and thence, not surprisingly, sufferend the greatest losses. As I am not a historian of this period, I have no way of knowing if this sentiment has merit or not. I just know what my father felt.

He describes how the war came to Skigersta on a quiet Sunday afternoon.

An Eerie Sabbath Whistle

One can easily visualize the hair-raising reactions of strict Sabbath keeping Skigersta's residents, so rigid in maintaining silence on Sabbath that dish rattling and loud conversation were repressed, when the piercing shrill of a whistle rent the air from door to door on one awesome Sabbath afternoon. I was eleven years old, and deeply awed, simply because my Christian parents for the first time of my brief recollections projected genuine alarm—even fear.

Back in those days, news of current international upheavals made little or no impact on the average crofter fisherman in our remote Hebridean islands separated from the mainland by the two Minches. Our first weekly newspaper was published in 1917, an era in which most of the old folks considered all newspapers evil conveyors of lies and iniquity.

This sharp Sabbath whistle, however, not only arrested everybody's attention but generated goose-pimples, even in staid Free Presbyterians. My sister Margaret, whose hearing was keen, at that age of twenty-one (as her eyes were alert to any form of filth within the *cagailte*) was the first to whisper a sinister sounding "Hush, listen everybody." To me, it was like hearing a loud spooky clap of a door with no one in sight.

In a while, we all heard it loud and clear. "Sounds like the post's whistle," mother exclaimed, rushing to the door. And sure enough, there was *Iain Beag*, Port, our current mailman, as horrified as the rest of us, with a message from the war office to all aligned with the armed forces that war was declared on Germany—as of August 4, 1914. In this message was Lord Kitchener's famous command to the army: "Fear God, Honour the King."

In the following sketch, the young Angus finds excitement in the grounding of a collier a stone's throw from his house, where a dangerous path to the boat, worried parents, frenzied coolies, shouts and shrieks were the backdrop for the greatest thrill of his life. The older Angus was both sorrowful and horrified at the end of this ill-fated ship.

MURDINA D. MACDONALD

The Ill-Fated *Poll Dubh*

During the First World War, while our age group, born in the early 1900s, was still in school, a tramp steamer of the collier type by the curious name of *Poll Dubh* ran aground in pea-soup fog, right smack into Philiscleatair's cliffs of dizzying heights, north of Celier head— not too far from *Taigh Iain Fiosaich*, Rev. Nicholson's summer home.

No pen could ever adequately describe the excitement this incident created, especially among us boys who literally went silly with emotional glee at the prospect of getting aboard. None of us were that close to an ocean-going craft before, and she looked immense from the high cliff towering over her in cold foreboding silence. From that vantage point, where a goodly crowd of old and young peered down in a curious mood, she appeared to us as a huge ship, even luxurious, a clear indication of our dismal ignorance of crafts' dimensions, designs, or displacements, even though born and brought up only a furlong from the open sea.

There were only two rocky tracks leading down the face of the cliff to reach the stricken vessel, and they were risky enough to keep our parents in a state of anxiety for many days. All the ship's crew except the officers were coolies, none of whom could communicate in English, but when grouped together to discuss problems, all talked at the same time in such excitable pandemonium that their noisy talks appeared to be one mass of garbled confusion. Scaling the cliff panicked the coolies, and their carrying on, scrambling up and down the precarious face of that high rock, screaming, whistling, laughing, and shrieking were to us at that age a carnival. This callous reaction, however, later came back to haunt us. Like wisdom, compassion comes late.

Amidst all this excitement, *Tarmod Ailean* came home, and as an experienced *seòladair* (sailor) volunteered to take all of us aboard. I can still vividly recall that I was so elated at Norman's offer I was shaking with emotion, as were all of us. I can't recollect any other moment in my whole life (and I am now approaching my eighties) to surpass in sheer joy my experience that unforgettable afternoon following Norman as he pointed out the various quarters, including the captain's, from stem to stern—a craft which to us was a veritable

Queen Elizabeth. *Tarmod Ailean* also enjoyed the whole tour, then a sophisticated world traveler and sailor, an experienced "man about town."

After several days of pounding by moderate but dangerous waves of easterly winds, in what was a touch-and-go of whether she could be salvaged, they managed to get her off and made for the nearest shipyard.

The next report we received concerning our *Poll Dubh* was that she was speedily repaired and being wartime was just as rapidly put into service. She was torpedoed in the Mediterranean where all hands were devoured by sharks. Horrifying reflections of the dreadful way they all perished lingers to this day.

Skigersta fishermen did not seem obsessed with the knowledge that German U-boats had been spotted patrolling around the Butt of Lewis. They continued to do what fishermen do—fish.

U-Boat Scare of World War I

During World War I, a Skigersta *sgoth* with a Knockaird gentleman aboard while on the way to *Cara Phìobaire* experienced a U-boat scare equally facing the gallant *Niseachs* in the many combat zones of the world. It happened on a late summer eve—a gloaming to remember in Skigersta.

The crew of seven are still recalled, five of whom, oddly enough, were MacDonalds from the *Baile Shuas*, including two sets of brothers. The Knockaird stalwart was the popular *Seonaidh Dhòmhnail a' Choire*, well known in Skigersta since the Tolsta-Skigersta road construction. While the shrewd *bodaich* were quite aware of traversing German U-boats in *Cara Phìobaire's* vicinity, twelve miles northeast of Skigersta, they nevertheless kept discretely silent on the matter, for obvious reasons.

On this particular evening, they all left in buoyant mood, especially my father who had just learned that cousin *Tarmod Ruairidh*, Habost, was home on leave from France following some frightful years of trench warfare. It was blowing a temperate northwest breeze which invariably dies down in evenings when they left the quay, and the sleek *sgoth Niseach* looked beautiful as she rounded the *àird* base in bulging full sail heading for the high seas.

About three miles short of their goal, the elements were becalmed and the sea flattened into pond-like placidity, glistening in gloaming splendor. Donald MacDonald of croft No. 10, famous since childhood for his sharp, observing faculties, kept peering from underneath the flapping sail when he casually remarked that a funny-looking mastless craft was looming ahead, the significance of which even he failed to grasp at the moment.

The alert *Seonaidh Dhòmhnaill a' Choire*, an ex-navy man, sitting back aft heard the comment and being familiar with submarines' outlines, scrambled out of his seat and made for the bow, remarking in Gaelic something to the effect that "if it's a mastless craft, we've had it." At first glance, *Shonni* knew he was staring at the enemy and shouted to the skipper that it was indeed a German U-boat, a mere eighth of a mile ahead. Instantly, *Iain Pìobaire* shoved the tiller to starboard while ordering the six oars into immediate service. And the panic was on.

At this point, it was assumed that the German commander, cold and cruel as most of them were, was laughing lustily watching the poor *bodaich* frantically rowing for their lives. As they desperately rowed on, they managed to lose him in the evening shadows. Suddenly, as if straight from heaven, a mild northwest breeze came to their assistance, and it was in that sailing condition, with six exhausted oarsmen, that they entered the safety of the old *Lòn Gorm* east of the parapet—grateful to be alive.

When *Eathar a' Baile Shuas* slowly worked its way toward our quay in that memorable gloaming after escaping a prowling German U-boat near *Cara Phìobaire*, the concerned villagers were stunned at the weird and sudden turn of events. Our first reactions were that either death or illness had struck down a crew member, which, strangely enough, though vulnerable like other mortals, rarely occurred among fishermen in our corner of the world. Our own age group couldn't recall even one such incident.

Therefore, when my uncle *Murchadh Buidhe*, the *Gille tòisich*, threw that painter ashore, all shook up and pale, with every head accounted for, everybody was relieved but still curious. Then, suddenly, as was bound to happen under the circumstances, the whole seven simultaneously burst out with their own version of the scary episode, and for a few hectic minutes, the old quay sounded like the ancient confusion of tongues. Pent up fear, bottled like a bomb within, freely flowed out of them in excitatory exclamations, releasing pressure like a valve on an overheated boiler.

Compounding the confusion was my young cousin *Alasdair Beag*, then a mere child, but a witty, pesky tease who kept reminding the *bodaich* that at least they broke all records in bagging the largest catch of ling within the shortest period of time in history. In the awful mood they were in, it's a miracle that one of them just didn't toss him into the brine.

When my father reached home that evening, an unexpected ordeal was in store for cousin Norman, home from years of bloody and muddy trench warfare in France, who calmly sat by our fire, when my father breezed in looking as if he had just survived the "charge of the Light Brigade." The gallant Norman patiently listened to my father's hair-raising adventure on the high seas when for the first time facing the enemy. This for years was the story of Norman's own life, but he quietly sat there unperturbed. The combat veteran listened to my father's sole brush with danger as attentively as if he himself had spent the last three years as a *Gille Bùth* (shop boy) on Cromwell Street—a classic in restraint.

On the following day, with everything and everybody back to normal, my mother, fostering a robust sense of humor all her life, teased my old man about the previous evening's ludicrous contrasts, when nephew Norman, engaged in deadly hand-to-hand combat for years, uttered no complaints while he spieled off all evening about one confrontation. My father kept shaking his head, obviously sensing that it was indeed ridiculous, but felt as grand and secure as Jonah when "vomited out upon dry land."

MURDINA D. MACDONALD

My father chronicles below the deaths of two men who formed part of that "lost generation" of the Great War: Murdo MacDonald and Malcolm Gunn. In the case of the former, Murdo and his shipmates became casualties of a well-intentioned act of kindness. In the latter, the zeal of a young man, and his sense of honor, brought him to a place of no return—and no rescue.

How a Beloved Kindred Perished

One becalmed Sabbath evening on the way home from church during World War I, a group of us Skigersta folks spotted this huge ship proceeding north just a mere couple of furlongs outside the Bragg rock. Fascinated, we kept our eyes glued on this big craft, obviously a man-of-war, as we walked along, but nevertheless puzzled by two valid matters regarding this particular vessel.

First, we wondered out loud why so close to shore, and secondly, why so slow, when even children knew that the waters north of the Minch crawled with German U-boats. Subsequently, and to our great sorrow, we learned the stark truth of it all. We were actually gazing at Murdo MacDonald's craft and coffin slowly passing by before our eyes. *Murchadh Tharmoid Bhuidhe*, a kindred of No. 9 Eorodale beloved by all Skigersta fishermen and the No. 7 household, was aboard. The following is a true detail of how Murdo perished.

It was reported to the commander while cruising along the eastern Hebridean coast, a well-liked shipmate who died of natural causes was buried in Tolsta, whose gravesite could be seen from offshore. Somewhere south of Tolsta Head, the commander slowed to a crawl to give shipmates a look at the grave.

After this foolhardy stall, he never picked up speed as he passed Cellar Head and Bragg Rock where we first sighted him as a made-to-order target for the Germans, proceeding at less than half speed. As the gloaming darkened, Murdo's man-of-war was torpedoed and Murdo perished.

Grenadier Hero

Malcolm Gunn, *Calum Mhurchaidh Ghuinne*, Eorodale, John Gunn's heroic brother, was one of the undecorated heroes of World War I. Calum's noble bones were forever abandoned to rot in Flanders field, undoubtedly due to his lowly background.

According to eyewitness reports, Malcolm's last fierce battle tends to read like an incredulous gruesome narrative of an overimaginative war correspondent. It was no military secret along early battle lines that kilted regiments were maneuvered into the hot spots of the French and Belgian frontiers where German onslaughts were anticipated. It was in these combat zones that Germans first learned about the deadly ferocity of the "Ladies from Hell."

Those fearful zones also became human slaughter houses during night hand-to-hand butchery of bayonet carnage, blood curdling to an uncommon degree. The eerie dying shrieks of gored gladiators bayoneting one another into eternity in pitch darkness filled the night air of frontline battle zones in the early phases of World War I.

Following one of these bloody nocturnal forays, as early dawn revealed the horrifying butchery of dead Germans strewn about in blood-spattered awfulness, the maddened Huns, infuriated at the sight and, just as the sun rose over the Fatherland, counterattacked in ferocious frenzy. Calum, the intrepid grenadier carrying his awesome, deadly devices in a frontal sack, was at them in cold, calculating fury, blowing the converging foe into kingdom come as one grenade after another rent the air.

In the heat of battle, however, our hero, oblivious to peril, advanced too far into "No man's land" and suddenly became hopelessly outnumbered, surrounded, and grenades well-nigh exhausted. With the odds of surviving now impossible, the thought of surrender never crossed Malcolm's mind, as he hotly pursued the slaughter until the very last grenade annihilated still some more of the charging enemy, after which he wildly lashed out with bare fists at the bayoneting killers—who quickly dispatched one of our greatest Hebridean heroes.

4

Grief Unutterable

On January 1, 1919, His Majesty's Yacht *Iolaire* crashed into the rocks known as the "Beasts of Holm." Onboard were 284 men returning from the Great War and the carnage of that war. These survivors were coming into Stornoway harbor on New Year's Eve, looking forward to the first peacetime New Year' day since 1914 and the faces and embraces of their loved ones. Only seventy-nine men survived while 205 died, a loss that is felt to this day.

Men had traveled from France to ports in southern England and from there were sent by train to Kyle in the highlands. There they became part of a tragic web of misjudgments, miscalculations, and errors. Most of the Harris men and civilians were put on board the *Sheila*. The Lewismen were placed on the *Iolaire*, whose captain accepted them knowing that there were only lifeboats for one hundred and life vests for eighty. In poor weather and bad visibility, coming into a port he did not know, he went below with no look-out posted and only half the crew the ship should have had.

The hero of the *Iolaire* was John MacLeod, a strong swimmer who swam to shore with a hauling line. There he succeeded in pulling a hawser over which a total of forty men were saved. The last man to survive was Donald Morrison, who clung to the mast all night until rescued the next morning at first light. Seven men had climbed into the masts seeking refuge, but six men in the night weakened, lost their grips, and perished.

No Court Martial was convened, only a Court of Inquiry, due apparently to fear that the former would imply blame on the part of the navy. The findings of that Inquiry, on January 8, 1919, were not released to the public for fifty years and concluded that due to the nonsurvival of any of the officers, no opinion could be given attributing blame to anyone.

This is how the Stornoway Gazette summed up the tragedy in its edition of January 1919:

> No one who is now alive in Lewis can ever forget the 1st January 1919, and future generations will speak of it as the blackest day in the history of the island, for on it 200 of the bravest and best perished on the very threshold of their homes under the most tragic circumstances. The terrible disaster at Holm has plunged every home and every heart in Lewis into grief unutterable.

My father was twenty days shy of his sixteenth birthday and asleep in a warm bed as men struggled with wind, waves, and treacherous rocks following the collision at 1:55 a.m. He talked about the *Iolaire* all his life, as did my mother, who had double roots in Lewis. Her biological parents were from Back and her adopted father from Skigersta. Surely we children growing up in New York City were among the few children in America who knew what the name *Iolaire* meant, a name just as well known to us as that other name is known to all the world—*Titanic*.

The most recent book on the *Iolaire* is by John MacLeod, *When I Heard the Bell* (copyright 2009). His bibliography points to other writings on the disaster, among them *Call na h-Iolaire* (The Loss of the *Iolaire*) by Norman MacDonald (Stornoway, Acair, 1978) and *Sea Sorrow. The Story of the Iolaire Disaster* published by the *Stornoway Gazette*, 1972.

Following are a series of my father's recollections on the *Iolaire*, including his overall view of the scene, the work of the hero John

MacLeod and a conversation John had after the disaster with my grandfather Norman; the washing ashore of his uncle Roderic dressed as perfectly as if he were going to a formal dinner and his thoughts on the skipper, Captain Mason, for whom he reserves his most scathing comments.

These reflections are followed by excerpts from Norman MacDonald's book. My father translated the whole of the document from Gaelic to English, which, to my knowledge, has never been published in English. I have included only those passages that speak to the human tragedy, not the technical details of navigation nor the minutia of the inquiry.

Reflections of *Iolaire:* 1919

It is now over sixty-eight years since the terrible *Iolaire* disaster. It occurred twenty days before my sixteenth birthday and can still vividly recall the evening well enjoyed in my old *Taigh dubh* of *teine-meadhan an làir* of long ago. Our evening *cèilidh* guest that terrible night was my cousin Donald Finlayson, just out of the navy. He missed the *Iolaire* by a couple of days.

Donald served on the mammoth *Queen Elizabeth* in the Dardanelles fiasco and had many interesting war stories to relate. I even remember that he left around 11:00 p.m. Upon opening the door, he turned and said to my father, "*Tharmoid, cha robh dùil agam gu robh an oidhche cho fiadhaich.*" (Norman, I didn't think the night was so wild.)

I looked out and the night was black as pitch and blowing a gale—ominously projecting a night of doom. As it had been established that the *Iolaire* crashed against the "Beasts" around 1:55 a.m., a period of time which obviously found me in sound slumber as 205 navy men perished. What a frightening reflection to live with.

The disaster area was about thirty-five miles from our own Skigersta *cladach*, a dismal ugly-looking shoreline which I passed in our Skigersta *sgoth* many times. The Stornoway harbor entrance is seven hundred yards wide. It has been estimated that the distance, as the crow flies, between the safety of the piers and the Beasts is less than a mile.

It has been established that Commander Mason, skipper of the *Iolaire*, was woefully unfamiliar with the maritime beacons leading into the Stornoway harbor. Bizarre conjectures as to why he abandoned the bridge at such a crucial time, on a moonless night no less, approaching a seven-hundred-yard entrance in near gale and heavy seas are still running rampant among Lewismen.

There wasn't a single lookout on the superstructure of the *Iolaire* when she crashed into the Beasts of Holm, not even one from stem to stern, except Lieutenant Cotter at the wheel. This deplorable, blatant breakdown of discipline on a British naval vessel is almost impossible to fathom in a navy that ruled the waves from 1588 to 1918.

Random Thoughts and Items—*Iolaire*

The Sabbath after the *Iolaire* disaster in which 181 Lewis navy men perished and seven men from Harris, the Rev. Kenneth Cameron, affectionately known in Gaelic as *Camaranach Steòrnabhaigh*, preached a sermon from Psalms 46:10: "Be still, and know that I am God."

Upon learning of this text which the esteemed parson selected to preach on that mournful Sabbath, it struck me right off that the very same line was one of my mother's favorites. It was over half a century later and deep in the heart of Texas that I read the line, probably in Calum's book *Call na h-Iolaire.*

Calum deserves credit for that book. It was a masterpiece of sad detail, concerning a tragedy which some historians consider the saddest maritime disaster of all time. Author Calum claims in his book that the naval brass in London concealed the real secrets of the *Iolaire*'s disaster in locked vaults for over half a century. Multitudes are wondering out loud if the deplorable shortage of life jackets and sailing on half a crew with the other half ashore getting an early start on a jolly New Year's eve had anything to do with a well-kept secret for almost sixty years.

This shocking disclosure would most assuredly give the efficient British navy a permanent black eye. On the other hand, it must be recalled that the mighty British navy policed and controlled the world's Seven Seas until the great American navy of awesome, almost unlimited power took over.

John MacLeod, Port—Hero of the *Iolaire*

The following is the exact English translation of John's reaction to the *Iolaire*'s fatal crash as told to my father within my hearing in the sad summer of 1919. "Norman," John related somberly, "I assumed when she stopped so sudden that she laid in some maelstrom of sea… neither rock, crag, nor cave entered into my mind—that's how calm and smooth she struck."

During that same evening *cèilidh*, John disclosed that he was almost certain he recognized William's voice shouting to him from some distance to try and swim ashore with a line. Young William MacKay was a popular Fivepenny schoolteacher, so well known and loved by Ness folks that most *Niseachs* forgot he had a surname. He was clearly the matinee idol of that particular point of time, partly because it was a rare and refreshing change of pace to have one of William's compassion and common sense teaching class in those dark days.

William knew John since childhood and was well aware of his swimming abilities and many wild escapades among the Port harbor waves and winds since a mere boy. It is truly sad to relate that the much loved schoolteacher perished—to the great grief of hero John.

Subsequently, John got married to a lovely Skigersta lass, raised a family, and lived into his nineties. His name will always make *Niseachs* proud. I was a few months past my sixteenth birthday and sitting right close to John at our *teine meadhan an làir* in our old *taigh dubh* when he made the above statements. I remember them as clearly as if it all occurred a mere fortnight ago.

Murchadh Iain: *Iolaire* Survivor

Neighbor Murdo Morrison's survival from the *Iolaire* was rather unique, like many of the other seventy-nine who barely escaped the jaws of death at the Beasts of Holm. Murdo, upon being tossed into the swirling surf, found himself blindly groping in the dark alongside the *Iolaire's* hull—just about to perish.

Suddenly, a hand from aloft, as if straight from heaven, reached down and completely yanked him aboard in one fell swoop. In the darkness and general frenzy aboard the stricken vessel, Murdo never laid eyes on his life saver but strongly assumed for the remaining part of his life that his gallant fellow passenger had been among the 205 who perished.

No sooner were Murdo's feet solidly back on deck than a do-or-die plan for survival propelled him into action. While pondering his predicament, he happened to peer over the so-called lee side and, to his amazement, saw a bare segment of rock within jumping distance from the gunnel.

Murdo blinked furiously and stared again, making sure it was no mirage, and there it was, a dry crag, protruding out of the foamy maelstrom and fury of that black night as if beckoning him to leap, which he did. No one followed.

What happened next clearly explains why. Before regaining composure after an awkward landing on the *sgeir* (reef), a huge incoming swell literally picked Murdo off, and on the crest of which, he floated upward all the way onto safe and higher ground. Exhausted and soaking like doused sponge, Murdo managed to crawl, at snail's pace, still further up, reflecting, not on one, but the two miracles which were instrumental in saving his life.

The Ill-Fated *Iolaire*: Lost Neighbors

Two of my Skigersta *Baile Shuas* neighbors, Murdo Morrison and John MacDonald, were aboard the *Iolaire* on the terrible morning of 1919. Murdo survived; John perished. My young Eoropie first cousin, Angus Morrison, also perished; his remains were never found.

My uncle Roderick Morrison, married to my mother's sister, Gormelia, on Back Street, Habost, was drowned. Roderick's body was found stretched out on the beach intact with gloves, navy hat, including chin strap, shoes, and topcoat in proper place—as if prepared to step onto Cromwell Street. Still a great mystery.

Skipper Mason: Commander of the Ill-Fated *Iolaire*

Throughout all of Ness rumors were heard that skipper Mason was pro-German and that his body was wrapped in two life jackets. This was never confirmed, perhaps because the naval authorities padlocked all negative information concerning the *Iolaire*. Mason told Commander Walsh in Kyle that he could carry three thousand passengers with ease. As it turned out, he sailed with 284 souls with half his crew on shore leave on account of the fast approaching New Year's Eve—thus eliminating 50 percent of assistance in case of emergency.

Commander Mason's conversation with Commander Walsh in Kyle prior to getting underway on that awful New Year's Eve was indeed puzzling and contradictory. Walsh inquired of Mason about barometric pressures. "The barometer is on the rise," Captain Mason assured Walsh. "It appears that we're in for a good night—a happy New Year."

It was impossible for that barometer to indicate rising tendencies with threatening, overhanging precipitations already covering the two Minches from Skye to the Butt of Lewis. Cold sheets of sleety rain sporadically descended on both Minches shortly after he took bearing off Rona Head. British marine barometers were the best and most sensitive to atmospheric turbulence known to man at that point of time.

On the night of the disaster, Skipper Mason went below for the night, no lookouts on duty, with half a ship's crew, inadequate lifeboats and life vests, with his craft, teeming with human beings, sailing toward a difficult harbor entrance seven hundred yards wide with which he was totally unfamiliar. Surely this is the unpardonable sin of ship's captains since Solomon's navy in 1000 BC.

One would imagine that the blackness of a moonless night would have sufficed to keep him aloft. This dastardly behavior of a British naval master abandoning his bridge under such precarious, adverse conditions has to go down in record as the most gruesome maritime crime ever perpetrated in the glorious British navy, which at one time policed the seven seas.

Excerpts from *Call na h-Iolaire:* How We Fared

The night was dismal, anyhow, and it's rather hard for me to start describing anything about it. The sadness of the matter brings fear that someone will be hurt as regards what took place, renewing matters of the past, though in a sense not passed for some. How it happened is known to those who read the records; the night was somewhat wild. There was a big breeze in progress, and the closer we came to Stornoway, the worse it got.

When we arrived at the back of the Light, it was very bad, but rather clear, though dark and pouring rain with a big breeze of wind. We came in quite good until reaching close to the back of the light. The Light could be easily seen as we came in, but we were too far to the north. I'm certain we were, because the course wasn't right according to the compass which was in the stand on deck, which I read. She was a point more to the north than where she should have been.

However, I did notice that the vessel did not keep on the usual course which I ordinarily took between Kyle and Stornoway. With that, upon scanning for "Lights," I could see that "Mileid Light" showed on our stern bearing, instead of the vessel heading for Stornoway with Stornoway lights guiding us in. She came that way every step of the way, and as she kept coming up, she came closer to Rudha's coastline, where she shouldn't have been at all—so far east toward Rudha's terrain that we came upon a familiar land mark which we call "Lamb's Island."

When it was discovered that the vessel was so far off course, he came down along the Rudh's coastline, so close to that land that she was by no means above danger. We were not below at all…we weren't, and we weren't alarmed at anything. We were reasoning that the craft was moving along as it should, and we paid no attention to what could possibly befall us.

There were some, we thought, much better at making their way into the approaches of the anchorage than ourselves. The wind was high—south southwest I would say—while crossing directly on our port quarter. But that vessel was making a good night of it just the same, and we were as happy on board as could be. I did not see anyone showing any signs of drink from the time I went aboard until I abandoned ship. People so courteous, asking us to make ourselves as comfortable as possible, clean ship, and us laying around anywhere we preferred—inside the saloon, on the floor and chairs in every space around.

The night was now as dark as pitch with soft sleet of snow. We did not feel that the night was wild, though it was wild, because comfort was so great, a ship so fine from all angles, we had access to all her quarters in the first and second class area. I was on the stairway leading up to the officers' quarters. It was there that many of our men gathered—everyone that could find room in good shelter and good warmth.

I was standing at the —— and I assumed the Tiger was with me when a man from Lochs hailed us with "A happy new year to you" which we returned in kind. The man from Lochs said, "Isn't he taking her rather close?" and the Tiger said, "Perhaps they created a new entrance since we were here"—and no more was said. I said to Malcolm, "We are almost in," and we put our oilskins on as we sat up in the bow, ready to step ashore.

I turned toward him, whom I always teased, and said, "Oh, Malcolm, we are almost on the beach here." "Ach," says he (teasing right back), "you are of the Harris breed." We weren't aware of anything when suddenly the ship raucously went up on the crag. Until we felt the slide, it was something akin to my boyhood days ambling on ice. Our first reaction was that she struck a mine, but then we knew by the manner in which she fell on her side, like she was high and dry, that she indeed collided with the crags. Then she listed; she was steeply positioned on a very sharp angle. We just couldn't stand up at all—we couldn't.

She slithered herself up upon the rock and dried herself, and as soon as she lost buoyancy, she went on her side in that spot and much material fell out of her. In the self-same spot that she hit, she keeled over on her side to starboard, and most of those that were with me there on the deck at that time jumped into the sea. I believe that they expected her to go over completely.

Then I inquired of a man if he had any idea where we were, and he said that he did very well: "We are on the 'Beasts of Holm.'" I said to myself at that time, "We are on the rock. It's on the rocks that we undoubtedly are but with a good chance of getting off them." I experienced great comfort at that time. I was saying to myself that she wouldn't break because she was solidly on the rock. We were close, she wouldn't come apart at least till daybreak.

It wasn't very long until all my ponderings came to naught. I would say that she took a quarter of an hour in that position. As for me, I had no idea where I or she was until I happened to go up toward the bow, and a rocket was sent aloft. There I saw the "Beacon" and I was familiar enough with the Beacon, and I knew it was the "Beasts of Holm." With that, land wasn't far away, even though the elements were rough and the sea in a bad way. At that time, I saw the land.

She went upright, and her stern end began to swing inside. It was her bow that kept hold on the rock. In a period of time, she came in on her side until pounding herself against the rocks. As she pounded on there, the night began to get worse and wind velocity increasing and the waves coming from both stem and stern. When she hit against the rock, it appeared that our stomachs mixed with our skulls. Every bone in your body was rattled.

Then began the turmoil, and many things occurred then that's impossible for anyone to remember entirely how it happened; besides the night was rough and so dark that no one could see anything. Everyone was trying to do the best they could and knew how—and we don't know what did occur. Providence was behind those that survived anyhow.

I hadn't reached the high deck when she hit, and they were laying there on the high deck the best they knew how, as close to one another as possible, some on top of others in bunches and deep slumber. When she hit the door in front of us leading to the outside got jammed, which a lad shouldered, opening the door, and I got out to the high deck. Those that were sleeping around there and woke up got out, and those that didn't wake up, it is my belief that they remained right there.

Everything around went upside down, with no course except everyone for himself. I looked every which way and there was no sight of Malcolm as I made my way forward. I did not reach the bridge, but there was a life belt there; I took it with me and kept it. Life boats began to be lowered and the sea commenced to smash them—the life boats—alongside. They began to abandon the boats.

We went up onto the Bridge. It was full prior to our arrival, as much as the Bridge could hold, including the skipper. They were working on the "Verey lights" at that time, sending them aloft. At that time, we commenced to watch those that launched the boats. The boats started to break on the port side, so many were pouring into them. Then we started to lower some ropes from the ship itself, and the men that were in the sea grasped onto the ropes and most of them came back up on board.

Upon looking around, there was this man yelling and I lost touch with everything, except this man. "Here," I said, "take this," and I threw the life belt from me and took off everything I could, and stood on the rail where I could see the shore very clearly as the surf washed against it. I was thinking that I could make it somehow but couldn't do much in comparison with others.

I could swim some without any doubt and let myself go then. I made for the shore but was forced to turn back. The sea was tossing me, and I couldn't grasp on anything. I turned away with my face down, and when I reached the shore, I was stuck right there. (Ambiguous line) I was set to go down through the end of this alley way, but it was so crowded with men that I couldn't get through, and I felt the water rising which prompted me to jump over the side.

I jumped out with my gray coat and everything on me; it was a rubber coat. I was out there a brief spell and saw that she wasn't going over and I again returned. She was now heaving so much it was easy enough to grasp her. I again returned on board. I was afraid of the shore, afraid that it could be very bad. It was now everybody for himself, and we took to the riggings.

She was fitted out with double riggings, and some climbed as high as they could possibly go but were all forced to come down. We had to, as we couldn't hold our grip because of the swing of her masts. Those narrow masts, so slender that they appeared to be of steel. I also believe their interior was of steel.

When the ship sort of uprighted herself, we came down from the mast, at which time two boats were launched from the port side. The forward boat was bigger than the one on the stern quarter. O, I did not know what to do. I held on to a stay and braced myself for jumping into it, but as I could see the matter, the men were jumping totally unaware of what was going to happen; she could either topple or sink. Fortunately, I said to myself, "It's best that I stay where I am than go into that boat."

Suddenly, two huge swells—one from forward and one from the stern barreled in. When they hit the forward craft, she turned over, and I don't think that one soul survived from that boat. Also the after boat got smashed, being holed, and most of those that were in that one got back on board again. The two boats were filled up, and when the ship turned, upon leaving the crag and came head-on into the wind, those two boats were awash with sea and didn't stand the pressure. Everybody that was in those boats as far as I know was drowned—except perhaps one or two. *Sgeul.*

At first, there was a small boat lowered at the far end of the poop deck, and I went into that one; there were six of us. However, she was swamped by the sea and all came out of her. Then I again came toward the ship and grabbed the rope, one of the save-lines dangling from the davit. I tried to climb hand over hand up the ship's side, and it helped me a lot when the sea threw her to starboard.

In this manner, the sea lifted me as I tried to ease myself up on the rope, and I was getting up, but at last some weight came on one of my legs and I had no idea what the weight was. At that moment, a rocket went off, and I saw then two black objects down in the water and instantly knew that people were hanging onto me. I then tried to clear them off me with my other shoe and managed to get one off and was somewhat relieved. But I had a frightful struggle with the other fellow—a struggle indeed—as I felt as if the rope was slithering through my hands, but in one more supreme effort, I cleared him off also.

I then managed to climb another mite, and someone grabbed me by the chest who asked me to let go of the rope, but I wasn't willing to let go. Another man took hold of me, and they brought me aboard on the forward side of the davit. *Sgeul.* At that time, I looked out on the port side and I was thinking that no rescue was to be had from that quarter. I saw the *Sheila* going in the loch.

I returned and went down on starboard again, and a boat was lowered there. Her blocks were still fast and a moustached man was on her stern end. I was quite young then and assumed that wearing a moustache made him a *bodach*, and I asked him, "Can we go in?" "You cannot," he said. No sooner I had turned my back on that boat than she went down.

I went down to the stern end, and Angus Morrison, Borgh, yelled at me, "Take your coat off, John." It was only two days before we left Chatham that I received the coat and hated to part with it.

When I went over to the ship's gunnel, there was some jumping overboard, and much naval black cloth was visible in the sea caught up in the water. I saw one man which the sea failed to carry off three times but finally took him right down toward the propeller. Subsequently I assumed that such a sight marred the confidence of those aboard watching their mates being swept away. *Sgeul.*

I was then up at the bridge, and they were lowering this certain boat. Now, just as they had her at sea level, in the excitement, I sensed everything that was going to befall that boat when I went in—but too late. We knew that that boat was not going to stand the pounding. I was then up on the after fall and didn't let go. I had a grip on the rope and sensed the rush of sea coming, and I swung myself up, having all my weight on the rope and that sea rush smashed that boat into splinters against the hull. I learned that only the man at the forward fall survived.

But I got back up on deck in hand over hand effort on the falls. I said to myself when I got onboard that I wouldn't now move from her until she went down underneath my feet, seeing I survived from that boat. *Sgeul*. After the vessel came alongside the shore, myself and another lad belonging to my own village went into this boat which was water logged—one of the lifeboats. We let go of her painter so as to get ashore and climb up on the rocks.

The rocks weren't awesomely high, and when the boat reached in, she stopped on a boulder and the other lad shouted to me that she was grounded. I then went down toward her stern end and let myself out, but a huge swell came and carried us both toward the shore. The second wave carried me back out toward the boat and took the other lad clear out of the boat. He kept swimming around there until they dragged him aboard ship but was exhausted—and went down with the ship. *Sgeul*.

Somebody threw me down a rope and tied his own end, and I went back hand over hand onto the ship. The men were in panic, and no wonder that they were, many of which were asleep when the matter occurred. It came so fast on them, it's no wonder that they behaved in such a manner. There were many of them below deck that didn't get up when it all took place. There was much turmoil; yelling this and yelling that dominated the scene, everybody shouting and no rescue for them whatsoever—no rescue at all.

If it had been daytime, I'm certain the panic would have been frightening. But people couldn't see the awfulness of the danger they have gotten into—and when they did, it was too late, as regards what to do—as they lost themselves. But the darkness, the darkness. Now the sea was so ferocious that you couldn't hear a word—not one word could you hear. Everybody was on the move without knowing where to go, but they were on the move. They were on the move nonstop.

All the upheaval was in keeping with the situation. Everybody looking after himself with intention to assist others the best they could. Everybody on board got panic-stricken, and small wonder. Oh yes, and panicky, indeed. The place got so dark you couldn't see anything but white foam, and with so much terrible phosphorus coming across, one could scarcely open his eyes. The wind's velocity was constantly increasing, and at last I was hard-pressed to survive within her as the raging sea swept over her—prior to slipping away.

Note from the editor: The Gaelic writer Calum of this book didn't see fit to identify the survivors who contributed to the many sad experiences they were part of in the sinking of the *Iolaire*. Therefore, the following glaring contradictory account of no panic must refer entirely to the men gathered around the famous rope the means by which about forty men were rescued.

"There wasn't, there was no frenzy on board at all." Everybody was considering the situation at hand—to wit, that the only comfort in store for all was to get on that rope. Well, one here and there shouted and talked, but most of them conversed with one another about what took place—how sad it was occurring on such a wild and terribly dark night.

At first there was no terror at all. You wouldn't think anything of the amount of turmoil aboard when she struck—except when they emerged upon the high deck. Anyhow, before I left the vessel, her riggings were like birds on a tree. They were as high as they could get on the masts prior to my rescue. They were high in both masts and riggings.

I didn't see any of the officers all the time we were there except the captain, and I went up onto the bridge where he was and asked him if he'd be good enough to tell me if the tide was in ebb flow or coming in? I reasoned that if the sea was going out, we could possibly be saved providing that she could stay listed inward. He said to me that the tide was coming in—"Still coming in," he said. There were two life belts alongside of him on the bridge. I asked him for one of them, and he said to me, "Don't dare touch any of them." He had the revolver at the ready. He did not fire it—he just held it in his hand.

There was a man from Rudha with him on the bridge at that time known as *Ailidh Mò Ailidh Mòr* Alasdair Tailleir, but he went outside before I left the bridge. When I left the bridge, I again walked up toward the bow and a heap of sea struck me in the side of my head, knocking my cap overboard, leaving me dizzy. I saw one man, the fellow that fired the rockets, and he was quite close to me. They were strangers to me, everybody on board was, but this was one of the officers for sure, sporting a Hama coat and an officer's hat.

There was no order there whatsoever, just do as you see fit. Because there was no order coming from the bridge, command of any kind was impossible. I heard one command from the bridge urging everybody to move back aft and go atop a hatch back there, hoping that perhaps she'd come back off the rock.

Another time I heard, "Let go the starboard anchor." Those were the only orders I heard while aboard. It so happened that I thought of bringing the line in my bare hand, and I jumped off the stern end in an effort to reach shore but didn't expect the rock's approaches to be so severe. But when I first reached in the rock was above me, and the sea's surge brought me back out again. If I had pounded against the rock, I'd have had it.

Then, that surging of the sea brought me further out than I was at first, and when three big billows rolled in, I rode on the crest of the third one and stayed atop until it left me high on the rock surface where I first aimed at with my chest solidly on "terra firma." That's how I got ashore, having the line in my hand all the time.

Now, when I got up on there, and the sea gone down passed me, I sat there until four came ashore on that thin line, moving me to shout back that the line was too short and too narrow, could not be effective, advising them to tie the sturdy heavy rope onto it, which they did. The rest got ashore on that rope.

MacLeod took off with that rope. I used what sailors call an *orling spar* [Spar: a stout rounded usually wood or metal piece (such as a mast, boom, gaft or yard) used to support rigging.] because I was convinced that the weight of all the people on that rope would sure topple me without the support of that stick between my legs. The efforts of one man ashore with the rope was indeed meager, and I said to myself—my father was living then—and I had a small two-pound bag of tobacco on me, intended for the local *bodaich* which I put in my mouth.

In those days, my mouth and good teeth were intact. I got to the rope but slid down some, far enough to go under and I let go of the tobacco, and he was desperately trying to pull the slack to him. That is how I got ashore. It just so happened that I was favored with a brief lull on my way in. Like they say, one can find calm in raging seas. At other times, the ship was in and out with the sea rising on occasion much higher than ordinary.

I reached John and the men were struggling on the rope, and we kept pulling the slack as she listed inward. Well, there was no place where that rope could be made fast, but even if we did find a suitable rock protrusion to hold fast that line, it would have snapped to smithereens. The ship was in and out—absolutely unstable. But I did ask MacLeod, "Where are you from?" "I'm from Ness," he said. "Well," I said, "I'm also from Ness." "Who do you belong to?" he said. "I belong to *Tarmod Donn*." "I belong to Murdo MacLeod," he said.

The first man to come ashore on the line was John Murray from Bach, one who is called *Iain Help*. He was the very first one. I recall quite well when he first came ashore, the first one to make it. He threw both arms around my neck as I sat at my post. As soon as everybody made it to shore, they'd grab the rope to help those coming across, some that were utterly exhausted when they touched on the rock.

Fortunately for me, it happened that I was near where the rope was first served out. It was down near her stern end that it was first served, and I assume that I was about the fourteenth to get ashore at that time on the rope. There were also many who, when they witnessed some getting sprung off the rope, as she listed backward, that wouldn't venture forward, and there were also many away back of the action who would have tried to save themselves—no matter what.

I've seen two or three who were pummeled against the rock and fell dead into the sea. *Sgeul*. The rope couldn't stand the high spray, and they had to ease it off occasionally. It was under much pressure, and when I went on it, I recall that I grabbed it with my right hand and stretched out my left. When the sea's backlash came on me, it pounded my head against the hull. I distinctly remember that incident.

Well, that did me in and I was knocked cold. It seems that the next inrushing sea put me clear behind a crag that was there. Now, there were times that we were almost high and dry as the backwater dried out. In that situation, a goodly crowd survived, among those who were ashore. The ones who were up ran down and grabbed those who lay around, whether dead or alive.

At that time, I felt the sea filling me inside, and I think that dying of drowning is the easiest of all, like falling asleep. I wasn't aware of anything after that until I threw out all that saltwater when safely ashore. *Sgeul.* It was on that rope that I got ashore—miraculously—with plenty of danger to get onto it. There weren't many staying on that rope. The fast motion of the vessel dropped them off.

Fortunately for me, I happened to put the rope under my arms, and as the vessel listed outward in water's turbulence, it saved me until I was dragged ashore. *Sgeul.* While standing around there, she at last started to take in water along the stern end, and a fellow from my own village took the rope down to midship and made fast. He himself was the first one to venture on the newly fastened rope, and he also made it but is now deceased—Malcolm MacLeod atop the *Creagean* of our own village right here.

When the sea came in to rock level and happened on the rope (if your hands could stand it) and when the sea returned again, you were then hanging onto the bare rock and had to hang on until the next incoming sea lifted you higher. That is how matters were ashore. Those that were a little higher grabbed the hands of those below to drag them clear up from the sea. That is how everybody that got ashore from her made it.

There were many waiting to go on the rope but lost courage, obviously had second thoughts on the risky matter. There were many who didn't even try—many more than did try. *Sgeul.* I said to myself that rescue from the open sea was highly unlikely and might as well try the rope, but I didn't think of going except hand over hand.

I didn't put my feet on the rope at all. I was in oilskins and never thought of putting them off, and when I reached the center of the rope, the backwater sea caught me—it was going in when I went on, and the rope's rattling shook me off. When I fell, I heard one of the boys who held the rope ashore saying, "He is also finished." But anyhow I wasn't, but the buttons of my oilskin burst with all the sea that poured inside. It was as if my two arms were snapping asunder. I went across on that rope to land, and that's how I made it, but in crossing, exhausted lads hung right onto me until they also made it.

Well, after that incident, I lost trace on who was where or how they subsequently fared. Not too long after the disaster, I happened to attend a wedding, and this lad came to me and said, "Do you know me?" "No, I don't," I said. "Well," he said to me, "I'm the fellow that you helped up toward safety—asking me if I were secure enough." The young lad was from Tolsta and is now living in Inverness. *Sgeul.*

As a boy on the moor, there were many times that I jumped further, but the problem was what was going to seize you, even if you did jump. The raging sea was catching them in the manner that you'd see a stick in the mouth of a wave in foul weather. The wave would surge up and leave the stick high and dry, only to be swept completely away by the next wave.

Her stern end was now closer to the rock than her bow, and I imagined that when the sea receded I could leap from her bulwark to land. When the sea rose, it surged, you might say, halfway up, leaving part of the rock visible. You could see the rocks when the sea went out and thought it an easy matter to jump ashore. But all immediate environment was awesome.

There we were, with some coming ashore and some getting drowned. She started to drift farther out and still farther out. At last, the waves began to sweep completely over her, and when she poured outward, snatching the rope from our hands, I don't assume that one living soul escaped from her after that.

I was at the extreme forward prow, and when I saw her listing outwardly, I just threw myself over her forward railings and went straight down head first into the sea. The anchor's fluke gripped onto my pants, and my weight happened to rip my pants open, thus relieving me momentarily. I then really went into the sea, abounding with wreckage—a world full of everything imaginable.

In that strait, a board came into my hands. I estimated it to be four feet long, which for a brief spell kept my head above water. But then, a huge series of sea advanced. "Oh, I remember it—and will forever." The series of big waves came and toppled myself and board upside down, leaving me in the midst of it all. When my head got up from there, one of those lads struggling for survival grabbed me by the shoulders and took me down under. We both went down under. I cannot say how long we stayed under—it couldn't have been too awesomely long. But I got up at that time.

Following that episode, I wasn't aware of anything further until I found myself on the bare rock with the sea enhancing my upward progress. I was thinking that she would last till day time; that big ship wouldn't break up at least until daybreak. But it didn't take more than an hour until nothing was left of her except the two masts. *Sgeul*.

Well, as she moved out, a sea broke in on her at that time, sweeping everything in sight, every single thing. Oh, it was breaking up everything but anyhow I kept my grip though the waves went over me. I still hung on. No sooner I had a moment or two of respite and breathing again than another one came, carrying me away.

It carried me off the boat deck. She was then listing inwardly toward the rock. I have no recollection of where I was carried or anything. I don't remember a thing except the noise in my head and in my ears. Anyhow, when I surfaced again, somehow, someway a rope came into my hands, and I tugged on it and surfaced, finding myself at her stern mast. She was listing seaward now.

She was first listing toward shore and had just reversed herself, and I couldn't see anything above water except her masts and the tip of the bridge. The funnel was gone. I was thinking that her boilers exploded because you could see a flame on the sea's surface moving back and fore for a brief spell.

Then, everything came to a complete silence. I then took hold of her mast's stays and hoisted myself up. I went up a goodly space and another lad followed. I was up farther, and he was just a mite below me. The first raging sea that came carried the youngster away before I had a chance to say one word to him. He was wiped away, and I have no idea who he was.

Anyhow, I again worked myself up until at last I reached as far as the stay allowed. I was holding right on to the mast good and tight as the elements passed on. I couldn't see a living soul but eventually began to see two survivors on the riggings of the forward mast. "Yes, they were there." I would say that they were on there from two to three hours anyhow, up there just as I was. But a huge sea again came rushing in, and although the ship had sunk to the bottom, the onrushing sea raised her masts up some and the backlash lowered them down again.

This man grabbed onto the mast as it went down behind the swells, which came up in fury and broke the forward mast, wiping off the two men. That was the end of the forward mast, and it also tossed me off to a point where I hung on with one hand. But I managed to get back on again. It was then that my fears were increased more than ever. The breaking away of the forward mast got me to thinking that the end of my own wasn't far away.

It was about the only part left of her—but was intact when I was rescued. At that time, there wasn't a living soul around except myself. From there on till daybreak, I hadn't seen anybody. When a lull occurred, I warmed one hand and kept hold with the other.

I was in a sitting posture somehow, someway. I think I was sitting on some kind of ring, with my feet crossing around the mast, holding a stay in each hand. I would let go one in order to warm my other hand. Well, I was kept so busy anyhow that I wasn't severely cold though after coming up out of the sea. The cold didn't affect me at all. Anyhow, I don't think it did. "If it did, I thought nothing of it." *Sgeul.*

There I was, and no one to come to me and couldn't do a thing for myself. I was stretching on the rock with downward elbows pulling myself in attempt to escape any more sea. There is no telling how long I stayed there, but anyway I got up to the local protuberances where sheep shelters in winter. I was underneath that shelter but managed to get up staggering. I was falling and rising. When I got up atop the shelter, I saw a light a good space distant and was saying to myself, "Oh, don't put out that light yet, at least until I can strive hard to stagger my way through."

I started to shout with might and main. Well, two women came along—two women came straight toward me—as straight as anything. By that time I was bogged, with my left leg down deep in the mire and the other atop the ground with both arms also in the mire with the leg. The women found me in that condition and took me to the farmhouse. It was Young's son that showed the light. He lived in Tolm at that time, and we made for the house, encountering much boggish terrain. But somehow, some way we got there.

When we got to the house and entered, the good man of the house was already up. There were some that reached his home before we did and some that barely made it. They were vomiting saltwater and every sort of matter. He then took us with a lantern, those of us who could walk, and guided us to the main road. Some Stornoway men with lifesaving apparatus met us on the way.

There was hardly anything of the *Iolaire* showing at that time except the masts; everything had gone under. *Sgeul.* They were telling me that when they fired the rockets, they did fire a rocket or two from the bridge—the battery attendance thought they were celebrating the New Year, due at 12:00 o'clock. It was a man from the *Sheila* who had just pulled in that inquired if the *Iolaire* had arrived, which had left Kyle long before they did. It was then that they knew the damage was done.

Sgeul—man in mast. Before daylight, I could see a light over to my left—the Patrol. It came out of Stornoway keeping on the lee side of the loch. They could not approach the weather side at all—oh, they couldn't. Even though the life boat in service today was available, she could not have come near either—a night as wild as ever touches these parts I reckon, with great gusts of snow at that time.

Anyhow, the wind began to ease down, and a tug and trailer came out of Stornoway with two boats in tow. I knew that they were coming to look for me. They had just received a report from the patrol about spotting a man in the mast. It was the trailer's boat that first came close. They were coming quite close to where I was but were forced to turn back. They were almost wrecked, and I was considering myself safer than they were.

Then, another boat approached from the other side, and the sea was breaking outside of me. They were telling me that oil was poured on the sea at this juncture. Then, the tug's boat approached; she came right in with a two banded officer in charge who shouted, "Can you come down?" I was right at the top of the mast with a stay leading from there down to the ship's bow. I told him, "If you bring the boat between the mast and stay, I'll come down."

He did just that. He backed the boat between the mast and stay, and when I found her directly underneath me, I came down on the stay like a cat, landing promptly inside. They rowed away and nothing harmful caught up with us. We were out of danger in moments of time, and they took me aboard the tug.

Coming down the stay, I felt as strong as a warrior, but on reaching the tug, I couldn't climb aboard—I just couldn't. My energy deserted me on the spot, despite the grand feeling of relief and safety. Peace was declared; it was our last lap of the way.

My Father's Concluding Comments

My father translated the rest of the book, which I hope to make available at a later date. On page 106 of his manuscript, he concluded with these comments:

> The foreword relates, among other statistics, the gruesome experiences of those who survived the *Iolaire* disaster, as told in Gaelic to author Norman M. MacDonald, which I translated into English in Texas for the benefit of my children and grandchildren in October of 1982. This sad sea disaster was no ordinary maritime calamity, as the reader will soon gather in its contrasting views, actions and reactions of not only trained seafaring men but of all involved from the highest Brass to the lowly R.N.R. It reads as if Satan himself, evil author of all mischief, had designed the perfect confusing blueprint for mass destruction.

5

Lord Leverhulme

In 1918, Lord Leverhulme bought the island of Lewis and Harris. As the means for his wealth had been soap, it is no surprise that he was referred to by locals as *Bodach an t-Siabainn*, the soap man. Can't help but think that his supporters called him this affectionately and his detractors—not so much. His ambitious plans for the economic development of the island centered on the fishing industry. Developments would entail the improvement of harbors, not only Stornoway but also Skigersta with canning facilities, the building of bridges, roads, and railways. It is said that he spent £200,000 annually on his projects.

Leverhulme took over Lewis just as servicemen were returning from World War I, men who had been promised land for their services in the war. As it became obvious to them that land had been given to others in the Highlands, they pressed for the same on Lewis but met with the disapproval of Lord Leverhulme. He was opposed to it on the grounds that he needed certain lands to provide milk for an industrialized Stornoway and felt that if the people of Lewis could wait a decade, the new economic boom he would bring in would change attitudes to land and croft ownership.

The result of these different views was a series of confrontations, the forcible takeover of crofts by ex-servicemen raiders, Lord Leverhulme's suspension of operations until his specific conditions had been met, unemployment of his supporters and employees, and, ultimately, Leverhulme's total abandonment of operations in Lewis when no workable compromise could be reached. What a total, unhappy mess. This tragic mix involved men desperate for land, an impoverished people, ineffective government representatives, a benevolent proprietor with a vision at odds with active segments of his people, and a sad destiny for many young men—emigration the only option.

Donald MacDonald, in his book *Lewis. A History of the Island* (1978), sums up this tale by saying:

> Therefore, due to the actions of a few ex-servicemen, a very small percentage of the ex-servicemen in Lewis, the actions of the Scottish Office and the Board of Agriculture, combined with that of outside organizations which knew very little of the conditions prevailing in Lewis at that time, and the stubbornness of Lord Leverhulme to modify his plans, the schemes for a prosperous Island came to nothing, and the Islanders were left destitute. Inevitably, emigration followed.

My father was a supporter of Lord Leverhulme. His sister Margaret worked for the baron in his Stornoway Castle, and he worked as a young man on the building of the road to Tolsta. He believed that mischievous forces, political and social, had combined to bring the lord down. That reality led to the economic disaster of the Isles which in turn led to the need to emigrate. He was one of 860 men who left the isles in the combined emigrations of 1923–1924.

Following is a typed version of a forty-six-page manuscript entitled "Benevolent Baron." Unlike the text of the *Iolaire*, which was a translation, this is, I believe, my father's own composition. It provides a piece of the Leverhulme puzzle which is not well known—his plans for the development of Skigersta harbor. Of interest is what it does not contain, references to raiders taking over crofts and the unpleasantness of all that, nor any condemnation of the Baron for his land policies. Surely what we have here is not just my father's views on the matter, who was a young man when all this took place, but, I think, the views of his community of Skigerstonians.

Benevolent Baron

William Hesketh Leverhulme was born in Bolton, England, in 1851, son of a grocer, in whose warehouse young William first learned the benefit of putting duty and hard work ahead of pleasure. It was here that the keen-minded innovative youth pondered deeply about a certain commodity, mentioned early in scripture, Jeremiah 2:22: "For though thou wash thee with nitre and take thee much soap, yet thine iniquity is marked before me, saith the Lord God," which humanity as a whole could never survive without—soap, equal to water and sunshine. From this scrupulous deduction, the man's bounce, leaps, and strides into prominence, wealth, and power were sheer phenomena.

When he purchased our island home of Lewis and Harris in the Scottish Hebrides shortly before cessation of hostilities of the First World War, he was considered one of the world's few billionaires. It is not so very long ago since it was almost impossible to find soap manufactured in any country on the face of the globe without the name "Lever" appearing somewhere in the fine print. His associated companies worldwide amounted to 250 when he died in 1925.

No other philanthropist on record—with the possible exception of Scotland's Andrew Carnegie—has done so much for the uplifting and enlightenment of the poor and disadvantaged as this soft-spoken, meek, and modest English baron, also viscount and MP. The baron's happy "Port Sunlight" employees, most contented laboring human beings on earth, can readily attest to the foregoing evaluation of the man.

By way of rendering a mere glimpse into the man's character, let us consider that as far back as 1909 he was busy laying plans for—not even improving on his share the profits scheme but toying with what is known today as "Social Security." It was no secret among the industrial world of that era, of many manufacturing millionaires wishing that the baron would drop dead. How ironic that his enormous wealth, influence, and especially his generosity were actually his downfall among us—in the Hebrides of all places.

It just so happened that when Stornoway's elite first learned of the transaction by an English soap tycoon who magnanimously shared the profits of his vast world-wide enterprises and loved the poor, suspicion entered, followed by envy—cruel as the grave. They felt like trapped peons with no place to hide. To them, the baron's bizarre attitude and conduct were like unbalancing the very forces of nature—a weird and blatant abandonment of the sacrosanct "status quo," some form of lunacy.

Their own combined wealth would be regarded by the baron at that particular juncture of his fabulous career—mere pocket money. The devastating effects of inferiority complex gendered an inner desperation of rare ugliness, as it always does. Sound sleep was now hard to come by among Stornoway's "powers that be," as if hearing the eerie seismic sounds of an approaching earthquake prior to the big bang. In equatorial status, it was like lofty Mount Everest settling down alongside *Mùirneag* and *Beanntan Bharabhais*.

All of a sudden, they felt like indigent dwarfs but lo and behold were quite capable of acting like demons, which they promptly did with a sinister craftiness worthy of shameless Sicilian mobsters. It was now time to put panicky heads together among those leading bigwigs most likely to be immediately affected by the new regime, and play a coy wait and see game in which the baron from his new dignified headquarters in the castle settled down to bring us Lewis peasants out of the deep slough of poverty in which we miserably wallowed for generations.

The baron loved the castle of attractive medieval design and greatly admired its quiet surroundings and beautiful trees, flanking the edifice as if expressly purposed for the comfort and delight of former distinguished Gael occupants. One of our talented Lewis bagpipe musicians from Arnold was permanently lodged in the castle's gate house for the sole purpose of soothing his lordship into a happy Hebridean slumber. It was nothing unusual for the baron to close his eyes enjoying the lively military twirl of one of our Gael classics reaching back to the romantic days of Bonnie Prince Charles, to wit, "Carry the lad that was born to be king over the sea to Skye."

Hebrideans were shocked to learn that the rich baron slept in a roofless bedroom, in Lewis no less, occasionally severely subjected to one-hundred-mile-an-hour gales and dampish sheets of penetrating mists as common as *Buntàta is sgadan* (potatoes and herring). He insisted on sleeping in this manner atop the castle, staring up into the night sky as the bagpipe music twirled through the air. Baron Leverhulme was much too deep and sensible a man to be eccentric, like many of our silly modern millionaires who think that nutty behavior is the status symbol of true success.

When my sister Margaret, who worked for the baron all of the time he occupied the castle, explained to my mother about that roofless bedroom, she was so astounded that she dropped a Gaelic cliché which was laughingly bruited about Skigersta until I left on the *Marloch* in 1924. She said to Margaret, sadly shaking her head, "Oh! *an duine bochd beairteach*." (Oh, the poor rich man), obviously concluding in her own mind that one of the brightest men of our age was nonetheless a mite daft upstairs.

In no time at all, the presence of the busy baron was felt all the way from Ness to Tolsta, Harris and even to Stornoway, the baron's nemesis. The slumbering Hebridean giant had just felt the initial effect of the first sharp shot in the arm, as timely as one grabbed by the scruff of the neck on the way down for the third time. Our Skigersta Tolsta road project for example was an immediate success, and any normal individual, whether able bodied or not, who wished to toil, could just throw the old spade on his shoulders and go to work.

There was no stuffy *panjandrum* snob reeking with self-importance and red tape in charge of hiring headquarters for the Skigersta Tolsta road of long ago. On the contrary, those in charge of personnel departments were specifically instructed by their humble billionaire boss to avoid silly strictures or any badgering of these hardy fishermen when applying for a job. How typical of the man!

It was common knowledge that in every project he ever owned or supervised since coming into prominence was a special consideration for those who toil, along with the underprivileged and unlearned. "Blessed are the merciful, for they shall obtain mercy." When we consider how contrasting this humane individual was to the modern, pompous employment managers of our own tumultuous times, we thank the Almighty that at least we can tenderly reflect on one warm industrial giant in a cold competitive world.

I shall now insert an excerpt from a piece that I wrote about those delightful days in Skigersta, written so long ago that I even forget the year. It is ancient and under the caption of "memories, memories." It is also a nostalgic reminder of how a lowly fishing village of the windswept Hebrides utterly captivated the affections of one of the greatest figures of our age—the Honorable Baron Leverhulme, Viscount and MP.

> Our fishing village of Skigersta, population 280, experienced the happiest and most buoyant period of its long existence during the prosperous Lord Leverhulme days. Actually our current posture of that brief spell was wonderful enough to make one think if such a grand euphoric situation wasn't just a mite too joyous to last.
>
> During that period, every Skigersta male from their late teens to the aged who wished to work was employed with a steady weekly wage arriving as regular as the incoming North Sea tides. The week's laboring chores at the Skigersta Tolsta road, which weren't by any means too rigorous to endure, did something grand to the village's crofter fishermen of that enjoyable era. Their self-respect was shored up afresh in manly, competitive, healthy outdoor labor building a supposedly MacAdams roadway link to Stornoway.
>
> This bleak eight-mile gap of moorland between Skigersta and Tolsta, which the baron wished to join in order to have a complete round

the Island roadway, is still a stretch of heathery wastes awaiting to be joined. The broken down borderline of Skigersta's finished mile to *Allt a' Mhaide* is still showing, and the road itself unusable to this day. A bit of the occult enters into this unfinished Skigersta Tolsta road. That curious prediction by one of our Hebridean mystics of long ago concerning that particular roadless gap is still recalled by old-timers. This so-called seer stated that he wouldn't want to be alive when this particular gap of moorland was joined by the "King's Highway." So there it is, a bleak eight miles still awaiting prophecy.

To link ourselves with Stornoway, our modest metropolis and headquarters of our distinguished benevolent benefactor, the Honorable Baron Leverhulme, was another stimulating incentive for us to keep busy on that road; in short, we were having fun. On Saturday evening *cèilidhean*, cozily relaxing around a blazing *teine meadhan an làir* peat fire, and the week's chores at an end, we Skigersta laboring folks of the Leverhulme days considered ourselves the happiest and most secure individuals on the face of the globe.

After all, wasn't the goose that laid the golden eggs now nesting atop our castle walls? Our biggest danger at this sensitive point of our prosperity was what ruined the foolish farmer of the parable—such was our confidence. Also enhancing our self-assurance at this time was the happy fact that three of our gaffers at the road were fellow Skigersta residents. They were Alex Morrison, *Lathamor*, who held the distinction of being one of the most single-minded, upright men of our time, and my own cousin Angus Murray, later of the Glasgow police, who also held the distinction of being the youngest gaffer in the entire Hebridean chain of the baron's progressive plans. To my own personal delight, my good-natured next-door neighbor Donald Mackenzie, *Pauil*, was also a gaffer and held the distinction of being the only Canadian on the Skigersta Tolsta road project.

Now, when we carefully consider this happy ideal situation, which undoubtedly it was, it is impossible to cease from deeply pondering if perfect security, like pride, comes before a fall. From what subsequently transpired as the following narrative indicates, it strongly appears that it works both ways. For example, just when our own anticipations and dreams were way up at zenith high, the heavy stroke of the mighty Leverhulme pen brought our blue Skigersta sky crashing down about our ears in the official announcement that all the baron's enterprises in Lewis were shutting down—finished forever.

Fortunately, Harris was spared, a blessing for which spunky brave Harrismen are grateful to this day. They not only showed more courage than us Lewis folks but also more savvy. Our benevolent baron was rudely rejected, harassed, and double-crossed by zealous Stornoway bureaucrats right out of our economic lives and right under our noses. Furthermore, and by way of adding insult to infamy, they ignominiously utilized the island's malcontents and "ne'er-do-wells" to do their dirty work, by hurling the fabled monkey wrench into the very heart of every progressive plan the baron came up with—and they were many.

The shocking and supine reaction to this dire disaster and insult by gallant Gaels, considered the bravest in battle, with the exception of American Marines in the whole world, are still greatly puzzling experts in human behavior. These scholarly individuals who minutely explain away the root causes of earth-shaking events are still scratching their heads, appalled at the cowardice of so-called Lewis stalwarts of storybook heroics.

They reflect on how incredible it is that descendants of proud clansmen who drew swords at the mere disapproving glare of an adversary could calmly accept such abject humiliation in mute silence. What did we renowned and legendary kilted warriors do to stave off poverty and modify an insidious insult? We just silently stood there, immobile, open-mouthed, and wide-eyed like common idiots—worse yet, hammily imitating craven cowards.

If such sleazy skullduggery had occurred in places like Iran or Iraq, Cromwell Street would have been violently razed to the ground. But we are a civilized, compassionate Christian people, someone proclaims. That indeed we are, and should be grateful, but if we scrupulously search the scriptures, we discover that God, under certain circumstances, appears to abhor cowardice on the same level of revulsion as any other ordinary sin.

We Lewismen sinned a big one, perhaps the unpardonable one, when we slovenly let the Baron Leverhulme slip through our fingers. Painful as it is to confess, reminisce, and accuse, it must be recorded here and now that it was on account of this uncharacteristic inertia and appalling apathy on the part of otherwise steadfast men our lovely Lewis moors, hills, and valleys, meadows, dales, and crofts are to this day sadly bemoaning the desolate vacuum and absence of that whole youthful generation, then in their late teens and early twenties.

Consequently and subsequently, we were all scattered to the four corners of the earth in the "Second Highland Clearing" of 1923–1924. However, in drastic contrast to the drag 'em and pull 'em down violent "First Highland Clearing"—a roguish raping for which jolly Johnny Bull never even apologized for to this day—our Second Clearing was done in style: three luxurious ocean-going liners wiped the slate clean. How subtle can you get?

The cagey British had now become smooth, mild-mannered experts in an area in which they excelled for centuries—transplanting human beings by the boat load. It is interesting to note how unsavory international publicity over the First Clearing forced brazen Johnny B. into mending his ways. He was now a gentleman: his most devastating role.

Our beautiful heathery Hebrides where I was born and abandoned amid poverty and despair in 1924 due to cowardice and corruption is a delightful chain of islands on the northwest corner of Scotland, divided from the mainland by the two Minches—famed fishing grounds before our time. Land mass of the Hebrides consists of 2,900 square miles from the Butt to Barra Head. Its population of crofter fishermen is about sixty thousand whereas the population of Lewis and Harris, northern region of the Hebrides bought by the baron, is in the neighborhood of thirty thousand.

To the historian, a few important items are still extant concerning our beloved windswept island home, which our many gifted Gaelic bards loved to extol. For example, Bonnie Prince Charles, on one of his many retreats, landed on a remote island in the southern Hebrides with £30,000 on his handsome head by stinking Billy Cumberland, fiendish royal son of George II. Charles was ferried across the Minch by the spunky Flora MacDonald, right under the redcoats' noses.

It just so happened that while touring our rugged island coastline shortly after his arrival in the castle, that our small Skigersta harbor caught the baron's fancy, a fact he immediately made known to his subordinates. It seems that he was so impressed with the natural, close, compact layout of our harbor entrance, he revealed something to his aides which startled not only them but shocked all those who later got wind of the matter, including Stornoway's town fathers already in quandary.

He was in fact seriously planning to build us Skigersta folks a modern harbor elaborate enough to accommodate ocean-going craft and dredge our Gil far into the pasture for wharfs, slips, and piers. Only a man of the baron's superb visionary capabilities could have even dreamt of such a colossal undertaking. But he could, and meant it, to the great concern of his financial advisors. It became quite obvious to those around him that the rugged, wild comeliness, and natural layout of our Skigersta bay strongly appealed to the baron shortly after purchasing the island from Mr. Matheson.

At that time, a story made the rounds that one of the baron's close advisors cautioned him that his grandiose plan regarding the Skigersta bay, if implemented, would cost him reams of pounds sterling. The baron, a fiercely independent man, allegedly retorted sharply that money could never be equated with beauty of such grandeur as the comely Skigersta bay. Many rich men desire to build mightily as a crowning glory to fabulous careers as lasting monuments to grand achievements.

The fabulous Baron Leverhulme was just that fabulous kind of fabulous individual. At this advanced point of his career, he had in fact to belabor the old cliché "money to burn," so much that he appeared to have had lost all interest in accumulating any more, especially now with the dreaded "three score and ten" looming in the shadows, and his favorite Scottish philanthropist and counterpart sixteen years his senior sadly showing signs of decline.

That the baron was seriously planning to transform our Skigersta bay into a showpiece of maritime elegance was firmly believed by most of our leading mentors of that generation. Those that really knew the aggressive background of the solid *Sasannach* were fully convinced that he meant to put our lowly but lovely fishing village of Skigersta on the map.

Be that as it may, rumors, truths, or half-truths notwithstanding, the mere vision of the matter sure raised havoc with our emotions, especially with us youngsters in our late teens who swiftly went sailing on cloud nine loaded down with hopes, anticipations, and dreams in a happy-go-lucky voyage into what turned out to be an elusive never, never land. It was brief, exhilarating, and even exotic, but oh how grand while it lasted—something akin to a beautiful dream, which at its most joyous moments suddenly and sadly fades into the mists of memory.

As regards our Skigersta bay, it was suggested later by our qualified engineers and lighthouse experts, one of which was Robert Louis Stevenson's father in his day, that the baron's plan was to erect two high mammoth storm bulwarks, parapets, extending at appropriate angles from the two eastern extremities of the harbor entrance, right into the teeth of the elements. In view of the severity of our northeastern waves and winds, in which thirty to forty foot waves are commonplace, this initial barrier, presumably of rock and concrete combine, expenditure wise, boggled the mind of frugal Scottish engineers.

In their view, it was reasonable enough to assume that a cool billion-pound sterling would be swallowed upright in this bulwark, just for a starter. Obviously, the two crucial points of bulwark foundations the baron had in mind were *Leac-Cousgair* on the south shallows of our harbor entrance, historical site of the sailing ship *Dùn Alasdair's* disastrous shipwreck of long ago, an exciting episode about which my talented next-door neighbor the famed Skigersta Bard composed his first *òran* masterpiece.

Apparently his northern foundation was to be solidly founded at the rocky base underneath Murdo Mackenzie's property, the *àird* area, slanting out into the mouth of the Minch for sufficient safety, the length of which was not divulged. This massive seawall would have to endure the ferocity of one of the wildest corners of the Seven Seas, the *Leac-Cousgair* breakwater, with an appropriate slant of its own, stretching straight toward northeast, leaving a calm entrance facing southeast, thus eliminating the dreaded unloved easterly breezes—*Gaoth an ear*—which so frequently kept our Skigersta *sgothan* in bay for days on end.

It would also leave the nostalgic *Cragichean*, our rugged and favorite boulder, unmercifully pounded by winter storms since Creation in calm lee waters forevermore. When the Baron Leverhulme, our unassuming billionaire benefactor, unexpectedly visited our Skigersta quay for the first time, it was truly an event of epochal proportion. So sudden was the first of three visits that the goodly crowd, including many *bodaich* who loitered around the old winch, felt moments of numbness, as if overawed in the presence of the man of gold. It was as if some prized curiosity had swiftly swooped down from out of space.

Of course being constantly bombarded by the rumors of an alleged new harbor increased our enthusiasm to a boiling point. Besides, no one in that crowd was that close to a real rich man before, and our weird nervous reactions to his presence must have bemused the cultured gentleman. But as a man of breeding, he remained almost as silent as the slip on which he stood.

However, we restless teenagers just couldn't resist gaping at the man, though gaping was strictly forbidden as utterly vulgar behavior by our rigid Free Presbyterian parents of those unsettled times. Moreover, so dismally ignorant of monetary matters were we at that daft age, we kept staring at the baron's pockets as if anticipating the pounds, shillings, and pence to pour out of him at any moment. We actually assumed that most millionaires lugged their profits in pockets as they moved along.

Though the baron remained silent most of the time, we took particular notice of how he minutely scanned the entire harbor and environs, all the way from the *Cadha* to the *àird*, *Lòn-gorm* to the *Seòlas*, the Gil to *Geodha nan Cnàmh*. Nothing of consequence seemed to escape those lively, expressive eyes. His interpreter, a fellow Gael, and unlike his boss talked a blue steak with the *bodaich* while exchanging dialogue into his lordship's ears so full of fancy semantics that the gist of his rapid-fire, nonstop chatter was going completely over our heads.

Right off suspicion permeated through us as regards this talkative scholarly linguist. We were concerned that he was somehow, someway attempting to persuade his boss against investing a mere pound sterling on the place. That current from rags to riches rumor—now getting more prevalent from *cagailte* to *cagailte*—was getting to us in a big way. The jolly idea of competing with snobbish Stornoway in luring maritime trade to our brand-new modern seaport at the busy mouth of the Minch, turning corrupt Cromwell Street into a veritable *fàsach* (desert) greatly appealed to us youngsters at that particular point of time.

Nasty news trickles of unrest between them and our benefactor were reaching us from day to day, and the gloomy climate strongly indicative of a brewing storm was increasing by the hour. Nonetheless, no one could tell of any disturbance bothering the calm baron that day as he bid us a happy arm-waving good-bye from his beautiful brown shiny sports car—smiling broadly at one and all. The usual letdown after excitement prevailed when the baron departed, as we all sat around the old winch in small groups staring into the placid *Lòn Gorm*—silent and exhausted.

Baron's second visit: That Lord Leverhulme was profoundly impressed by our Skigersta bay on his second visit was quite obvious to all of us—who again were caught somewhat by surprise. It must be admitted, even by the most biased, that our small Skigersta bay is indeed of rare rugged beauty, which even littoral artists greatly appreciate.

Such calm days without a ripple showing from *Leac-Cousgair* to the *Lòn Gorm* could easily remind a world traveler like the baron of dreamy faraway places which he and his lovely Lady Leverhulme so frequently enjoyed. Except for the concrete quay and parapet, nostalgic reminder of mason *Dòmhnall Weir*'s handiwork, the natural wholesome quality of our Skigersta harbor was intact since creation, as our distinguished guest astutely scanned every boulder and crevice.

His keen interest was quite evident in the searching expressions of his calm countenance, occasionally nudging his interpreter and pointing out a certain spot which arrested his attention. That poignant urge of "I can hardly wait" exuding out of him was manifest to all, so graphic we could almost taste it. Also on this propitious day, the green vale of the Skigersta *Gil*, designated by the baron for huge dredging diggings, was a tranquil dale of soft rural loveliness, winding its way past *Taigh Eithig* coming down through the village pasture from its meager confluence of the southwestern moorlands.

Its sloping green banks, gently sweeping into the valley bed, were virtually blanketed with dazzling daisies of fragrance and beauty on both declivities all the way from the old *Taighean Sailidh* to *Lios Dhòmhnaill Tharmoid*. Some contented cows leisurely grazing along its green banks enhanced its pastoral loveliness. The *Gil* itself, a mere *sruthean* (small stream) in dry weather but a roaring river in winter storms, languidly murmured along on this delightful day toward the *cladach* to expend onto the pebbly beach and into the bay.

Luckily for us, *Dànaidh* Mackay, always in command of fluent English and refined manners, was available that day for exchanging some dialogue that made sense to us impatient youngsters, weary of that interpreter, a man of a million words. *Dànaidh* explained to the baron about certain spots in which he seemed to be most interested, such as the crumbling *Taighean Saillidh*, now dormant and in shambles, along with *Taigh Eithig*, the lone house on the *Gil*'s crest, which somehow caught the baron's fancy.

It is quite possible that as a shrewd businessman, the uprooting of this one home, *Taigh Eithig*, the lone house on the entire *Gil*, would stand in the path of his colossal dredging plans. He was aware of the tedious, long drawn out legal complications that could emerge in the Crown Courts of the land. Even *Dànaidh*, with higher than average IQ, was puzzled, shaking his head and wondering as to why should a man of such enormous wealth and power be so curious about one lowly squatter's home on less than an acre of soil.

Eithig herself, widely known as *Eithig Aonghais Ghuinne*, a pious, hardworking widow, was in good physical condition at the time and her only son Angus employed by the baron. If things had gone well, Effie would have most assuredly lost her home but in return gain five fortunes. Meanwhile, most laymen throughout the universe keep wondering if there are any obstacles anywhere in this whole world capable of standing in the way of an innovative billionaire, viscount, baron, and member of Parliament. Herein lies power and prestige, hard to hinder or subdue. Be astounded and learn how a weak cluster of crude, illiterate Lewis crofters, sophisticatedly instructed by miserable merchants met power head on.

The baron's interpreter continued explaining away to his boss about matters here and there, so complex that only *Dànaidh* could understand. We again got nervous that the loquacious scholar, though a fellow Gael, wasn't exactly rowing on our side.

Again, suspicion mounted, and when a group of prying Free Presbyterians gets edgy, that old maxim of *far am bi ceò bithidh teine* (where there's smoke, there's fire) gets into play, infusing their natural mystic talents into discerning trouble looming in the distance. For example, shortly before the turn of the century, they, almost en masse, became the gazing stock and oddballs of the whole Ness community when they scrupulously sensed heretical encroaching mischief in ecclesiastical high places and from which they wisely and promptly separated themselves forevermore.

It was shortly after the baron's second visit to our Skigersta quay that we learned to our sorrow about the incredible fact that long before this great man had crossed the Minch to commence his progressive schemes, nobly aiming at rescuing us from perennial poverty, unsavory rumors concerning his character ran rampant. Lewis gossip is not only the swiftest media system on earth but also the most thorough.

Few *Cagailtean* are immune from its devastating impact and sleaze from the babe to the *bodach*. The more deadly the gossip, the faster it travels; the more unsavory, the sweeter it sounds. We are born gossipmongers. Even to this day, well over half a century later, the few surviving Lewismen of the Leverhulme days are still puzzled as to how and where was that vicious and damaging diatribe concerning a gentleman of the baron's sterling character hatched in the first place.

The outlandish innuendoes were that the baron was overbearingly domineering, to the point of tyranny. A more distorted image of this meek, unpretentious man couldn't have been depicted but by Satan himself, archdemon of all wickedness and father of the lie. Subsequently, however, the pieces began to fall into the puzzle one by one until the moment of truth awesomely and clearly dawned on all of those interested in justice and fair play.

It had been established by reliable sources, of neutral stance, that leading rebels throughout Scotland and Ireland got timely words to Stornoway's business key figures with axes to grind, warning them of the grave problems an arrogant billionaire *Sasannach* could create for rural, naïve illiterate Hebridean crofters. From this small cloud, first the size of a man's hand, came the flood.

Immediately, evil whispers were disseminated among the vulnerable, unlearned masses about how this powerful Englishman, an experimenting fanatic, would eventually deprive crofters of the rights to own an acre of soil. The well-trained tale bearers even had the gall to suggest that as a member of parliament, he could negotiate the Crown's untouchable Crofters Act into shambles. This devastating propaganda weapon took on deadly overtones for the baron's progressive plans as regards our island home. It was instantly effective, lethal, malicious, and triumphant. Cold, stark fear swiftly inundated the land all the way from the Butt to Harris.

Their crofts mean everything to Hebrideans; their very lives depended on them back in those days—vital as water, breathing, and sunshine: an insurmountable barrier that even a billionaire could never hope to override. It was now obvious to all and sundry that Stornoway's evil geniuses made a "bulls-eye"—straight from the demon's den.

The shrewd and calculating Stornoway evil fathers found the jugular and knew it, an occasion for which they ardently celebrated in grand style. All of Cromwell Street was agog with glee in discovering the very instrument by which a towering giant could be floored forevermore. Another spate of negative innuendoes were now widely and wildly afoot among a people well versed in the cruel history of the first and infamous Highland Clearing by callous English lords who ruthlessly raped our land to confiscate our salmon and grouse—unashamedly as of this day.

Therefore, it goes without saying that the cards were stacked against this marvelous man even before the ink was dry on his ownership documents. As a matter of record, Lord Leverhulme was no *Sasannach* per se. He was a humble, compassionate Jewish gentleman about whom the scripture declares: "Blessed are the meek, for they shall inherit the earth." Real Jewish people, on account of their being chosen of God as his own precious people from among all the nations under heaven do not consider themselves anyone else but Jews, no matter where or when born.

Marvel not at this gross and gruesome gentile because these people were the "apple of God's eye," carried on eagle's wings, and fed by food of angels, by whom came Christ who is over all—God Blessed Forever, Amen.

Now that the beastly bureaucrats had skillfully acquired for themselves an unbeatable propaganda weapon, they quickly added more sinister punch to their arsenal by using the island's "ne'er do wells" for harassing and embarrassing the baron's progressive plans all the way from the Butt to Harris. Slow retreat here and there, along with a marked defensive posture, was now beginning to show in the baron's behavior—a dismal stance which in all likelihood the great man had never before experienced in his entire illustrious career. It was also one that he most assuredly would not tolerate.

It was also a factor on which his sharp Stornoway foes staked all and hit the jackpot. From that point on, it became quite obvious to all that the patient baron was having second thoughts of ever rescuing us from the counterproductive apathy which overwhelmed us at that time. We became hopelessly divided, another factor which greatly enhanced the cause of his enemies. It saddens me to record it was during this gloomy climate that the baron paid his third and last visit to our Skigersta quay, and though uncertainty abounded on all sides, his appearance was almost as exciting as his first.

As in former visits, the baron just calmly stood beside his interpreter minutely scanning the harbor scene with the shrewd gaze of the trained tycoon. Again, as in former Lord Leverhulme visits, *Dànaidh* Mackay, with intrinsic diplomatic flair and calm approach, was communicating, while Murdo MacDonald, *Lathamor*, a man of depth and keen grasp on local consequential causes, elucidated in Gaelic to the baron's interpreter—a boring babbler to us teenagers.

One strange aspect of the baron's visit on that day which greatly baffled us was the happy fact that he never showed up in winter months, when the bay was frequently subjected to lengthy high waves in frothy fury crashing across the whole entrance, one behind the other. In fact, his absence during severe winter storms greatly encouraged us—accepting it as a good omen. It became quite obvious that we were in fact leaping for straws, with no other visible object available to keep our heads above water.

It just so happened that about this phase of matters concerning the baron's enterprises, more dark bits of nasty negative news began to reach us about some sharp unpleasant verbal disagreements erupting between the baron and his Stornoway antagonists. Deep underlying worries began to rumble within us as regards the fearful prospect of the independent baron abruptly pulling up stakes and leaving us to our own devices—poverty.

I had just obtained my first promotion at the road project, and one for which my good neighbor, gaffer Donald, must receive credit. He placed me in as a helper to his brother-in-law *Tarmod a' Bhàird* in the big shed which housed the cable winch that dragged the Bogey wagons uphill from the gravel pit down below. Neighbor Norman, also with higher than average IQ, learned how to operate that winch like a veteran machinist.

Duke Bhery, Port—a born wit—who was the lively sprag man of the wagons, kept everybody amused. *Seonaidh Dhòmhnaill a' Choire*, a fine gentleman from Knockard, used to drop around occasionally just to hear the duke's hilarious remarks about the easygoing old *bodaich* working the road. One frustrated young gaffer asked a certain immovable old *bodach* if it was on account of the plank attached to his back that he was unable to bend down? No gaffer ever dared to complain to the office about the slow *bodach* in fear of Mr. Leverhulme's great consideration for the elderly.

I can still recall quite vividly one particular sad incident regarding the baron's woes which occurred at this time, even though I'm writing this piece deep in the east of Texas, sixty-four years after the *Marloch* migration of 1924 (1988). I relate the matter for the sole purpose of making those interested in reading about the benevolent baron fully realize how much he meant to us in Skigersta of long ago.

It concerns *Dànaidh's* younger brother, Norman MacKay, a sailor crony of my brother Donald who had just arrived from Stornoway with the startling news that the rebel Irish with whom we never quarreled, our own Celtic cronies, had recently informed the Baron's enemies in Stornoway of their full support—logistic or otherwise—in ousting the ambitious land grabbing rich *Sasannach* immediately from Hebridean soil.

Never will I forget Norman's depressive visit to see my brother Donald on that dismal day of long, long ago. He walked straight up toward our door through the bare crofts of early spring with the slow monotonous gait of a man burdened down with anxiety. We both watched him as he ambled uphill toward us, and the moment he stepped onto the road my brother pointedly asked him the obvious, "Norman, have you got bad news?" "That I have, Donald," was the gloomy reply, "news that will probably affect the happy lives of many Skigersta residents forevermore."

"The brutal fact is that the baron is losing his grip," Norman continued, "and the restless Irish—brave and skilled in local uprisings—have just offered all-out assistance to thwart every progressive plan on the baron's drawing board. Their strategy is to reinforce the local malcontents which the opposition utilizes to harass all of the baron's schemes—from the Butt to Harris, shaking his confidence probably for the very first time in his life."

We heavily walked inside and sat down by our old *teine meadhan an làir*, being joined by my sister Annie and Millie who sensed at a glance by our downcast expressions that woeful tidings were in the air. As Norman outlined the uneven struggle between the baron and crafty Stornoway merchants, our small party huddling around the peat fire took on the melancholy appearance of a somber 3:00 a.m. wake sadly bemoaning a parted pal.

We quickly sensed that the end of our prosperity and even security was much closer at hand than we dared to ponder. We were all certain of one thing, however, and that is that the powerful baron would not be humiliated—he just wasn't that kind of man. For what reason would this great man engage in dirty dogfights with corrupt Cromwell Street pipsqueaks, none of which was even a bonafide millionaire, though loudly tooting themselves as such, for obvious reasons.

At that particular point of the baron's career, Lord Leverhulme could buy and sell the whole pack of retail rascals ten times over and still remain a billionaire. All of their grief centered on this one factor. His enormous power and wealth were driving them bananas. However, it is highly unfair to include all of Stornoway's businessmen in this dark disorder. There were, for example, the big *Uigeach* and the *Tìr Mòr* gentleman, along with merchant William MacLeod "Canadian," formerly of Back and *Tarmod Bàn*, formerly of Carloway—four staunch and devout Free Presbyterians who would sooner part with a limb than participate in mischief.

There were also at this time two revered ministers of the Gospel preaching in Stornoway: Rev. Neil MacIntyre, FP, and his equally pious Rev. Cameron, FC—known as *Camaranach Steòrnabhaigh*. Both *Dànaidh* and the Baron were well aware of the Stornoway setbacks that day on the baron's last visit to our shores. They both kept their cool, however, probably because they shared much in common—calm and cool by nature.

Whether the baron was sufficiently impressed at this point regarding the construction of a modern seaport in our Skigersta bay, a project which he most assuredly was determined to accomplish, shall never be satisfactorily known to us in view of his last and sad visit to our quay. People of his breeding have their own way of concealing emotions, and the baron didn't show any signs of enthusiasm—or lack of same—as he waved a last cheerful farewell to a group of eager *bodaich* and teenagers who steadily watched him taking off in a shiny sports car, fit for the king of England.

Shortly after the baron's final scrutiny of our beautiful Skigersta bay, this great Jewish gentleman was rudely coerced by jealous, corrupt creatures in high places to abandon all his busy enterprises and future progressive plans throughout our island home, and into which he had already sunk a big fat bundle of pounds sterling. This obvious monetary loss on the baron's part greatly elated his enemies by way of adding insult to injury, or, as medical experts would evaluate matters, something akin to the sick sadist enjoying the torments of his lash.

It is futile to compare this Lewis loss in Lord Leverhulme abandoning us to our own stupidity, cowardice, and poverty to any of our other disasters, because there weren't any. Not even the *Iolaire* and Great Drowning could be compared to this terrible tragedy in sadness, hopelessness, and despair. Nearly a whole generation of strapping Lewis youngsters, ranging in ages from their late teens to early twenties, was lost to Lewis forevermore. It was without a shadow of a doubt our darkest day.

It must be noted that Stornoway itself, population four thousand at the turn of the century, was teaming with hardworking folks of common honesty, most of whom were embarrassed at the Leverhulme debacle of those unhappy days. Its meager beginning reaches back to the reign of King James VI, when Stornoway was only a scattering of small dilapidated-looking grocery and retail shops along Cromwell Street and their great hero Oliver making himself obnoxious bullying and bossing neighbors as a tumultuous tyke of five years old when James came to the throne.

It has now become quite clear to anyone wishing to read my history of the baron's tribulation among us that my young generation became the deplorable victims of envy, greed, fear, and cowardice, concentrated evils of sufficient devilish density to cause our scattering to the four corners of the earth. "The evil that men do lives after them" (Shakespeare).

Now, it was also quite obvious, or as we say, stands to reason, that the impending economic repercussions of the benevolent baron leaving us to our own devices was bound to make waves and arouse interest throughout the land, which of course immediately occurred, rumbling all the way to the British Parliament. Even though badly suffering from blunted claws and minus a couple of front teeth from the severe pummeling received in the First World War, the British lion was still sharp, adroit and coldly practical—as of yore.

In quickly sensing that dangerous pockets of unrest would most assuredly mushroom throughout the Hebrides when confronted with hunger and despair in the wake of the baron's disastrous departure, the lion—in typical demeanor—stirred and snarled. Freshly demobilized, hardened Hebridean veterans, bitter survivors of a four-year abyss of abuse and terror in what General Sherman called "hell," were in no mood to twiddle their thumbs and starve after rescuing the so-called king of beasts from being mauled to death by the heinous Hun.

Who else turned the tide of the First World War 1914–1918 except our kilted Gael warriors—mostly Hebrideans—who stopped cold the on-rushing German hordes thirty miles outside of Paris when the demoralized, disorganized, retreat-prone French army miserably failed to protect their own capital? It was here that the horrid Hun first learned of the fierce ferocity of the skirted "Ladies from Hell," especially in close hand-to-hand butchery which the Germans feared more than death itself.

No one was more aware of this cogent fact of life than the sagacious *Sasannach* in Parliament, who, as history clearly bears out, relished wiping their swaggering shoes on us so-called ingenuous, dumb "Heeland men" for generations. This does not by any means include or involve our present lovely and most gracious monarch, Elizabeth II, of Scottish forbears, and adored by most of the civilized world as a True Sovereign of genuine integrity, beauty, and common courage. Nor does it by any means include or involve the average English en masse, who, with the exception of Americans, are the most compassionate people on the face of the globe. Besides, a world without the English is unthinkable—even impossible.

Therefore, in view of this dark, ominous, explosive economic potential, especially among tense Gaels whose proud Clansmen ancestors lived by the sword, a hasty legislation was schemed and quickly implemented for the sole purpose of spewing the young human surplus onto the colonies, as a release of the safety valve prior to explosion. However, it took the powers that be until 1923 to get their act together, when the first young group sailed on the *Metagama* in a voyage of no return.

The baron's hold on the island lasted about five years, at which time he gifted the castle to the Town of Stornoway in a thanks-but-no-thanks gesture—and was also off on a trip of no return. In 1925, the year following our own mass migration on the SS *Marloch* in 1924, the benevolent baron was no more. It is reasonable enough to assume that a man of the baron's tender sensitivities was fatally bruised in mind and body upon learning of our mass migrations to the four corners of the earth, a tragedy he fervently wished to avoid when he bought Lewis/Harris.

It was many, many years later that we miserable roving migrants, ranging from New Zealand to Australia, British Columbia to Brooklyn, Toronto to Texas, California to Connecticut, and Florida to Phoenix first learned that our banishment was in fact the bird-brained rationale of our own supine elective Gael gentry. They were as perennially useless as breasts on a bull and just as ludicrous, condoned by the wishy washy Ramsey MacDonald, the political flop of the ages, labeled the "boneless wonder" by that great warrior Sir Winston Churchill, who saved the world from the Nazi boot.

The second Highland Clearing was also at the behest of monocled English monsters, reeking with indolence and arrogance. It is now sixty-four years ago this past April since we gathered on the Stornoway pier in sorrowful groups of weeping women to bid goodbye forever to our own native land. Nostalgic gazes at the empty castle across the waters aroused bitter memories. It looked dreary in its dormant state like some monuments of great men.

It was a mere few years back since all our hopes and dreams centered around this attractive edifice, a mecca and panacea rolled into one, greatly boosting the morale of insecure Lewismen who loved the baron. On my own last day in Stornoway, sister Margaret served as my able escort on a grand tour of all the castle's rooms and grounds, affectionately recalling and pointing out certain cozy spots which became favorite lounging and recreation areas for the great man.

It was indeed a most depressive tour for both of us, in which room after room luxuriously adorned was entered, still and silent as tombs of the dead. To worsen matters, my sister, as if swallowed up in double sorrow, was so downcast at my going away that she could scarcely walk more than a few steps without suppressing the tears, as we moved along. She did smile, however, when showing me the baron's roofless bedroom, remembering mother's remark, still amusing village residents, when she labeled one of the world's richest men— *Oh! an duine bochd beairteach!*

Also, on that last doleful day, Cromwell Street, where all the vicious mischief against us was hatched and skillfully implemented, was teaming with rural strangers from all corners of Lewis to bid a loved one good-bye. It was impossible to walk more than a few steps without seeing a woman in tears. Ironic, is it not? That old *Sràid na Bùth* (street of the shop), center of our downfall, greatly benefited by the two massive migrations of 1923–1924.

This weird twist of matters in their favor came about by the brisk sale of keepsake, going-away artifacts for the so-called sentimental pleasure of the hapless young victims which they themselves deprived forever of enjoying an acre of their own native land. They were, not even sleeping better now, but making money at the expense of the vanquished—fully enjoying that buoyant heady thrill of victory which tyrants relished down through the ages.

There was no doubt whatsoever as to who was severely suffering the agonies of defeat on that sad day of long ago, as we awaited our turn to board the barge which ferried us onto the *Marloch*, looming beyond Goat Island like some mammoth monster of the deep, eager to swallow us up alive. *Cha chreid Mac Leòdhasach a' chreach gus an ruig i an doras aige.* (A Lewisman will not believe his misfortune till it is at his door.)

As I look back on it now, I keep wondering if the heavens either frowned on the unhappy occasion or shed farewell tears as the evening suddenly darkened and light mist moistened everything from Cromwell Street to Chicken Head. Dreariness, dampness, darkness, and gloom descended simultaneously, as if we didn't have enough problems.

It was not by any means a happy departure, with so many crestfallen countenances and sad faces within an easy glance, shattering morale, and emotions about to explode. I was under the impression that my own sister was the most crushed of the lot, having virtually raised me as the youngest of five, but there were others sharing her loneliness. There were some real old men wandering around the pier whose pitiful expressions clearly exuded the conviction that they'd see their young offspring no more—and most of them didn't.

The compassionate Mary Ann Matheson, our favorite Ness schoolteacher, famed for piety and generosity, supported my sister and strained to hold back the tears. I can still vividly recall that our barge group went straight to the *Marloch*'s dining room table. It was supper time, and the steward, a Glasgowegian, who else, seated us around the large table in the selfsame British exactitude and precision required in the presence of Lord Nelson.

I can also recall that after a long quiet spell staring at the numerous shiny pieces of fancy utensils around my plate, wondering what the heck was what, a fellow seated very close to me shouted to the steward, "Steward, are we underway?"

"Yep, anchors aweigh," was the snappy reply.

"Oh, oh," I mumbled to myself, "these two salties have been around"—their crisp maritime idioms gives them away.

As a matter of fact, we were under way at that very moment. Angus Graham, Back, sat next to me in the dining room for the eight days crossing. Angus was short and wiry with much more social spunk for demanding to pass this and that at the table than I had. After dinner, we all went aloft to look for fires along the dark coastline.

There were some in Rubha, but we couldn't locate their exact areas. One was either in Tolsta or Back, and one in Ness, but couldn't tell whether it was in Skigersta or Port. I was trying to spot the beautiful *Camaisear*, our favorite Skigersta fishing grounds where I spent so many happy summer days fishing for *Lòbag*. We estimated that the old man was sailing about three miles above the Bragg Rock but was farther out at the Butt where he swerved to west in order to take a bee line bearing for the mouth of the St. Lawrence.

The revolving flash of the Butt lighthouse was intensively watched by the Skigersta Angus until its last flicker slowly diminished into the black moonless night, leaving all the immediate Atlantic around us looking blacker than the proverbial pitch. While socializing a little before turning in, we came across a small group, mostly Rubhachs, listening to a young black-haired fellow Rubhach singing that famous nostalgic *Oran* composed by another gifted *Rubhach* while preparing to emigrate on a voyage of no return.

It was devastating, particularly at that stark moment of time. When I now look back on that sad evening of long ago and only a handful of us *Marloch* migrants now surviving, the somber verse from Jeremiah 22:10 sorrowfully comes to mind: "Weep sore for him that goeth away: for he shall return no more, nor see his native country" (Texas 1988).

6

My Own Dark Ages: 1908–1917

My father's memories of school appear to have been, in the main, unpleasant ones. He mentions only two of his comrades who actually seemed to enjoy school. All the rest, like himself, lived for the day when they could escape the classroom at age fourteen. It would seem that part of the explanation for this feeling, if not all of it, was the rigorous treatment that students received at the hands of their teachers. Corporal punishment was tolerated at the turn of the century, and teachers could use these methods of discipline either gently or fiercely, as they saw fit.

Angus's first teacher apparently had no interest in teaching, only entertaining, while his second threw him out a window. So, at the ripe old age of five, he had been both ignored and assaulted in a classroom—hardly an auspicious beginning.

I Remember *Seonaidh Tharmoid*

In the spring of 1908 at the age of five, on my first year in the little Skigersta school with easygoing, come-day, go-day Kenneth *Coinneach Bhreascleit* as teacher, I got to know *Seonaidh Tharmoid*, *Danaidh's* brother. He came into class every single afternoon just to raise Cain. He was a close crony of Kenneth, a pair who had much in common. Neither gave a Scotchman's hoot about teaching anybody anything except fun and games. *Seonaidh* left for Canada the following autumn, probably in his late teens.

Our whole afternoons were preoccupied with just having fun. We loved to see *Seonaidh's* smiling face coming through that classroom door, for obvious reasons. Teacher Kenneth sported one of those old-fashioned, huge, golden watch and heavy golden chains hanging loosely across his chest—the status symbol of success in those days. As a teacher, he was a disaster.

On sunny days with *Seonaidh* present, Kenneth had all of us noisy tykes chasing shadows. He'd take out that big yellow watch, open it, and flash the round beam all over the classroom floor as we scrambled like mad to catch it, sometimes piling on top of one another, as in football scrambles. Who needed education? We didn't want any and received none, so everything was even-steven.

Seonaidh, who loved to laugh in those young days, enjoyed that floor show and roared with laughter. About half a century later when I read that *Seonaidh* came home as a dying old man, I was bombarded with flashbacks of the old schoolhouse and *Seonaidh* passing by as a very old man who, I'm sure, had many nostalgic memories of his own.

A Celebrated Window Toss

It is almost certain that I am the only *Niseach* on school records who, as a child, was unceremoniously tossed through an open schoolhouse window onto the grass below by an angry female teacher—and survived. It occurred in the latter part of 1908 in our little Skigersta schoolhouse which still stands, and so did the window and iron swing gate in 1952 when I made a special walk to see both on my first visit home after the *Marloch*.

After Kenneth's departure, in breezes a fiery female from *Coinneach's* neighboring community of Carloway by the strange Gaelic sobriquet of *Luag Aonghais Beef*. *Luag* was obviously a corruption of Lucy. She was slender and beautiful, but her explosive temper aroused our village *bodaich* and *caillich* (old women) into an uproar, especially the mothers, who took an instant dislike to her.

I was seated in the front row along with my restless young cronies when some noisy commotion erupted, and *Luag*, probably determining that I was the instigator of the bedlam, seized a firm grasp of my pants and buttocks with her right hand and another fistful of my jersey between the shoulder blades with her left and tossed me clear through the open window—as the whole class gasped in horror.

I ran toward the gate and could hear Lucy racing through the front door in a desperate dash to keep the cat in the bag. She was reaching for me just as I squeezed through the old iron swing gate by mere inches from her outstretched arm. I wildly raced home, scared and panting, to the horror of angry parents and outraged neighbors. They all wholeheartedly insisted that I would not return to class until the tinder-tempered *Luag* was dismissed—which she promptly was.

Annual Visit

In the Skigersta and Lionel schools of my time, 1908–1917, a local clergyman paid an annual visit to all classes, obviously to gather a general idea of how matters stood between the current teachers and the educational powers that be. However, we never did bother at that age to find out whether the board of education or the church sponsored the tour.

To make the exam easier and less embarrassing all around, the minister examined the class as a group and not individually, a feature which those of mediocre marks loved. Our teachers always informed us a day or two prior to the parson's visit about the matter—some betraying concern.

In my time, the brilliant Reverend MacDougall, Free Church, Cross, was the selected inspector for two of the tours that I recall. Regrettably, however, only one of his topics, a geographical study of the Zuiderzee Sea and environs, do I remember. Perhaps the prime reason that I so vividly recall that particular topic is because our answers concerning the famous Netherlands' body of water left much to be desired. Mr. MacDougall was such a lovely gentleman however that he graciously overlooked our dismal unfamiliarity with that part of the world.

My uncle Murdo, *Murchadh Buidhe*, a most veracious storyteller, told us youngsters a most interesting tale concerning a predecessor of Mr. MacDougall who made a startling discovery on one of his inspection tours in Ness and elsewhere. On commencing his tour of the local schools, the old esteemed pastor decided to ask his young pupils, among many other questions, a certain cogent query in every class, not to trick anyone but just curious to learn for himself how many of the children were aware of that momentous time period in which Christ was born, a date dear to his soul.

According to my uncle's report, it appears that the old worthy went from class to class, patiently inquiring from school to school without as much as a guess from a single student until reaching the Lionel complex, last on his itinerary.

Our headmaster of the complex in those days was the proud *Seòras Ruadh* (Ginger George), George Milne, a rigid disciplinarian, but happy with any positive reports of his young charges. Just about when the old parson was getting discouraged and upon presenting his pet query in a certain class, young Norman Mackenzie of Eorodale, *Tarmod Fhionnlaigh*, stuck his sturdy little arm unhesitatingly into the air and clearly said, "The year one, sir." The minister was pleased, probably considering Norman an answer to prayer. *Seòras Ruadh* was ecstatic and wanted to make Norman a school celebrity, which the shy Norman wanted no part of.

I recall my father at the dinner table talking about the incident of the Zuiderzee Sea. I wondered then, as I do now, how many elementary school children would be able to identify this spot on the globe? How many adults could do it? My guess is, few to none. I only know the place because of my father's story.

Dark Ages Continued

Most of our Ness schoolteachers of my age bracket were not schoolteachers in the proper sense of the word. In fact they were sick sadists in much need of psychiatric counseling and behavioral observation.

These bombastic so-called pundits relished rigidity and a cruel censorious stance for the dual purpose of bolstering their own inflated ego and inspiring terror in scared children, flaunting a four-fingered cowhide strap while strutting across the classroom floor like Nazi goose steppers.

Sad to say, however, they did manage to scare helpless children, not even adroitly but very thoroughly, because the largest portion of their pupils were much too terror stricken to absorb even the rudiments of elementary learning. Their tender minds went blank upon entering class, and a mere look at their tweedy tyrants sent them hopelessly on the defensive. Our masters enjoyed corporal chastisement in the sick manner a sadist takes pleasure in afflicting pain on his victim.

Our scholarly Ness youngsters of today need proof, and I don't blame them, so consider the following. Some twenty-three years after leaving school, a bunch of Ness men, including myself, enjoyed a *cèilidh* right in the heart of New York City and Lionel school days were recalled. Norman Mackenzie, the "Broxy," Habost, a devout gentleman not given to exaggerations, made the following statement: "My year with the *Giagan* was a total loss, because my fear of him was such that from the moment I entered class, my whole mental and physical being froze—nothing could penetrate. I was just a sitting zombie."

Most Lewis teachers of my day, because of a prestigious social status obtained via a smattering of education, assumed the haughty airs of super citizens. And were they the Toffs! Great Caesar, these tweed covered twits were conceited. They strutted around the Ness community as insufferable snobs in baggy, ludicrous-looking plus-fours, positively the ugliest attire ever designed by man, or most likely hastily patched up by some inebriated bird-brained Scotchman upon dropping his regular pants on a Lost Weekend. There are no pluses associated with that atrocity: it's all minuses. Its worst feature is that it is almost impossible to determine whether the creature inside this shapeless blob is male or female.

Not until the marvelous Mary Ann Matheson and William Mackay, Fivepenny, two sane and sensible teachers, entered the

Lionel complex did the place lose its barracks complex and came to take on a compassionate feeling toward tender tykes. To the great grief of all, the kind and gentlemanly William was lost on the *Iolaire*.

When our crop of 1903 matured in the little Skigersta school and moved to Lionel, a two-mile trek, that militant defense post was already in an uproar, and not for the first time. George Milne, the redheaded schoolmaster, *Seòras Ruadh* to us and a *Tìr Mòr* scholar, was under a guilty cloud for thrashing a male pupil to within an inch or two of his life. Angry *Niseachs* demanded everything but his scalp, but the cantankerous gaffer survived the storm, touchy and irritable as a rogue elephant.

On top of this gloom, we learned that the dreaded *Giagan* was going to be our first teacher on class 3. Two generations of my own family shuddered at the prospect, having received their own baptism of fire at the hands of this bandy-legged beast, known as the "teacher terror" of that age. Fortunately, *Giagan* reformed and became a gentleman, but before old age and common sense reversed his attitude, the man was a snarling devil on two crooked legs.

His paranoid dislike of Skigersta's residents, as rebel Seceders since 1893, was a legend of our time. This coming from a man who cared not a Scotchman's hoot about any belief under heaven, puzzled even his own family, one of which became a lovely and devout Skigersta mother, loved and respected by all.

It also aggravated matters that Skigersta's *Iain Bàn*, a physically powerful fisherman, at one time in Stornoway swung from the hip and landed a stevedore swipe right on the teacher's chin, sending him sprawling on the sidewalk. We all knew about these matters as we nervously walked into his class on that memorable morning as the prancing spider watched the five Skigersta flies...

First of the Lionel School

When our age crop of Skigersta's children first walked into the *Giagan's* class in Lionel, he was already a living legend as the teacher terror of our generation. His partisan, prejudicial mind was keenly felt and loudly heralded by preceding pupils, such as my sisters and brother for example, who were more than glad to escape his abuse at fourteen.

In all fairness, that particular group saw John Gunn at his worst, fresh out of college, in the heady high gear of self-importance, with only a handful of educated figures in the entire region, and a mere three or four in all of Ness, at that dismal point of time. He loved that prestigious posture, being surrounded by illiterate multitudes—peasants—who couldn't even write their own names. This suited his burning ego to the mark.

It was in this explosive climate that we, the shy Skigersta bumpkins, walked right into the spider's web. I can still vividly recall how his nostrils, stretching to capacity in obvious revulsion at our arrival, immediately impressed me deeply. He looked like some ravenous, ferocious bird of prey about to swoop on carrion.

John Gunn: Teacher Terror

When the young, irrepressible John Gunn, Eorodale, the dreaded *Giagan*, first breezed out of college to commence teaching in the Lionel complex, the social and educational face of our Ness community was so drastically rearranged that it could never again be the same, something akin to Humpty Dumpty. Today, almost three quarters of a century later, the mere mention of his name, the *Giagan*, among his few surviving pupils immediately arouses interesting reactions, caustic comments and rueful reflections. Such was the impact of his powerful personality on old and young.

Only a meager few, including his mother, could stomach him; the bulk of the population loathed him, and all children, including his own two brothers and sister Mary, trembled in his presence. At that fiery phase of the *Giagan's* career, he was without question the epitome of conceit: well educated, handsome, fiercely partial, and acrimonious, considering all Skigersta's Free Presbyterians heretical rebels, way beyond the pale of sanity, common sense, and even common salvation.

The *Giagan* arrived at the zenith of his fury and prime of life simultaneously, a fierce phase in which he exuded cold, stark fear akin to *Righ nan Uamhann* (the king of terrors). By a strange twist of fate, the effect of losing a brave brother, *Calum*, unrecognized grenadier hero in World War One, was obviously the root cause of the first crack in the *Giagan's* roily mentality.

In the aftermath of this great change and loss, John Gunn matured into a soft-spoken congenial gentleman. Subsequently, he established a night class for navigation, a term in which he majored in college, and from which two Skigersta stalwarts emerged with flying colors. Both *Dànaidh* Mackay and *Dòmhnall Mòr Mhurchaidh* graduated as expert mariners.

Whence the *Giagan*?

John Gunn, my fiery former teacher, known in Gaelic as the *Giagan*, was reared by grandparents, just a mile north of Skigersta, downhill from Eorodale proper, in a bleak, peaty terrain which his hardworking parents developed into a modest homestead. His sailor father, *Murchadh Guinne*, was a well-liked old salty who saw much service as a tough youngster before the mast in the rugged era of wooden ships and iron men.

John's mother, a witty, down-to-earth woman, was equally loved by all. Her frequent visits to our house were delightful occasions because her quaint clichés had everybody in stitches. Her gallant son Malcolm perished as a grenadier *Gaisgeach* in Flanders Field. Donald, youngest of the family, inherited his mother's wit and was grand company and a gentleman all his days.

Three other sisters, the eldest of whom became a staunch Skigersta Christian mother, completed John Gunn's family, as normal, upright, and nice as could be found north of the "Solway." The foregoing is a glimpse into the background of a young schoolteacher, who, prior to reaching maturity, was the most censorious and ornery teacher that ever paced a classroom floor, exuding terror, breathing vengeance, savoring cruelty by insulting parents of backward children in savage sarcasm.

Who can explain it? What went wrong? Why had the gender gone awry, or the genes askew?

Childhood Cowardice

Ever since we discovered that all our parents were angry at Miss Miller, our schoolteacher, we rowdy tykes went all out to harass her in class, just to get her dander up. It was cowardice in its ugliest form, but children have a history of being both cowardly and cruel, and we were most assuredly both, as the most miserable pack of incorrigibles ever raised in Skigersta. Our favorite piece of deviltry was the mud marbles.

The following is an explanation of how the tiny mud marble almost drove the beautiful, volcanic-tempered Miss Miller to madness. We'd pack a wad of mud into the sharp angles where sole and heels adjoins, enough to make a few round mud marbles while Miss Miller was preoccupied with class curriculums.

She always sat facing the class, at the huge classroom table, at the back of which hung on the wall a large map of Scotland, our target for mischief. As she sat concentrating and the whole room as silent as a tomb, bang went the first mud marble against the map behind her with a whack loud enough to startle her almost clear out of her chair. A lightening angry glance at the class revealed nothing because all eyes were now staring downward on a prearranged signal from culprit to culprit.

This terrible form of torture was repeated on the comely lass until she was dismissed by the Board of Education, at which time she was dangerously near breakdown. What makes this true tale so unusual is the fact that it was over our muddy shoes the nasty brouhaha with our parents commenced, right on her arrival. She complained on her first day in class, remarking that our condition was an affront to hygienic progress. The *bodaich* and *caillich* went wild.

How ironic that our shoes became instrumental in driving her to the wall. Most amazing of all was the fact that that highly intelligent, well-educated girl, with higher than average IQ, never figured out how we got that mud into class, though minutely examining each one of us at the door every single morning.

Nevertheless, with all her faults and failures, she was the victim of pressure groups against one who couldn't read, write, or speak our language, and felt lonely and miserable confronting hostile parents, almost from day to day. She never made any friends in Skigersta, probably because she had no great love for Free Presbyterians. She always seemed to be on the warpath—mad at the whole world.

We rowdy young rascals took full advantage of her miserable plight, and her awkward stance among us wasn't lost on us creeping young cowards who made the most of a perhaps scared girl on the run for survival. A sense of shame fills my soul to this day—seventy-four years later.

John Murray: *Iain Bàn*

Of those born before the "Great Drowning" of 1862 among our village fathers, only one could read, write, or speak English. There were quite a few of this crop in Skigersta and elsewhere. For example, my own father couldn't write his name. John Mackenzie, our next-door neighbor, could read and write some English but was unable to communicate.

Then, *Iain Bàn's* age bracket emerged, much younger than the former, and John made the most of the deplorable hit-and-miss meager schooling available back in those days before compulsory education became mandatory. It was obvious, however, that most of *Iain Bàn's* learning was acquired through diligent self-training and hard study in the manner that merchant Norman Murray, Habost, no relation, accumulated his vast knowledge, and both of these men were excellent scholars. Both men were also endowed with higher than average intelligence quotient.

Iain Bàn, a ruggedly built six-foot fisherman, was also quite gifted in many aspects of the common struggle for survival eked out of the ocean and a small plot of land. He was exceptionally alert to the various changing occurrences of the world around him: happenstances on which he kept on top with the zeal of a roving reporter. His eagerness to pay heed to the latest press and wire releases kept him way ahead of his fellow fishermen in general information. Moreover, the fact that he was a forceful speaker in both languages greatly enhanced his clout and prestige in all community and village entanglements which cropped up from time to time.

It was *Iain Bàn* who found himself in the center of the most emotional upheaval ever to erupt within our so-called bellicose Skigersta since the attempted ecclesiastical invasion of the archvillain Robert Rainy in 1892–1893. As was previously recorded, one lovely lass, a teacher from *Tìr Mòr*, complained bitterly about our arriving in class with muddy shoes, and the stormy petrel was looked upon by the parents as a threat, challenge, and a nuisance. *Iain Bàn* immediately volunteered to head off the gale.

Verbal clashes between *Iain* and Miss Miller ensued, with John gaining the upper hand, mostly because of her volcanic temper generating incoherence as she groped for proper words in pinkish defiance. She always turned pink when aroused. Finally, in order to thrash out and finalize the whole sordid matter, the Board of Education called a special meeting in which Miss Miller and *Iain* were pitted against one another in naked debate, as the powers that be looked on, refereeing the contest.

This sensitive situation put *Iain Bàn* exactly where his temperament fitted into the circumstances like the hand in glove. He was articulate and knew it, and like most men of the era, he was not averse to accept positive publicity now and then. In a final able speech, *Iain* minutely enumerated Miss Miller's utter unfitness for her chosen profession, impressing the board members with his command of flawless English and keen grasp of the delicate relationship between child and teacher. Miss Miller was dismissed, and the fighting firebrand took off angry, pink and breathing vengeance, presumably wishing a swift toboggan slide for all Skigersta Seceders into oblivion.

Beauty and the Beast

While most *Niseachs* were shocked to learn that the *Giagan*, our fiery teacher of long ago, was human enough to love anyone, they nevertheless secretly admired his taste when rumors made the rounds that our vixenish Skigersta teacher, Miss Miller from *Tìr Mòr* (the mainland) was not only his favorite but his first romance in a thrashing pull-'em-up, drag-'em-down career.

The *Tìr Mòr* lass, a striking-looking brunette, was truly someone special in looks, attitude, and attire. Miss Miller regally paced our classroom floor looking like a queen. Two piece navy-blue ensembles were her favorites, invariably laced in narrow white fringe encircling bottoms of skirts and cuffs, with a white silky blouse overlapping the lapels of a snugly fitting jacket of perfect bodice form.

Occasionally she'd step into class with her shock of shiny, brown hair smoothly cascading straight down her back, loosely tugged a mite below the lovely lobes and neatly affixed by a big, beautiful brooch in dead center. Adding these adorable beauty features to her slender, pinkish high cheeks and large, luminous blue eyes, spreading black eyebrows, shapely full lips and thin, attractive nose, and the *Giagan's* favorite, despite a volcanic temper like her admirer, was a vision of loveliness.

Though kind Providence decreed that these two firebrands never got together in holy matrimony, they nevertheless richly deserved one another. Subsequently, according to reports, the *Giagan* married a lovely woman and raised a family. Miss Miller left Skigersta in a blaze of pinkish fury.

Our Schoolmaster: *Seòras Ruadh* 1916–1917

Scarcely a day past during our last and lost year while attending Mr. Milne's class that he wasn't deeply embroiled in bitter arguments with the educational powers that be. They kept him in a daily state of turmoil, so acute that he often walked through the complex with both hands clasped behind his back mumbling to himself. For all we learned in our last year in Mr. Milne's class (six) from thirteen to fourteen, we could have gone fishing.

It was absolutely cruel what he endured throughout that year, and his consummate hatred of Germans in general and Kaiser Bill in particular compounded his miseries and greatly added to his already tortured soul. So great was the pressure that he was literally betraying the eerie symptoms of a man going mad. It was quite obvious that what really ired him to the quick was the fact that those who exercised autocratic power over the purse strings of the educational board were fellow countrymen, even promoted college cronies, all Scotsmen to a man.

His old living quarters, housing a wife and large young family, was actually crumbling down about his ears, but allocations for repairs and improvement were held back by what he used to call "Scottish snobs." Whenever *Seòras Ruadh* mentioned his so-called highfalutin superiors in class he turned red with rage, and with his shock of red hair, pinkish-white skin and blazing eyeballs—a fearsome image emerged.

The scholarly schoolmaster would be scrupulously accurate in affirming that while Irish snobs are unbearable and English snobs intolerable, Scottish snobs symbolize the capricious ass with more ludicrous finality than any other cluster of creatures of God's creation.

Seòras Ruadh

Nothing enfuriated Mr. George Milne, our redheaded schoolmaster, as much as supercilious people, a strange side to a man who was reared among toffs on *Tìr Mòr* but that's the way he was—the haughty panicked him. Our age bracket of 1903 were thirteen years old when first we joined his class, a dismal year for the schoolmaster. Protracted pressures and hot hatred of the kaiser found him tottering on the brink of physical and mental collapse.

Grapevine gossip made the rounds to the effect that the vigorous Edgemoor preacher, Rev. John Nicholson, perturbed him no end, because of his alleged liberal approach to scriptural fundamentals and obvious rejection of the Shorter Catechism. This attitude projects another strange side to the man, who wasn't by current standards even a religious person.

Nevertheless, Reformation precepts were deeply ingrained within Mr. Milne's personality, who since childhood boned up on the powerful publications of his three-famed fellow Scots: the divines Thomas Boston, John Brown of Haddington, and Robert Murray MacCheyne. Also, according to rumors of those days, Mr. Nicholson's jaunty cosmopolitan trappings, and supposedly superior airs gadflying among the peasants gave vent to Mr. Milne's pet peeve as regards such behavior.

Therefore, there was no way of averting a verbal clash between those two articulate intellectuals, except that one would either die or disappear. Like two prized bulldogs kept apart, they managed to evade each other until the law of averages caught up with them and suddenly collided at the school gate.

There were no reporters, tape recorders, or even witnesses to jot down the interesting high points or low points of that touchy dogmatic dispute, between an arch conservative and liberal Baptist, both short fused as a smoking grenade, both clever and convincing, and immovable as Gibraltar, with exegetical knowledge of scripture, locked in a fierce verbal give-and-take battle at our old school gate for a whole hour.

Mr. Milne disclosed later, much later, when both got older and perhaps wiser, that he opened debate with a blazing broadside concerning his opponent's utter disrespect for the Shorter Catechism to which John the Baptist, as he used to call him, countered with the following gem, in equally blazing form: "Mr. Milne, may I remind you of the imprudence and crude judgment of nonswimmers who brashly step into deep unfamiliar waters way over their heads."

Looking back on it now, Mr. Milne tolerantly observed with a chuckle, many years later, "It still baffles me how, where, and when did John the Baptist learn that I couldn't swim?"

God and the Schoolmaster

Any pupil reckless enough to exude indifference while Mr. Milne, our stern schoolmaster of long ago, was in a preaching mood had to be confused above the collarbone. There was no escape from his searching, disapproving stare. Mr. Milne's piercing glance actually carried weight, in the sense that whenever his large expressive eyes coldly concentrated on some unruly child, invisible heaviness buckled the knees, such was the psychological impact of his stare, not only on children but adults as well.

For a so-called secularist, Mr. Milne harbored great affection for scripture and the Shorter Catechism while prudently avoiding any embroilment in the schismatic tumult of the time. One day in class, the schoolmaster, in a fervent desire to explain, by way of illustration, a potent point regarding the eternal existence of the Creator, which he knew all children down through the ages pondered with some perplexity, rationalizing that because all tangible matter has a beginning and end, God also must be of like mold and makeup.

Subtle, audible scraping of his larynx always preceded momentous moments of such classroom climate—a storm signal which all and sundry ignored at their peril. With great ardor, he solemnly charged the class to pay heed, while he explained something of colossal importance about God. Then, facing the blackboard, he unclasped the right hand from behind, leaving the left, as usual, reposing along the belt line awaiting quick reunion, and, with chalk in hand proceeded to meticulously draw a big round circle on the board.

When he turned to face the class, obviously it goes without saying that everyone sat stiffly in mute silence as he commenced to articulate. "Consider that white line," he admonished sternly, "it is symbolical of the Eternal God—no beginning and no end." That ended the sermon. After this, the right hand again cozily joined the left, to perpetuate his perennial posture in triumphantly striding to the nearest exit and out of sight.

Teacher Trauma

Following Miss Miller's torrid tenure in our Skigersta school of long ago, our age category had matured enough to move into the Lionel school complex. Many years previous to this event, the current schoolmaster, Mr. George Milne, a redheaded intellectual known in Gaelic as *Seòras Ruadh*, had joined the complex as headmaster to the children of nine Ness villages.

Mr. Milne, from Nairn on *Tìr Mòr*, was a rigid disciplinarian but difficult and immovable as Gibraltar. He could not speak, write, nor understand a word of Gaelic and cared less. Only redeeming qualities that we could see in the old curmudgeon were his lovely wife and lovely large family.

Prior to our Lionel enrollment, however, a disturbing event occurred in the Lionel complex which old and young deeply pondered with trepidation, besides shocking the whole community. One memorable afternoon, our redheaded schoolmaster, in a fit of unbridled fury, dismissed class early, locked all doors and windows, and strapped a willful lad whom he detained for punishment to within an inch of his life.

The public's violent reaction to this hitherto unheard of brutality was instant outrage, and the clamor for the schoolmaster's professional scalp ran rampant, from Eoropie to Eorodale, Knockaird to *Cnoc a' Choilich*. Consequently, this local brouhaha put the erudite giant woefully on the defensive and touchy as a rogue elephant. Under these circumstances, who needed education? What we tremulous new Skigersta kids needed at that point of time was an around-the-clock bodyguard.

Another agitating aspect concerning the school was the awesome presence of the teacher terror, John Gunn, the famous *Giagan*, whose weird oblique strides throughout the complex so psychologically affected the children of all classes that they imagined him to be everywhere—like an apparition in a graveyard. Such was his consummate conceit that he worked hard at maintaining his ferocious image and loved the "teacher terror" label. His frequent unmerciful beatings of his own younger brother Malcolm in class (who subsequently perished as a fearless grenadier hero in France) was to him sheer delight.

While lacking normal equilibrium, he was nevertheless begrudgingly handsome, in the sense that many deliberately closed their eyes on his so-called good points, which were nil, in fear of mellowing toward him and deprive themselves of the jolly diversion of loathing him from day to day.

The *Giagan* was tall and rangy, with shiny black hair stretching straight upward, projecting the belligerency of a Cossack on the warpath. His thin, shapely nose housed a pair of such flexible nostrils that they became the pupil's storm signals, widely expanding prior to erupting into temper tantrums, as the large, blue eyes, like twin lasers, probed body and soul.

In the following two sketches, my father deals with a school yard prank that almost turned deadly and a visit of young men, liberated from the schoolhouse, who went back to witness the instruments of their former torture. The last two sketches shed a positive light on the world of education in the portraits of a beloved teacher and two admired schoolmates who actually loved to learn.

Teen Tragedy

In my early teens, not too far from our liberation from school at fourteen under the British system of the Victorian era, our closely knit family of seven, on No. 7 Skigersta's *Baile Shuas* was involved in deep tragedy. Prior to this dire event, our well-adjusted family was one of ordinary, hardworking residents who liked nothing more than to avoid notoriety of any form or hue, love our neighbors and be at peace with the whole world.

Capricious fate, however, decreed otherwise, or was it Providence, whose ruling rod "raises one and lowers another"—in fine, whose ways are beyond finding out. This tragic event occurred in a sling skirmish at the walls of the Lionel complex, in which Murdo Morrison, Lionel—*Monstran*—a family friend of ours, was foolishly fired upon while returning from lunch.

The crofts were dormant and Murdo was shortcutting his way across from his nearby home, adjacent to *Bùth Iain Chaluim*. One of our restless group, comprising mostly of Skigersta and Adabrock boys loitering away our lunch hour at the southwestern corner of the complex, fired on Murdo as he advanced toward the school gate, and pronto, Murdo fired back in self-defense.

In a mere few moments of time, all of us were firing on Murdo, though utterly outnumbered, as if he was our mortal enemy—sheer madness. Just as Murdo dashed into the wall's eastern segment, advancing several feet within its shelter, my sling stone fired over the wall hit him squarely in the left side of the head with such force that he laid motionless for almost an hour before Mr. Milne, the schoolmaster, decided that he was alive.

Return of the Rebels

In Skigersta of long ago, one particular event that guaranteed a capacity turnout of adults was our meetings of the minds. Occasionally the village fathers—*bodaich*—decreed to thrash out local problems in our erstwhile detention den, the old schoolhouse of lingering and sad memories. For our age bracket, who had just gleefully escaped its doleful confines, with only a scratch or two and hardly any knowledge whatsoever, this hastily devised assemblage was of course a carnival.

Our little schoolhouse still stands off the main road, qualmishly and shameless facing a sacred prayer house, unrepentant, despite its strapping sessions of sequestered young Skigerstonians since compulsory education was de facto implemented. The lone square classroom of bleacher crude design, elevated rows of seats each representing a class, was in our day a dank, cheerless hovel, more reminiscent of a covert of chastisement than a cozy elementary for tender tykes.

That special macabre appeal to us recently liberated rebels in gathering at our old alma mater was threefold. First, it boosted our previous sagging self-confidence to realize that the stuffy pundits-in-residence were now, since our permanent parole became effective, reduced to our own level. Our freedom brought them down a peg and raised us one, in an eyeball-to-eyeball ugly confrontation. Their former superior airs and autocratic aura were forever gone by the board, as we walked tall all the way to the Lionel complex.

Secondly, like all transgressors wishing to return to the scenes of their sins, we likewise in morbid curiosity enjoyed coming back to the site of our previous disobedience and disorder. Finally, our grand get-together was a welcome antidote in a somewhat dreary repetitious existence, in which rubbing elbows with a cross section of the most interesting assortment of colorful characters that ever decorated landscape was a refreshing change of pace.

In a village of approximately 280 souls could be found worthies, wits, wags, and oddballs, the laconic and loquacious, saints and sinners, along with a perennial *amadan* (fool) or two like myself, all of whom converged on the old schoolhouse at such excitable events.

Immediately upon entering our former classroom, mute evidence of the bygone penal instruments so ardently and adeptly utilized by our former masters were glaringly visible all around. That dreaded familiar long wooden pointer, which so frequently and resoundingly crashed on my equally wooden skull, rigidly and brazenly stood in its traditional corner, craving to be called into service.

His culprit counterpart, the shiny brown ferocious-looking cowhide strap, a quarter inch thick and over a foot long, with sufficient slit fingers to suit the particular propensities of the current creature in charge, shamelessly recoiling from the rigors of overwork on a table nearby looking like a loathsome reptile, aroused shuddering memories. Just to stare at the immobilized monsters and not feel incarcerated anymore was a joy defying description.

Mary Ann Matheson

Tall, distinguished-looking Mary Ann Matheson, affectionately known to us *Niseachs* for many years as "Mary Ann" was to our age bracket, born shortly after the turn of the century, no ordinary, run-of-the-mill schoolteacher. Her impeccable, maidenly demeanor, enhanced by unassailable Christian conduct, raised Mary Ann's image in our mind's eyes to a cherished pinnacle not attained by any other schoolteacher or young woman of her day.

To her pupils and scores of friends throughout the Ness community, Mary Ann became a symbol of everything that is noble in a cold, competitive world. She stood out as someone special even among a churchgoing populace, where circumspect multitudes perennially bear the stamp and influence of the Gospel message from day to day.

The Mary Ann that we knew back in the early twenties was painfully shy, but not by any means ambivalent in significant matters pertaining to her religious beliefs and laudable behavior, in which she constantly and conscientiously disassociated herself from the careless and foolish, while maintaining a quiet, delightful sense of humor. It was obvious that this girl of sensitive breeding and outstanding gracious qualities fostered the "roots of the matter" since a mere child.

Sad Reflections: Wallace and Percy

In retrospectively viewing our own schooling days in Skigersta of long ago and considering how unimportant educational advantages appealed to us, it's nothing short of phenomenal that any of our age bracket managed to absorb even the fragments of knowledge we now claim. To our particular age category, born shortly after the turn of the century, the only real enjoyable moments that we experienced in class were looking forward to our fourteenth birthdays and grand liberation from it all.

This indifferent attitude is hard to fathom, considering that we were all brought up in Christian homes where wise parents never ceased to point out how apathy invariably warps the sense of values, a gift without which one stood in peril of forever remaining as the tail and never the head—in essence, an invitation to perpetual failure.

Luckily, however, as often occurs in extreme matters, an exception emerges. In this case, they were the Nicholson cousins, Wallace and Percy, who found their schooling days a pleasure, simply because they both loved to learn.

Not until I became Wallace's shipmate on the Great Lakes did his superior learning and general advanced knowledge dawn on me in embarrassing awareness. I felt completely out of his league, which indeed I was—on the defensive—a disposition which invariably means disaster.

7

Duncan Macbeth: Divine of His Day

The subject of this chapter is a man my father never met, as he died in 1891, twelve years before he was born. It would seem that he was loved and revered by everyone in Ness. No one, with the exception of Lord Leverhulme and the Bard, occupies so many pages in these memoirs as this preacher, saint, and reputed prophet—certainly a legendary, perhaps even a mythical figure.

Duncan Macbeth was born in Applecross in the West Coast Highlands of Scotland and according to a recent book by Norman Campbell (*One of Heaven's Jewels*, 2009), had a ministry in Inverness before establishing himself in Ness. His sense of calling led him to routinely traverse the whole area of his responsibility on foot, visiting the sick, the shut-ins, and others in his care. Despite the obvious seriousness with which he took all his duties, he had a healthy sense of humor, one example of which is provided below.

The Saintly Duncan Macbeth

Among the many eminent ministers who preached in Ness over the years, none gained the affection of the populace to the extent that the Reverend Macbeth enjoyed in his thirteen years of powerful preaching, instrumental in the conversion of multitudes. My mother, who got married the following year after his death, never ceased to talk about the man in such glowing terms that his image some way, somehow, abides with me to this day.

That whole generation carried Mr. Macbeth's image to their graves. They just could not forget him, and when he died, the whole Ness community, according to reports, went into such a state of silent mourning unheard of before or since in that corner of the world.

He spoke to his young servant Isabel Morrison shortly before he died of the clouds that were thickening and the gathering storm about to befall the Free Church. It happened two years after he passed on. He made it plain to Isabel that he did not wish to be alive when the storm burst forth and advised her not to be carried away with the greater numbers. If only three made a stand for truth—"be one of them"—admonished the great man. Isabel was true to his memory and sound advice.

Macbeth

"Air chuimhne gu bràth bithidh am fìrean" (Ps. 112:6: "The righteous shall be in everlasting remembrance").

Reverend Duncan Macbeth, the saintly south Dell clergyman of long ago, an epitome of dignity, was of average height and statuesquely formed, somewhat akin to the comely biblical personality of flawless, physical frame "without spot or blemish." Like the famed prince of sacred chronicles, Mr. Macbeth was favored with an impressive shock of straight hair (mostly fair), beautifully blending into soft, lustrous aspects of golden hue smoothly dropping to the collar. Here, in a neatly clipped, curved trim covering the nape, his shiny hair suspended a mite above the shapely shoulders in pale-yellowish splendor. One pious woman, whose deep motivations for adoring the eminent minister was of much greater significance than just physical appearance, put it this way: *"'S e duine bu bhrèagha air na leag mi riamh sùil."* (He was the most handsome person I ever set eyes upon.)

Macbeth: Credentials to Preach

Long ago, around 1878, *Niseachs* were almost deprived of Reverend Duncan Macbeth's invaluable ministry, in the midst of prevailing illiteracy, because, of all absurdities, the young clergyman's scholarly achievements didn't quite come up to par. At once, this appears to be both ludicrous and improbable in view of Ness men's fabled common sense, besides living with four towering spiritual giants of the age, such as MacDonald of Eorodale, Morrison of Fivepenny, the *Gobha* of Swainbost, and *Seumas* of Skigersta.

In all fairness, however, the majority of Ness folks were blameless in this respect because ever since they first heard Mr. Macbeth preach, their genuine affection for the saintly parson never deteriorated. At that point of time, the few scattered learned men entrenched within Stornoway, Barvas, and Ness exerted tremendous influence on the general mass. It seems that one or two prominent parsons of power decried the fact that Mr. Macbeth failed to obtain sufficient seminary training befitting a minister of the Gospel.

Meanwhile, something very extraordinary occurred, a startling turn of events which *Niseachs* of that generation never forgot. At a special meeting, with many ministers present, an articulate Macbeth supporter, sensing that something drastic was about to transpire, bounced to his feet and unloaded his soul in poignant Gaelic metaphor: *Tha sibh, ars esan, 'a' cur an aghaidh seirbhiseach Dhè do bhrigh 's gu bheil sibh làn mhothacail air gun tilg e 'n dòrnag seachad oirbh.* (You, said he, are going against God's servant because you are well aware that he can throw the hammer way past you.)

That did it. The opposition relented and Mr. MacBeth was chosen.

MacBeth: Dedication and Deference

Perhaps there are only a mere few *Niseachs* alive today who can verify the consistency of the following incredible but true anecdotes concerning one of the great clergymen of the past. These are only two of the many related to us by truthful parents, upright uncles, and veracious neighbors, many of whom would almost as soon part with a limb than peddle an unfounded tale.

According to their reports, the Reverend Duncan MacBeth, saintly South Dell minister of long ago, considered by most of the elderly the greatest Gaelic preacher of all time, was so totally devoted to prayer that the toes of his bedroom slippers were the first to show signs of wear and tear in his entire modest wardrobe. Such dedication would appear to concur with the old saying which affirms that truth at times can be stranger than fiction. Now, in view of the austere and hardy construction of shoes and slippers in the frugally oriented era of the late nineteenth century, it's rather astounding to realize the enormous amount of time that Mr. MacBeth devoted on bended knees. Without any doubt whatsoever, Mr. MacBeth was also a prophet.

In all likelihood, the following authentic story concerning Mr. MacBeth will be equally hard to accept. Nonetheless, the noted storytelling expert *Iain Pìobair* loved to tell it. Like all faithful ministers, Mr. MacBeth, an exceptionally compassionate man, made routine rounds of his huge Ness parish to visit the shut-ins and pray for the downtrodden with the same serene constancy that he preached on Sabbath—seldom missing. However, able bodied as he was, he couldn't possibly cover all the scattered villages in the course of a day, but five of Ness' towns are so closely linked that they appear as one grand thoroughfare in a direct sweep to the sea.

In the course of an ordinary day, Mr. MacBeth, in that weighty, measured gait so commonly practiced by parsons of his day, walked the entire route from Cross to Lionel with a visit here and there to pray in troubled homes. So genuine was the reverence for the man of God, however, according to *Iain Pìobaire's* report, that throughout this long stretch of thickly populated highway, no one remained outdoors, including juveniles, and none loitered by the roadside in fawning fashion and brash attempt to strike up a conversation while the esteemed figure, impressively attired in vestments of his lofty calling, serenely strode by.

MURDINA D. MACDONALD

MacBeth: Sabbath Observances

Except in cases of sickness and dire emergencies, the Reverend Duncan MacBeth, South Dell pastor for thirteen years, was unapproachable on the Sabbath day. This rigid stance was particularly aimed at those wishing to discuss a mundane matter or two of so-called immediate urgency, a sly, secular stratagem common to worldlings weary of Sabbath strictures. Mr. MacBeth's stern disapproving glare at the talkative knave quickly aborted any such approach.

He strongly held the opinion throughout his ministerial career that those who wearied of Sabbath's sacred exercises were still serving the world, the devil, and the flesh. As a special gesture of affection for the fourth commandment, Mr. MacBeth's Sabbath at the manse, an abode which still stands, commenced Saturday at the stroke of 10:00 p.m.

After 10:00 p.m., every single thing and phase within the walls of that manse took on a different character. Shoes were shined and put away. Garments were dusted and dishes designated for Sabbath servings remained unwashed until Monday morning. From thereon, with all matters in order, a holy hush descended on that dwelling until 7:00 a.m. Monday, a hush that only the furtive mouse in search of a morsel dared intrude upon.

My father would never hear Duncan Macbeth preach nor would he ever have the opportunity to participate in a worship service with undivided Free Churh men and women, but he could imagine such an idyllic scene in Ness of long ago, as indeed he did.

Twin Dells of Long Ago

That unimposing-looking strip of grass stretching northward from the base of the Dell river bridge was a sacrosanct spot to our Ness parents of long ago. Here, in favorable weather, the great minister Duncan Macbeth conducted outdoor services to a harmonious, happy congregation, representing the fourteen villages of the closely knit Ness community of other days. Peaceful *Niseachs*, in accord and of one mind, joyously sat here on balmy evenings, contentedly absorbing the divine deliveries of the saintly clergyman.

On this modest plat, Mr. Macbeth on numerous occasions sorrowfully reminded his faithful followers of the "brewing storm," an impending church turbulence which constantly preoccupied his mind, frequently trembling with emotion cognizant of its awesome aftermath. While still intact and in one assemblage, however, it staggers the imagination to visualize the sublime scene on that river bank, when a singing multitude in Gaelic unison sweetly responded to the grand precentors of long ago, as the sacred crescendo voluminously arose out of the tranquil dale, heard for miles—and reaching to heaven.

Lewis, as an island of crofter-fishermen, had many men who went down to the sea in ships and were routinely exposed to the dangers therein. Macbeth felt their danger and appealed to heaven for their safety.

Lone Vigil

When the Ness fisher folks of long ago encountered a menacing night breeze many miles offshore, Mr. Macbeth's manse windows, like the sacred temple of yore, glowed continuously. At such a time, the saintly pastor Duncan Macbeth never closed an eye. On the contrary, the renowned clergyman and prophet apprehensively paced back and fore in a strange identical pattern which, perhaps inadvertently, subsequently became the fixed mode of his behavior whenever danger on the high seas became obvious.

An anxious spell at the window peering into darkness, with lips moving in silent devotion, like Hannah at Shiloh, began his lonely vigil. Then, gravely returning to his favorite chair, he invariably knelt down in front of the seat, folded his hands, and closed his eyes to offer a brief prayer of praise and supplications.

In concluding this somber rite, he usually stood rigidly upright, enthusiastically stretching in an exercise or two, after which he'd slowly walk toward the open Bible affixed by the bedpost. Here, prior to resuming his next walk to the window, he solemnly leafed through scripture pages, softly quoting the famous line, "Watchman, what of the night?" "Watchman, what of the night?" *Fhir na faire, ciod mu'n hoidhche? Fhir na faire, ciod mu'n hoidhche?* (Isa. 21:11).

While it is common nowadays for teachers to encourage their students by asserting that there is no such thing as a "stupid" question—and that may be the case—the esteemed Macbeth, however, had no trouble discerning a truly silly prayer request and reacted accordingly.

Colin Macritchie

Because the Reverend Duncan Macbeth of south Dell always dealt with weighty matters of great concern, his general appearance was inclined to look rather somber, but not too severe. This despite the fact that he was a man of rare warm disposition and an easy smile. At any rate, the great clergyman's occasional laugh was both a relief and delight to his many friends who frequently felt a mite overawed in his presence.

Therefore, it might be of interest to recall that Mr. Macbeth's heartiest laugh ever was evoked by a visiting Canadian, who to this day is remembered in Ness as the rash, foreign unbeliever who made the reserved pastor laugh out loud. As a young man, this happy-go-lucky kinsman from Quebec, born and brought up there, braved the North Atlantic elements to look over his many worthy relatives scattered throughout the Ness community, most of whom lived in Knockaird, Habost, and Skigersta.

"Crossing the pond," as he used to call his voyage, was quite a feat for cousin Colin, because he candidly admitted to anyone wishing to listen that visualizations of massive ocean waves and sharks haunted him since childhood. With a chuckle, he marveled at his own daring. Understandably then, his return voyage was of utmost importance, especially as that crucial day loomed closer and closer. When it finally arrived and while bidding tense good-byes, Mr. Macbeth unexpectedly walked right into his path on a stroll of his own.

Young Colin Macritchie wasn't the type of individual to fool around in dire emergencies. To him, as a brash, rugged child of the forest, a desperate situation demanded a more desperate, head-on approach. As re-crossing the "pond" was now irksomely uppermost in mind, with a man of God so close at hand, a bold solicitation for the clergyman's assistance made sense to Colin at such a stark and late hour.

With the practical urge of a pressed person hastily ordering an exigent piece of merchandise, Colin immediately confronted the saintly Macbeth, beseeching the minister to earnestly pray for him, as he put it: *Bithibh ag ùrnaigh air mo shon gus an ruig mi null.* (Pray for me till I reach over yonder.) Upon hearing the young Canadian's incongruous request, in seeking only the Lord's temporary succor, Mr. Macbeth laughed so lustily that Colin's plea, especially *gus an ruig mi null* became a Ness household expression, frequently quoted to this day.

In case the very young missed the point. It was quite obvious to the minister that Colin's prime worry was to set foot solidly on Canadian terra firma, after which he'd presumably manage very nicely on his own, in which all prayers for his future safety and well-being could end at the waterline.

Prophet Macbeth

During winter storms, pounded by roaring breakers from all sides and unceasingly punished by sleet and hail, frequently in gale-force violence, the tiny Isle of Rona, jutting out of the North Atlantic, has to be the most forbidden spot of God's vast and comely cosmos. Yet two Ness Christian cronies of long ago peevishly took off in an open *sgoth*, fully determined to live out the remaining part of their lives on this undesirable speck of arable land, but perished in so doing.

Rona is a seal's breeding ground, where countless harems concentrate in late autumn to deliver pups in great numbers, and the eerie moans and spooky nocturnal groans of these animals hauntingly disturbs the soundest of slumbers. Nevertheless, these two Ness men, both pious men and esteemed pillars of the church, went there to fulfill unavoidable destiny.

Their problems stemmed from a rather heated dispute, never quite fully clarified, with the saintly clergyman and prophet, the Reverend Duncan Macbeth, south Dell, probably the last of the great divines. James Andrew Finlayson, the worthy Skigersta church elder and warm friend of Mr. Macbeth, was also involved.

It seems that the pastor, a rigid disciplinarian in all matters pertaining to church direction and ordinances, declared to all and sundry (his vindication would be manifested) as a distinct sign from heaven, by the discomfiture of their demise, that all three were to be deprived of any bedfast consolation or pillow comfort. The exact Gaelic words the minister applied in his prediction regarding these eminent figures were familiar to my generation: *Chan fhaigh duine dhiubh bàs a' chinn-adhairt.* (None of them shall die in their beds.)

Shortly after settling down in a miserable, crudely constructed *bothan* (small hut), woefully lacking nutriments and hardly any comfort whatsoever, the two Christians died, presumably simultaneously, obviously striving desperately to reach the makeshift bed, the desired goal which neither achieved, just as the clergyman foretold.

Some pious person, whose identity is obscure, but who apparently was familiar with that sad imbroglio, was divinely informed (either by dream or prayer) of some dire tragedy taking place on Rona, but strangely enough failed to specify or elaborate. Immediately a crew took off to investigate, who, upon finding the Christians dead, took particular notice of the fact that their prompt arrival favorably coincided with the condition of the corpses, verifying the perfect timing of the "One" whose "ways are beyond finding out."

Prophet Macbeth: Part 2

When James Andrews's God-fearing cohorts perished in Rona, deprived of comfort or consolation, as Mr. Macbeth foretold, the whole sad episode was now viewed by the Ness populace in a more awesome perspective than before. With the resolute *Seumas* of Skigersta still hale and hearty, sole survivor of the three church members under the parson's portend, the morbid curiosity of that strange colony who relishes the weird ponderings of such matters was aroused afresh. Pious old James had hosts of friends throughout Ness and elsewhere, multitudes of which now zealously prayed that nothing unusual would befall the grand septuagenarian, the *Lathamor* sage of No. 18.

One day, Annie Mackay, James's young next-door neighbor and later mother of the widely known *Dòmhnall Anna*, was busy drawing water from the crisp, cold bounty of the *Fuarean*, hard by the *cladach*, when she noticed James some distance ahead ambling down the steep gravel footpath leading to the popular spring, gushing out at the foot of the small gulch dividing *Lathamor* from the *Baile Shuas*.

Annie, losing sight of James on the decline, followed his footsteps downhill, and upon reaching her father's workshop site opposite the *Fuaran*, old *Seumas* lay dead where her artful parent, *Dòmhnall Mac Fhionnlaigh*, built sleek *sgothan* of other days.

James's demise, dying without a vestige of human comfort, just as the minister predicted, not only fulfilled the prophecies of an offended clergyman, the great Reverend Duncan Macbeth, but also concluded the saddest and most baffling church crisis of that generation.

All Flesh Is Grass

Never before or until the *Iolaire* disaster was there such profound, far-reaching grief felt in Ness as when the famed clergyman Reverend Duncan Macbeth died. When the popular minister passed away, the populace, young and old, immediately sobered into a penitent spell of mourning, as if the removal of such a saint signified that some divine judgment was at hand.

Rugged seafaring *Niseachs* who looked upon any effusive display as a mark of some basic flaw in the personality, along with the most callous, strained to hold back the tears. During these depressing days, a tomb-like hush fell on the whole region, from Stornoway to Skigersta and beyond, with multitudes subduedly conversing as if their whole world could never again be the same. And to many it never was.

Shortly after the great pastor entered into his rest, all of Ness became bitterly embroiled in professorial mischief, which he characterized as the "brewing storm," thereby alienating his many ardent admirers one from another.

Our parents, uncles, and veracious neighbors who adored the clergyman nostalgically related interesting items concerning Mr. Macbeth, whose image as a special saint, super preacher, and prophet that whole generation carried to their graves. For instance, they pointed out that the unusual large turnout for Mr. Macbeth's funeral was by far the most massive in Lewis records.

One can visualize, with male attendance from all over Lewis and Harris, in two abreast order slowly moving toward Swainbost, the extent, aura, and solemnity of that procession of long ago. For a brief spell, the howling winds of the North Atlantic and gentle summer swept across the minister's lonely, unadorned grave while awaiting the honor and recognition due a divine.

Fortunately for concerned *Niseachs*, a small band of influential followers dedicated themselves to the noble idea that Mr. Macbeth's worthy name and memory should be remembered by Nessmen forevermore. With great ardor, they went about the task of deciding on a suitable stone design befitting the clergyman's conservative character. To their great credit, they managed to come up with a modest, beautifully outlined near-white monument, at the base of which the appropriate verse from Daniel 12:3 was neatly engraved in Gaelic perfection. (And they that be wise shall shine as the brightness of the firmament; and they that turn many to righteousness as the stars forever and ever.) And there it stands to this day, while underneath, reposing in the perfect security of a warm Christian grave lies the sacred bones of the great Macbeth—"until the day dawns."

Agus deàlraichidh iadsan a tha glic mar shoilleireachd nan speur; agus iadsan a thionndaidheas

mòran gu fìreantachd mar na reultan fad saoghail nan soaghal.

Air chuimhne gu brath bidh am fìrean. (The righteous shall be in everlasting remembrance.)

Mortifying Silence

In south Dell, a little north of the main highway, on the western slope of the beautiful Dell River, flowing its way through the twin Dells onto the open sea, can be seen the decaying façade of what once was the most respected and cherished abode of our Hebridean heritage. Here, piteously on its last legs and barely holding on, stands Mr. Macbeth's former two-story dwelling—manse—obviously abandoned to the elements for generations.

This onetime imposing-looking manse now appears to be an anachronistic, weird, unwanted object, incongruously looming out of the modern, spruced up terrain of today, like a gloomy nightmare refusing to go away. It's utterly impossible to disregard this incredible sight, especially in view of the deep affection our elders harbored for the former divine.

The manse's onetime bright and charming exterior, fittingly signifying the renown and goodwill of its yesteryear occupant, considered by our parents the greatest Gaelic preacher of all time, has completely surrendered to the inevitable. While awaiting extinction, however, he has fallen victim to dark, unattractive accretions of repulsive-looking hue, and like a longsuffering patient, weary and wasted, he is ready to crumble and perish. Meanwhile, its doors and windows, forebodingly shut tight at all times, eerily stare out at a cold, indifferent world in grim, mortifying silence.

MURDINA D. MACDONALD

Dad described his sketch of his black house in the village of
Skigersta with the words, "Think of the days of yore and years
that have long gone." Translated from the Gaelic.
Notice the person carrying a load of peat on
the far left of the main black house.

Rev. Duncan MacBeth, 1879–1891
Old Established Church

William Hesketh Lever,
First Viscount Leverhulme (1851–1925)

MURDINA D. MACDONALD

Norman Morrison (1859–1932)
The Skigersta Bard

Angus's brother Donald and mother, Christina

BLACKHOUSE GOD'S HOUSE

Angus's sister Annie

Angus's sister Millie

MURDINA D. MACDONALD

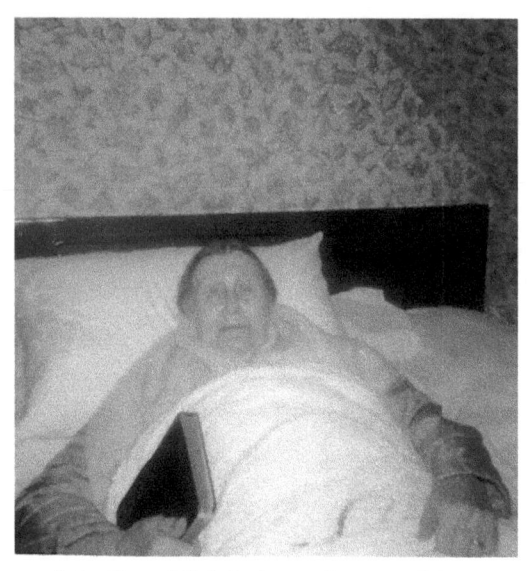

Angus MacDonald's Mother, Christina MacDonald

Sister Margaret, daughter Isabel, and friend

BLACKHOUSE GOD'S HOUSE

No. 7, Skigersta, 2012

View to Skigersta Bay from No. 7, Skigersta

MURDINA D. MACDONALD

D. B. MacKay (1867–1950) of Skigersta and owner of a shoetree factory in New York City which hired many Lewisman over the years.

BLACKHOUSE GOD'S HOUSE

17 Skigersta, site of D. B. MacKay's house

Across the road from 17 Skigersta, workshop
of D. B. MacKay's father.

MURDINA D. MACDONALD

Robert Burns. 1759-1796.

All men will remember him
As the earth slowly turns
Auld Scotia's Son.— The Immortal
Inimitable Robert Burns.

Dad's sketch of Robert Burns. He recited Burns' poetry in the Broad Scots when he was courting my mother, Effie MacKay.

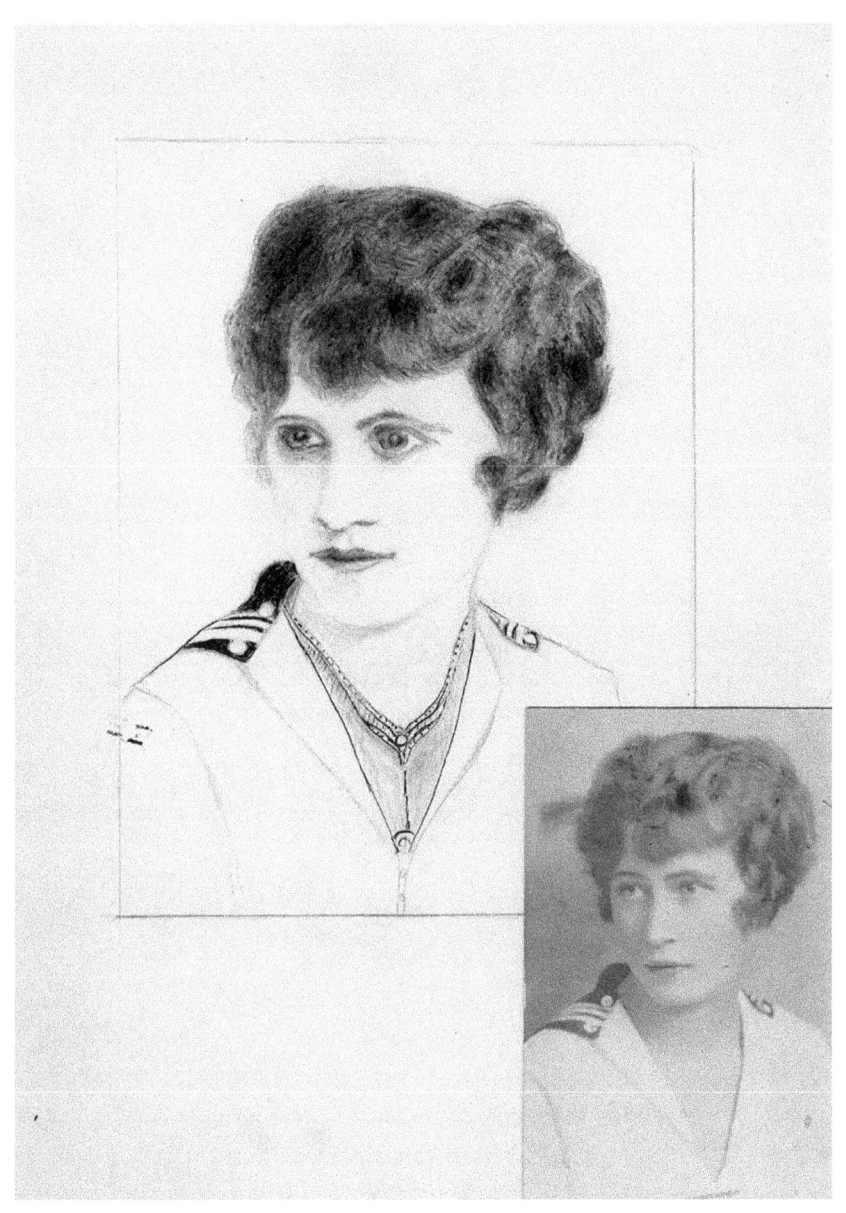

Dad's sketch of Murdina Prather, my mother's favorite sister.

MURDINA D. MACDONALD

Effie Buchanan MacDonald MacKay and
Angus Morrison MacDonald
May 1936

Norman, Murdina and Christine–1954

MURDINA D. MACDONALD

House in Bayside, NY

Norman and Lucky

BLACKHOUSE GOD'S HOUSE

Family Portrait
Bayside, NY–1958

House in Flushing, NY–1960

Scattering of Dad's ashes, Elgol, Skye, 2012

A whisky tribute to Angus by Captain Alex
of the Bella Jane, Elgol, Skye.

8

The Ablest Man of His Generation

Norman Morrison, the Skigersta Bard (1859–1932), was my father's next-door neighbor. By all accounts, the man was extraordinary. He seems to have had it all—knowledge, mental and physical strength, poetic powers, commanding oratorical abilities, superb seamanship skills, and, as if these were not enough gifts for a single person, he evolved into a deeply spiritual presence after his later-in-life conversion at about age fifty. The *Free Presbyterian Magazine* ran a brief account of his life in its issue of December 1935 which is reproduced here in Appendix 4.

Birthplace of *Bàrd a' Baile Shuas*

Upon walking the *Lathamor* road from the quay's sloping incline toward our *Baile Shuas*, the stretch of road is relatively level until reaching the schoolhouse. At the schoolhouse environs, all of *Lathamor's* crofts end. From there, the road steadily climbs until joining the main road at *Tarmod Pìobaire's* intersection.

However, the *Baile Shuas'* arm sweeps south toward *Cnoc a' Choilich*, passes *Taigh Chalum*, and climbs over croft No. 4, curving on croft No. 5 to decline at croft Nos. 6 and 7. It levels off somewhat at the Bard's home of No. 8. The narrow road continues on past No. 9 croft and at croft No. 10 begins to slope downward into Murray property of No. 11. Here the road expends itself into the Skigersta pasture at the old *Cabhan*, which is now only a memory.

The Bard's father, *Dòmhnall Mac Tharmoid*, skipper of the Skigersta *sgoth* lost in the drowning of 1862, lived in an old thatched *taigh dubh* of those days. In this humble thatched home, overlooking the comely *cladach* in unpretentious environment, one of the ablest figures of our generation, or any other generation, first saw the light of day.

Following is the third of my father's sketches to make mention of portends or prophecies or predictions, if you will. The first such note was sounded in the wedding of John MacDonald who perished on the *Iolaire*. The second mention was the prediction of Duncan Macbeth regarding the deaths of three colleagues which was taken as prophetic. Below my father describes the prediction of a passing preacher about the bard based on his physical appearance as a young boy.

Marks of Genius

In Skigersta of long ago, an unusual male child was born in a lowly three compartment thatched *taigh dubh* overlooking the sea who, according to the midwife, showed, upon opening the matrix, four teeth (two in upper and lower front gums). This boy, healthy and handsome, was just another exuberant village lad until something astonishingly puzzling regarding him occurred when he was about nine years of age. Strangely enough, however, the incident wasn't exactly heralded from the housetops, mostly because the modest parents frowned upon making much ado about the matter. This attitude, probably a wise one due to the boy's immaturity, explains the neighbor's reserved reaction regarding a most extraordinary event of Skigersta's past. The story got out in the open, however, as most do, and was repeated to us by our elders, who loved the truth.

It happened on a day when a noted preacher made routine rounds of the village, and while passing No. 8 on the *Baile Shuas*, he slackened his pace some to watch the lively Morrison lads, Norman and John (later the pious *Iain Beag*), frolicking outdoors. On being informed of their names by the mother who stood by, the perceptive parson attentively affixed his gaze on both boys, as if spellbound in discerning something of note, and for a few silent moments, he just looked on, apparently absorbed in deep meditation.

It soon became clear the good reverend had something profound to reveal, and turning to the mother, he remarked as follows: "I will not comment on John at this time," he said, "but the proximity of Norman's ears to his shapely skull arouses my curiosity. In considering the impressive inward curvature of his ears, I'm prepared to conclude that with the emergence of maturity, he shall, in my judgment, flourish into a remarkable scholar."

Without any doubt, the foregoing prophetic, analytical probe was scrupulously accurate, because the lively lad grew, learned, and prospered to become, according to many erudite, observant experts, the ablest man of his generation—who was none other than my illustrious next-door neighbor.

Neighbor Norman

My immediate next-door neighbor, the Skigersta Bard, was truly endowed with extraordinary mental faculties. For example, his young contemporary, the gifted poet Alex Nicholson, once conceded, "In my opinion, Norman Morrison is the ablest man of this generation." It was affirmed by some veracious village *bodaich* that he memorized the entire Shorter Catechism in the course of one Sabbath day. Obviously Norman was in command of a phenomenal photographic memory, which was the happy lot of the great Winston Churchill.

Perhaps another mark of Norman's mental superiority was the way most men shied away from entangling themselves in any of his disputes. They wanted no part of his caustic wit and searing semantics, which, when he was aroused, were awesome. On more than one occasion, we village youngsters witnessed Norman in the middle of some complex local imbroglio, when tempers flared and sharp, weighty words rent the air. What would I exchange right now to have a tape recording of that vocal, poignant give-and-take innocuous squabble while compiling brief sketches of our colorful village fathers of long ago?

Some of the Bard's other able contemporaries, gifted in poetic renderings themselves, readily acknowledged that the Skigersta Bard was no average, run-of-the-mill man of letters. On the contrary, his unique Gaelic wording and semantic mastery of the mother tongue clearly placed him in a class by himself.

As he sat quietly by our fireside at *cèilidh*, I couldn't resist the temptation of sizing him up in my own limited way when I became of age and reached the early twenties. While looking quite unexceptional, even nondescript, with hardly any outward appearance of possessing the super-skills for which he was famous, there was, nonetheless, a certain unmistakable mystique about the man which I, of meager education, find impossible to define.

Of the fact that it was there I was quite certain, because the more I looked him over, the more convinced I became that he was no ordinary mortal. Even a glance at his picture, one of which I have carried in my wallet for generations supports the point I wish to make. Never exceeding five feet ten inches in height, the Bard was of slender, dynamic frame with thin, light-brown hair which he combed to the right eye.

When in somber mood, his blue eyes exuded a brooding Abraham Lincoln expression, but which quickly lighted up in merriment when amused. His occasional lusty laugh was different, simply because it exposed the most prominent-looking, massive set of even white teeth ever created in a human head. These teeth became famous because, as a young man in his prime, he could sink them into a full boll of meal sitting on the *being* (bench) and gently place it on the floor with both hands clasped behind his back.

It has been suggested by many literary experts that *Oran Dhùn Alasdair* was his masterpiece, perhaps because it embraced nearly every phase of existence in Skigersta of long ago.

Dùn Alasdair

The poem is about the boat *Dùn Alasdair* which went aground near Skigersta before my father was born. Despite the complete loss of the ship, there was evidently no loss of human life. Finlay MacLeod reads a portion of the poem in Gaelic online.

Among the many grand attractions Skigersta's harbor had to offer us village lads of long ago was one of utmost historic value, exciting enough to inspire our local Bard into composing a Gaelic classic commemorating the event. According to literary experts, the humorous lyric is still one of the great masterpieces of Lewis lore. The artist of course was none other than my neighbor Norman—known all over Lewis as *Bàrd Sgeadharstaigh*.

On the treacherous southeastern shallows of our bay, known as *Leac Cousgair*, the ill-fated sailing ship *Dhùn Alasdair* crashed onto the *Low Leacs* and right into maritime records. On impact with the shoreline, in thick fog, spars, canvas, rigging with their attendant profusion of blocks and tackles, tumbled into the surf, followed by the complete smashup of the vessel from stem to stern. Its utter ruin inspired the Bard to write the classic line: *Thug carachan Leac Cousgair an ceann às an amhaich aic'* (The rocks at *Leac Cousgair* tore her apart).

In our young days traipsing up and down the *cladach* by the hour, we occasionally stumbled at low tides on rusty iron fragments protruding from underneath the dulse-covered boulders—mute evidence of the shambles. *Dùn Alasdair's* watery gravesite fascinated us at that age, even though it all occurred long before any of us were born. What bothers me to this day is that we didn't keep even a small splinter as a keepsake. Born dumb.

Some Are Born Great

Two of the most startling events in the Skigersta Bard's career occurred so swiftly that village residents were both shocked and elated. In the brief period of a mere few days, this extraordinary man, whose light could no longer be contained, became the leading Bard of his day and within a few years thereafter, just as rapidly, became a devout Christian of unassailable conduct. His conversion was sudden, effective, and believed in—even by his critics.

When the Bard's first classical composition made the rounds, the residents were amazed and for a plausible reason. Up until the sensational release of his introductory rendition, even his closest friends weren't aware of such hidden talents, though witty remarks always sparked his daily repartee. No one expected the oral and literary gems which overnight became public property.

Unprepared for such a sudden flash of light, the village folks were somewhat dazzled but very proud of their newly found genius. Lowly Skigerstonians, whose separated stand on church tenets culminated in a protracted trauma, were now visualized in an entirely new perspective. Contrasting northern neighbors no longer quoted their favorite derogatory cliché, to wit: "Can anything good come out of Skigersta?"

Subsequently, the creative poet Alex Nicholson, a junior contemporary who loved the village and whose lovely romantic verses shall always enrich Lewis lore, set up a home and grocery shop combine on the beautiful *Baile Àird* overlooking his favorite village, next to Lionel, his birthplace, and, as scripture promised, the last became first.

Shakespeare, greatest secular writer of Christendom, wrote, "Some are born great, some achieve greatness and some have greatness thrust upon them." Norman Morrison, the Skigersta Bard, unquestionably belonged in the first category.

One of a Kind

In his father-in-law, D. B. MacKay, who was also his employer for many years, my father found a rich source of further information on the Bard and gained some new perspective on him.

Thinking that as a next-door neighbor I was somewhat aware of the Bard's many faculties, one can imagine my surprise when in

1928, right on the edge of New York's notorious "Hell's Kitchen," D. B. Mackay, formerly of Skigersta, explained to me about the Bard's least publicized aptitude—his enormous physical power. D. B., of whom I had heard so much but never met till then, arrived in New York from Glasgow shortly before the Spanish–American War. His workshop at that time was on the third floor of a tenement area.

D. B.'s first bit of startling information on my first meeting was that he knew more about my father and the Bard than I did. "They were my constant pals during my apprenticeship years in Stornoway," he boasted with the elation of one referring to royal personages. For the next twenty-three years of almost inseparable relationship between us, these two cronies, especially the Bard, dominated most of D. B.'s conversations.

He never ceased to point out how the Bard bested massive fishermen in weightlifting contests, men who towered over him like giants—Norman never exceeding five foot ten inches and slim as a board all his life. It appears that the current big men were as puzzled as to wherein his great strength lay as Delilah was regarding Samson.

However, not until difficult spells of exigencies on the high seas occurred, which I witnessed, did the Bard's real fiery self come into play. Watching his performances in such situations was both awesome and inspiring. When those brooding blue eyes flashed furiously and arms flailed fast and adroitly in all directions, the rest of the crew, skillful seamen to a man, seemed to be clogging his path.

It is rather astonishing, human nature being what it is, that none of these tough, sea-faring stalwarts, in years of accepting his disciplinary guidance as their skipper on open waters, ever indicated a tinge of jealousy regarding his superior qualities and no-nonsense, harsh exercise of prerogatives in times of stress. On the contrary, even as retired landlubbers, they still admiringly looked up to him, cautiously awaiting his final opinion concerning all weighty matters of local and national consequence. Fishermen in general are a versatile, talented breed, but obviously recognizing leadership qualities among themselves is the most astute feature of their numerous mores.

So modest was neighbor Norman amid all this respect that he even disdained the common praise which is the inevitable lot of great men, partly because of his perennial fear of becoming victim to gaudy adulation, which, as a Christian, he considered the province of the lewd and foolish.

The following three sketches provide further insight on the Bard as skipper-sailor. In the first, his mastery of mathematical computations is highlighted. In the second, he exhibits all those qualities one would want in a capable captain at war. He is supremely confident, decisive, skillful in all things necessary, has perfect timing, and is ferociously aggressive. In the third, he takes his large, fully loaded *sgoth* out into deep waters under very nasty wave and wind conditions in Skigersta harbor—and prevails.

Superiority

Without any doubt, the Skigersta Bard surpassed all his fellow fishermen in arithmetical ability during our youthful years in Skigersta of long ago. His superior skill in this particular field became glaringly evident when on-the-spot estimates, sans paper and pen, were desirable among the *bodaich* in determining the crew's share of the catch prior to touching on shore. Many of our fishermen participated in this pastime when looking over a hefty catch, but the slow ones in mental calculating never divulged their conclusions—for obvious reasons.

There were several Skigersta fishermen who were experts in this mental exercise, of which four besides the Bard come to mind: Alex Murray, *Dànaidh*, *Iain Bàn*, and that sharp-eyed stalwart Murdo Mackay, who could appropriately be called the "fisherman's fisherman" because he never took to sea without his emergency box containing everything from stimulants to bandages.

However, without attempting to negate the talents of these able men, let's consider, by way of stressing a point that they were of a younger age bracket than the Bard and somehow managed to obtain the basic system of arithmetical subjects, especially *Dànaidh* and *Iain Bàn*. None of the Bard's age group ever attended class and neither did the Bard, which of course is another story and puzzlement to villagers to this day, including his own son Norman, our best informed resident.

In regards to instant estimates of catches on the high seas, it suffices to point out that the Bard, in a mixed crew of good-natured competitors, was the first to arrive at the exact figure. Superiority excels no matter what the circumstances might be. To the fishermen's credit, all the Bard's fair-minded rivals readily conceded that such was the case.

While these were no isolated instances, proving the Bard's higher than average degree of intellectual powers, perhaps the hallmark measure of his sturdy manliness can best be analyzed when, on one embarrassing occasion, we Skigersta lads witnessed in horror the Bard, our alter ego, grossly entangled in one of his rare mathematical errors in the cruel glare of public scrutiny.

It is one thing to stumble on an error of our own making, with no one aware of the matter, and pulling a public blunder within the critical gaze of village residents. What happens when an expert of the Bard's caliber, rarely on the wrong side of any current topic, finds himself enmeshed in a maze of wrong computations in front of a shocked audience at our old schoolhouse of long ago? It is related in another anecdote. Read about how men are separated from the boys.

Camaisear Confrontation

The Skigersta Bard's casual demeanor was very misleading. His raw courage and fierce determination came to the attention of his young crew one early morning on a routine fishing errand south of home base, our own comely *cladach* of long ago.

Back in those days, the poaching trawler, especially the *Sasannach*, was generally equated with abject humiliation, an affront to traditional Gael pride and courage. As the carefree young crew, bristling with the spirit of adventure, rounded the vantage point upon clearing the Bragg strait, where a clear sweep of our favorite fishing ground, the popular *Camaisear*, came into focus, there was a bold black trawler hugging the coastline along the beautiful *Cladichean geala*.

In the tense climate of those days, a more obnoxious object couldn't be encountered sufficient enough to arouse the dander of seven young Skigersta stalwarts aboard *Eathar a' bhaile shuas*, a sleek *sgoth* of yesteryear. Moreover, the fact that the poacher stealthily scraped the ocean floor in search of the *Leòbag* and *Cròdan*, special Skigerstonian delicacies—added fuel to the fire. A more propitious hour for a splashing skirmish, come hangings or high courts, could never again emerge—*Cum rithe thall* (keep at it).

Donald Thomson, *Dòmhnall Mòr*, the junior member of the crew, famed for his descriptive accuracy in detailing matters of importance, recalled what occurred when, almost simultaneously, they spotted the common enemy. As usual the Bard, svelte and supple as a cat, held sway on the stern end, with tiller firmly grasped and eyes alert. He was running full sail in a temperate northwest breeze when he spied the culprit.

Abruptly, while yelling for a shortened sheet, he shoved the tiller to port as the slick *sgoth* smoothly swerved to starboard until the brazen bounder was in clear frontal range of vision. The trawler, with full gear in working order and registration marks concealed under canvas, like a masked bandit on the prowl, slowly headed due west obviously anticipating to complete the sweep and turn at *Quiseadear* to head for open waters.

They were in for the biggest surprise of their poaching careers, on suddenly becoming aware of seven Skigersta wild men stalking their trail, eager for battle in the David and Goliath clash of the century. The freakish head-on *Camaisear* confrontation which quickly ensued was probably the shortest but most decisive of all maritime conflicts, the story of which contained more excitement to us youngsters of that era than tales of great sea battles of the past.

The details are related by *Dòmhnall Mòr*. As the baby of the crew, he recalled with a chuckle that he became acutely apprehensive as the lawless intruder got bigger and closer, but one look at the Bard's fearful combat countenance quickly convinced him that jumping overboard and taking his chance on swimming to shore was his only alternative.

Suddenly, on becoming aware of peril, nervous heads began to appear along the trawler's railings, some quickly vanishing, obviously terrified at the wild looks of the Skigersta warriors itching for battle. Not so the skipper, however, who in apparent curiosity, owlishly looked out of his wheelhouse window sizing up the manic-looking young fishermen (in disdain, no doubt), when, abruptly, he was startled clear out of his wits.

The Bard, ired beyond control at the composure of the shameless villain calmly peering from aloft, fired a hefty stone missile which, in perfect aim and timing, resoundingly crashed just a mere foot below the skipper's face. The awesome whack reverberated from stem to stern as the skipper's weather beaten face and serenity vanished simultaneously.

Within seconds, dire panic erupted aboard. Bells clanged, whistles shrieked, with the old man belaboring feverishly to abscond fast and furious into open waters. Just when the scared skipper finally got his cumbrous craft on the move, the Bard, on catching a glimpse of his frightened face, shouted up through cupped fingers, "*Biodh fhios agad, ars esan, 'nach ann ri gealtairean a tha do ghnothaich*" (May you know, said he, that you are not dealing with cowards) as the panicky poachers streakily headed for the three-mile limit, ostensibly vowing, never again. Subsequently, the trawling limits were extended to twelve miles.

Ladysmith

Late in the fall of 1923 Skigersta's youngsters witnessed one of the last spectacular performances of a twenty-one foot *sgoth* just prior to our migration the following year. It was a precarious race against the menacing waves which, on certain storm-bound days, rapidly rolls into Skigersta's narrow harbor, one behind the other in stiff easterly breezes. This daring deed demanded a fast escape during the occasional lull between breakers—a quick get-a-way right into the teeth of the elements. It was the kind of maritime feat where skilled seamanship made the difference between survival and complete disaster.

The *sgoth* was the noted speedster and beautifully lined *Ladysmith*, skippered by my illustrious neighbor, the famed Skigersta Bard. *Dànaidh* MacKay, of respected memory, was the able *Gilletòisich* (fellow at the front). The occasion was transporting solidly packed ling, dried and cured, to the Stornoway market.

Following much elaborate preparation, including launching the large *Eathar mhòr*, as her type was called, all the way from the high berth, the sturdy crew, in typical Skigerstonian tenacity, hated to turn tail and admit defeat. So great was the risk involved, however, that when the perilous event was successfully accomplished, and the men safe in open waters, a retired mariner, who apprehensively watched from the shoreline, remarked, "That was by far the most foolhardy episode that I've seen in a lifetime at sea."

On this particularly rough day, every minor and major detail aboard the *sgoth* was smoothed out to perfection, in which extra precaution was prudent and a margin for error intolerable. At a glance, the crew's expressions indicated the importance of the moment, as each member, expert seamen to a man, tautly awaited at his post, with wary eyes on waves and weather.

As all local fishermen know, the navigable gap of water between the craggy north and south entrances leading into Skigersta's harbor is cramped enough to allow only two short tacks by means of reaching the safety of open waters in adverse weather. The southern tack toward the boisterous *Cragichean* abruptly terminates in its immediate vicinity, in a swift swerve to northeast, whilst guardedly avoiding the treacherous alee hazards of the *àird* base to the north, which of necessity must be negotiated at close proximity as the last formidable obstacle in a dash for the "Deep."

Suddenly and simultaneously, everybody standing around on the quay became aware of the anticipated lull, and tension mounted as the old *Lòn Gorm* looked smooth and inviting, in that brief, deceptive calm so well known to men of the sea, and just as quickly, the Bard's shout to "let go" echoed from the *Leac* to the parapet.

Instantly, that open *sgoth* became a beehive of fast, adept activity, an unforgettable display of human effort and flawless performance. In mere seconds, the big angled sail on the cumbrous gaff was tackled to peak high by three stalwarts amidships—two for the long pull and one below for the slack, so rapidly the canvas was already bulging and the *sgoth* gaining momentum as able hands made fast.

With a generous breeze and protuberant sail, the speedy *Ladysmith* now streakily headed south, rakishly slicing across the bay with a massive white bone in her teeth and all hands in "heads-up" vigilance. At top speed, she approached the roaring south shallows in moments of time, and the Bard, in perfect timing, sharply swung to port and plowed right into an onrushing high frothy swell, part of which wafted over the bow, spraying the crew in their first Baptism of brine for the day.

During the crucial subsequent "hove-to" seconds available, canvas was lowered, switched to port, and hoisted aloft with the smooth, magical speed common to trained mariners since antiquity. After this, *Ladysmith*, regaled in bulging, full canvas glory, was off in typical fast form toward the high seas of northeast, bypassing the *àird's* foamy surf by a comfortable margin, furiously splashing through angry white caps, looking like a mammoth sailfish assailing the elements.

After his midlife conversion, the Bard became an elder in the Free Presbyterian Church and a spiritual force in the community. My father describes both his conversion and the subsequent effect he had on participants in worship. In the third sketch, he addresses the issue of why the Bard often seemed so sad. Mrs. Morrison's sadness, though, was no mystery. We see this last reflection of the Bard's home life through the eyes of the two Anguses—the young and indifferent one and the older, more sensitive one.

Conversion

No episode in the Bard's exciting career was more noteworthy than an esoteric experience which should be related with some trepidation because it enters the sensitive aspect of his conversion to the faith. In our corner of the world, with the outpouring of the Gospel message available to all and where within a five-mile radius nearly everyone knows everybody else, personality changes through the power of the Word are commonplace.

When this drastic change occurs, however, the weird assessments and spurious speculations of gossipy idlers regarding the background and general behavior of these "other sheep" referred to in the Gospel goes into high gear. The Skigersta Bard, with one cogent difference, was no exception in this sinister scrutiny—of *Siol nan nathraichean nimhe* (the seed of poisonous serpents). In contrast, Norman's startling conversion low-toned the tale bearers to guarded whispers because no one dared to mouth out loud a derogatory remark about one of such searing vocabulary whose weighty words carried a certain clout all of their own.

Therefore, doubtful worldlings and skeptics had no choice but to mutely wait and wonder if Norman's sudden about face was the genuine "call." They waited a whole life time only to witness spotless Christian conduct amply rewarded at the age of seventy-two upon entering the "saint's everlasting rest," having endured his share of tribulations, disillusionment, and discord.

Like most sinners, the Bard as a young man was a careless worldling but was upright, a hardworking and adroit skipper, quite satisfied with current conditions as they were, not wishing to rock the boat or make waves on either side of the sacred or secular climate of the day. This seemingly secure, happy-go-lucky state prevailed through several fishing seasons in which he and my father indulged in an occasional animated *smùid* (intoxication), consisting of more innocuous noise and loud laughter than harm to anyone.

It seems that in the wake of one of these tumultuous outbursts, the arrow of conviction, unobtrusively and unbeknown to the world, found its mark. According to my Uncle Murdo's report on the episode, the aftermath of the Bard's complete reversal of his former behavior was an astonishing appraisal of the man's enormous strength of character regarding his solemn obligatory duties toward God and man. Not a single fishing day was lost or one hour of croft chores avoided prior to or following one of the most unassailable conversions of that rigid and skeptical generation.

The Bard on *Là na Ceist* (Friday)

I couldn't help but wonder how one individual held such a spell over an entire community for a whole generation as I watched neighbor Norman slowly and methodically fill up his pipe sitting unperturbed by our middle-of-the-floor fire of long ago. That was exactly the Bard's posture for many years in the sense that nearly everybody awaited his opinion in consequential matters of crucial import ever since I, in my early teens, became aware of the man's multiple talents.

For example, what prompted a crowded church at communion seasons on *Là na Ceist* to eagerly await with awe his poignant discourses in which he graphically outlined the conspicuous marks of the true Christian and those of the unbeliever in terrifying terms and clarity for all to understand? It was nothing else but the singular power of his personality that created this unique situation when all, including the ministers, made a point of hanging onto his every syllable in the manner the divines and sages of old were listened to in hushed silence.

There were many articulate and fine speakers commenting on Christian experience on *Là na Ceist* in our day, but none held a congregation as spellbound as the Bard. Furthermore, only the most deluded and dullest of that solemn gathering on *Là na Ceist* in our day with the Bard as chief speaker harbored the slightest doubt as to whether he or she served God or mammon—especially after he sat down. To our own age group, going through the impressionable phase of the late teens, it was a frightening experience to hear our alter ego, mentor, friend, and next-door neighbor ripping off our self-righteous rags piece by piece until stark naked, so to speak.

Without any doubt, it was the Bard's strong and aggressive approach to all obstacles and problems, which he attacked with the fervor of a charging Cossack that was primarily instrumental in gaining the respect of the populace. He was the epitome of mental and physical power, amply proven by the way his presence was felt wherever he went. That Norman applied this rigid, no compromise, no holds barred approach to his own religious life was evident in his daily deportment and general relationship to his fellowman.

For example, few people ired him like the lukewarm Laodicean communicant, whom he equated with one living with a lie. His motto was, "Be a good Christian or none at all." This unpopular stance frequently plunged him into hot water, but who was going to dispute or argue with a man of such searing vocabulary?

A Somber Bard

While growing up next door to the famed Skigersta Bard, I often wondered why he always, or nearly always, looked so sad. As I look back on matters now in my early eighties, several major reasons for gloom clearly come to mind. First, his son Donald, the apple of his eye, emigrated to Canada sometime between 1907 and 1908, the big migration era, and immediately forgot that he ever had parents—not even a postcard showed from year to year.

Second, his beautiful daughter Annie, able and intelligent like her father, was crippled from birth. Third, death removed his third daughter Mary when in her twenties, acknowledged a foremost beauty of our Ness community. Exact words from her own lips, not many moments prior to entering into heaven is worth recording. She told her mother, who stood over her in her last moments, as follows word for word: "I could not stay for a thousand, thousand worlds."

Fourth reason, his second son Norman, who still survives and was equally loved, well known throughout Ness as probably the best informed and erudite of his generation, had severe health problems after leaving the militia. For a few years, it was touch-and-go, as people worried and of course likewise his father, who almost despaired of ever seeing Norman well again. Norman recovered and retained his higher than average IQ to this day.

However shocking as it might seem, none of the abovementioned reasons for gloom cut into the Bard's soul as sharply as the one I'm now about to reveal, and one which is unknown to any soul on earth at this point of time except myself—and possibly his only surviving son.

Back in the Bard's reckless, carefree days, in command of terrible, vilifying Gaelic adjectives, he brought a cloud of shame on local personalities in verses of savage semantics, shocking a Christian community. It was a black blunder of the deepest dye. After his conversion, the impact of this utterly sinful abuse of talent hit him doubly hard and he never, never forgave himself. This miserable mistake stuck into the Bard's conscience like a knife until the day of his death.

Next-Door Drama

Looking back on my twenty-one years of living on the beautiful *Baile Shuas* of long ago, from the lofty vista of three score and ten, I find it more impossible now than before to shake off the sad image of my next-door neighbor *Bean a' Bhàird's* (Bard's wife's) daily dismay. Mary Morrison endured the daily trauma of rejection and sorrow for most of my young days, almost within a handshake from my door.

While myriads of the sins of omission rear their ugly heads in my long and turbid track record, now too clearly in focus, callous insensitivity nonetheless to a neighbor's suffering also gloomily peers right at me as a grim reminder of youthful indifference to other people's woes. I refer to my adolescent apathy as regards *Bean a' Bhàird's* perennial perplexity, a lovely, compassionate mother of two sons and four daughters—whose sorrow could never be weighed. In Mary's case, it wasn't any lack of common amenities, friends, or sympathetic adults, all of which she, as a popular Skigersta mother and spouse of renowned Bard enjoyed to the fullest, that brought grief and loneliness to her heart, but a prodigal son in faraway Canada who ignored her from year to year.

It was shallow pleasure as usual for us four *Baile Shuas* males near the same age, as the mailman whistled from door to door, dropping a letter here and a package there, advancing toward Mary's door where for years she listened to that whistle getting closer and closer as she awaited by the *ursainn* (doorpost) in ecstatic anticipation. In the absence of a Canadian postmark, Mary plunged back again into the abyss of despair, wishing for tomorrow.

What powerful drama can daily and quietly enfold so physically close to us, and yet find us untouched and remote as if it all occurred in the farthest corner of the world? It did not move us youngsters one whit to see our elders agonize with Mary every day at mail delivery time because of our utter inability to fathom the depth, height, and width of mother love in our mad adolescent *Amaideas* (foolishness) in which we reveled with abandon.

Looking back on it now, it strikes me as rather strange that the largest portion of local sympathy centered on the distraught mother more so than the father, our famed Skigersta Bard. Neighbor Norman, though probably one of the strongest men of his generation, was also a man of tender compassion who unashamedly wept when deeply moved, as I have witnessed.

Upon returning to my native strand, after an absence of almost three decades, that door, a mere few paces from my own, the sad site of Mary's long and lonesome vigil over the years awaiting the postman, revived somber memories. The God-fearing Mary and her equally pious spouse had previously entered into that "prepared place" where neither sorrow nor tears shall be their part evermore.

9

Working

How people in and around Skigersta made a living was not the focus of my father's writings, but in his celebratory sketches of people he most admired, he simultaneously lets us peer into the world of work at the turn of the century. In addition to the skills represented below, we know there was a tailor in Lionel because he hurled insults at my father and his Separatist chums on their way to school every day and a blacksmith and smithy in the same village.

Fisherman Murdo

Murdo Mackay, an interim skipper and inveterate fisherman of our young days in Skigersta, could, with his steel-trap mind, emerge in our modern jungle of technology as a top-notch astronaut. No item, momentous or minimal, escaped his attention as regarded his crew's safety in his final inspection of the *sgoth* when about to head for the open sea.

Murdo was the first *sgoth* skipper in our fishing community of Ness to lash a first aid kit abaft the after thwart for emergency. The dreaded tetanus and treacherous *Dubhan mòr* (hookworm) were Murdo's prime concern in these precautionary measures.

Murchadh Dhòmhnaill Ruaidh was one of the most spirited and supple of our many vigorous village fishermen. His powerful pair of arms were frequently commented on by fellow fishermen, among whom were many physically powerful men. I was about five years of age when Murdo first impressed me, as we watched his lively gait and catlike moves on the old quay, where we tykes shared the excitement of those colorful days of long ago.

The salty Murdo was then in his prime, and he looked every bit of it, briskly maneuvering from stem to stern with the agility of the trained mariner. His bristling crop of reddish-brown hair, lively blue eyes, and trimmed red moustache cut an unforgettable figure while issuing last-minute orders to a crew who greatly respected his sound judgment and renowned expertise on the high seas.

It was estimated by our local seafaring experts of Skigersta and elsewhere that no one in these parts made the scientific study of the treacherous currents which daily and furiously flow in abrupt changing courses along our island coastline as Murdo Mackay did. They are known among fishermen as the *sruth sear* (eastern current) and *sruth siar* (western current).

It seems that the keen-minded Murdo was aware of the phenomenal elements of those strong currents right down to the time of change and their effect on open waters in conjunction with prevailing winds. This knowledge gave him, as a skipper, tremendous advantage, especially when tacking along the shoreline. Nearly all our fisher folks were skillful seamen, but *Murchadh Dhòmhnaill Ruaidh* surpassed most of them in natural alertness, in which his uncanny predictive gifts hit the mark every time.

Murdo's annual trip to *Sùlaisgeir* was the joyous high point of his whole seafaring career, and no sooner was he back with a hefty load of sweet-smelling *gugaichean* (*guga* is a young solan goose or gannet) than he combed the community arranging for next year's crew—an amazing, energetic individual.

Murdo Mackay was also a tenderhearted man of compassion. For example, when his gallant young next-door neighbor, John Morrison, was missing in action during World War I, so deeply touched was Murdo in watching John's father *Alasdair* suffering in the abyss of despair that he found attending Sabbath services impossible. He agonized with his brokenhearted neighbor from day to day. John Morrison's supreme sacrifice in Flanders field brought out a soft side of Murdo Mackay which even his closest friends weren't aware he fostered down deep in his soul.

Curer Murdo

On the sunny days of a prosperous past, a large portion of our modest Skigersta beach was utilized in curing the noted and nutritious ling for the Stornoway market. Today the ling, the basic means of support for our hardy forbears, has in value and prestige plunged to the market level of what the dogfish and mackerel, scavenger fishes, maintained in our young days. "How has the mighty fallen."

Three twenty-one-foot *sgothan* on a round-the-clock ling fishing routine to *Cara Phìobaire* and elsewhere kept the curer and the nostalgic *Taighean saillidh* (curing houses) bustling with activities for six solid days. Atop the white pebbles on our *cladach*, the split, flattened ling in drying process were cautiously and evenly laid side by side in straight, lengthy rows with only a narrow footpath between sections.

Tall, gray-haired Murdo Mackenzie, *Lathamor, Murchadh Chalum Pìobaire*, was for a spell following *Ailean Bàn's* retirement, the curer for the *bodaich* when our age bracket was about ten years old. Murdo, affectionately known as *Murchadh Chalum*, was a retired fisherman who loved boys and who entertained us youngsters with exciting yarns about his long life at sea.

Murdo's conversation, which poured out of him nonstop, didn't deter him a whit from deftly slicing away at gills, caudals, and innards with a long razor-sharp blade. It was obvious that the fish's gall worried him no end, because he gingerly stabbed around them like they were explosives—reminding us of the volatile swiftness in which the burst gall entered the ling steak, contaminating the lovely ling beyond anything meaningful except a grand soiree for seagulls.

Knowing our fathers well, erstwhile crew members, he never failed to inquire about their health and everyone's well-being within each *cagailte*. I can still recall how at that tender age we just loved that warm bit of intimacy, especially his genuine concern regarding indisposed members of our families.

Other people's problems laid heavy on his mind, perhaps explaining why few *Niseachs* in our day were regarded with more respect than *Murchadh Chalum*. Murdo was a deeply religious man of a tall, straight frame and impressive, lively gaited bearing for one of his age. Not much given to laughter, he nevertheless could laugh lustily when his comical neighbor *Seòras Sheumais* came out with his daily budget of hilarious observations concerning his wife (my aunt), his brother Norman, and spinster sister Christine living next door, all three being his first morning targets for generations.

When old age infirmities confined Murdo to home and bed, the Skigersta *cladach* appeared deserted. His delightful approach and engaging, magnetic personality virtually filled our compact, comely beach all the way from the *Seòlas* to the *Taighean saillidh*.

Skigersta's *Taighean Saillidh*

As youngsters roaming the Skigersta *cladach* from day to day, the dank and dark interiors of the *Taighean saillidh* never failed to impress us, as we examined the overturned *sgothan*, speedsters of other days. Curer *Murchadh Chalum Pìobaire* Mackenzie and *Ailean Bàn*, Allan Mackay, two *Lathamor* old-timers, recalled the background of the upside down crafts which provided roofs for our curing shacks where the *sruthan Gil* flows into the bay.

There was something pitifully incongruous and sad about the *sgothan's* overturned, awkward position in contrast to their glorious speedy performances on the high seas when our sturdy grandfathers caught ling in copious quantities just a mere three miles offshore. Around 1908, when I started school, there were about two of our salting shacks in service housing three large wooden tanks invariably full of ling in the salting process.

After a certain spell in the oblong tanks, curer Murdo would flatten the split ling all along the pebbly beach, row upon row, sometimes covering the entire south corner of the *cladach*—a beautiful sight to behold. In our young days, the flat corner housing the *Taighean saillidh* looked beautiful from *Bàrr a' Chladaich*, especially in the summer season with the old upturned *sgothan* snuggled against the grassy, daisy-covered green slopes of the *Gil's* former grandeur— as the nostalgic *sruthan* slowly murmured its way into the sea.

Alasdair Ruadh

Offhand, I can think of no other *bodach* in Skigersta more visible every day than Alex Murray, *Alasdair Ruadh* of High Street. Alex, a remarkable, energetic fisherman, could be seen moving about the village ranging from the quay to the *Baile Àird* and the *Baile Shuas* seemingly nonstop from morn till night. Boats and fishing, in which he was passionately involved since his teens, were the story of Alex's whole life.

In a broad sense, there was no other *bodach* in Skigersta just quite like *Alasdair Ruadh*. While lacking even grammar school education, he could speak English fluently and was so adept in mental arithmetic that the crew's share of the catch was calculated by able Alex prior to touching on shore.

Ever since my age bracket could recall, Alex was off to the east coast herring fishing: Frazerborough, Peter Head, etc., every season with the regularity of incoming and outgoing tides. He never missed. Such were the demands on his services that he immediately obtained a place on a drifter. His expertise was such that he felt equally comfortable on a drifter, *sùilea*, or *sgoth*.

It was among the skillful east coast fishermen, the *Bucaich* (people from Buckie), that versatile *Alasdair* first learned the rather complex art of net mending, a craft of deceptive intricacy requiring more skill than meets the eye. It was in this particular field that *Alasdair Ruadh* became such an expert that no one in our Ness community could even hope to match, especially in speed, corner patching of badly torn herring nets, the acid test between the expert and the bungling amateur. The knitting in of a corner herring net patch, especially a large one, demanded cunning forethought in which absolute perfection of detail was imperative prior to the first stitch, like buttoning the overcoat with the top button in the wrong hole.

In this phase of net mending, Alex Murray was, to belabor an old cliché, in a class by himself. It was sheer delight for us youngsters to watch *Alasdair Ruadh's* fast moving hands finishing off one of those complicated corner patches, feeling as confident of the positive final outcome of his handiwork as an expert trained seamstress feels in sewing buttons on sleeves. He was absolutely sure of his skill and showed it as he closed up that corner to perfection.

When we left Skigersta in 1924, there were twenty-five of the village *bodaich* surviving. Only Alex and Norman MacLean were around when for the first time I arrived back in 1952. What a grand group of worthies those hardy men were! We loved them all. Their witticisms, harmless shouting matches and frequent eccentric strays from the norm kept us youngsters amused from day to day. When old Alex walked onto our *cagailte* to greet me with an outstretched hand and familiar grin, the thought struck me that such a warm experience was in itself worth the journey.

Skigersta's Quay

At Skigersta's quay of long ago, when the big *sgothan* heading for berth were safely inside the calm, manmade lee cove, touching on the slip, four fishing stalwarts, two on each side in hip-high solid leather boots waded out a few feet and in back-to-back unison eased the receding bow clear out of the water onto the slip. Sounds easy. Why report it? Well, read on.

The round built-in keelhaul, a fat inch in diameter and a mite abaft the stem's joint which, with a few hefty heaves became high and dry, was of course the objective of the four fishermen. Then, a sturdy steel bar was shoved into the hole equally protruding on port and starboard where a twin fingered cable was hooked, which the strain from the old winch on high ground held fast.

In calm weather, all this was relatively easy, but with a running swell, common enough in Skigersta's *Lòn Gorm* that brief task demanded swift and thorough performance. On many occasions, it was touch-and-go because the inrushing swelling waters frequently raised the Big Sgoths, *Eithrichean mòra*, as they were called, again to floating level which, in the following ebb flow dried the cumbrous craft past midships—inviting disaster. Hence the urgency of attaching that cable with the special expertise and piercing reflexes of the trained mariner.

The tedious uphill drag which followed was a trying project in itself because so much manpower was required to keep the big, heavy *sgothan* on even keel in a steady steep climb all the way to the modest but secure berth, whose sole claim to notoriety was the fact that Lord Leverhulme stopped to chat with the *bodaich* at that very spot on his first visit to the Skigersta bay which he adored.

So severe an incline was and is our quay's slip that to tread upon it on wet days is rather risky. Nothing embarrasses a sure-footed fisherman like landing on the seat of his pants, but it frequently occurs, even in Skigersta. In the 1860s, the era of the great drowning (1862) when thirty-one *Niseachs* perished, there was no Skigersta quay, no parapet, no slip or winch, just a wild cove, similar to any open roadstead constantly exposed to the elements. How our grandfathers managed to maneuver the *sgothan* in such severe surroundings is something to ponder. There was one favorable feature going for them, however, that fact that ling, their prime support, was to be had in great quantities three miles offshore.

When the ingenious mason *Dòmhnall Weir* signed the contract for constructing our present L-shaped quay, the current *bodaich* were as elated as we were back in the twenties when the munificent multimillionaire and soap mogul Baron Leverhulme planned to build us a seaport.

Who would guess that there was a connection between a Skigerstonian joiner/shipbuilder and the famous clipper ship *Flying*

Cloud? That connection is explored in the first sketch below. In the second, this craftsman emerges as a favorite of my great-grandmother, who commissioned him to build her a *dreasair*—one more beloved object my father would remember leaving behind. In the third, the joiner of my father's generation is highlighted, but as usual, it is the Bard who "steals the show," emerging as a master at yet another skill.

Dòmhnall MacFhionnlaigh

Slicing through frothy whitecaps in full sail with an occasional ripple dramatically wafting over the bow, the famed *Sgoth Niseach* was a vision of nautical beauty. In Skigersta of long ago, such exciting scenes were commonplace. Hardly a day passed that *sgothan* weren't visible from our favorite vantage point, the onetime imposing eminence *Cnoc a' Choilich*.

Perhaps unknown to our current youngsters is the fact that we in Skigersta at one time boasted of a noted *sgoth* builder of our own, a bona fide Skigerstonian artisan. He was the sturdy craftsman Donald Mackay of No. 17 *Lathamor*, *Dòmhnall MacFhionnlaigh*, who claimed distant relationship to the most famous shipbuilder of all time, the American Donald Mackay of New England, who helped design the world's fastest sailing ship, the immortal *Flying Cloud*. The well-known D. B. Mackay of New York, Donald's son (who made it big on his own as a successful shoetree and last manufacturer), amassed some knowledge of the intricate blood relation existing between his family and of the famed shipbuilder. The latter's background is recorded in the *Encyclopedia Britannica*.

No records are extant to determine how many *sgothan* the dexterous *Dòmhnall* built in Skigersta, hard by the *cladach*, where launching was easy in high tides. The unusual location of Donald's boathouse never failed to arouse our interests as boys, who spent a large portion of our young lives in its immediate locale. His workshop was directly opposite the fast flowing *Fuaran Lathamor* at the eastern bottom of the small ravine which divides *Lathamor* from the *Baile Shuas*. A small languid stream meandered past the *Fuaran*, freely flowing out of the western bottom of the gulch until a concrete keep was provided.

On the eastern side of the tiny *sruthan* was a flat, earth-packed natural protrusion which provided Donald with sufficient leveled area to lay his keel. None of our age bracket, of course, remembered these colorful events, and the oblong segment of soil where Donald shaped the sleek *sgothan* was just a flat patch of grass in our time. Today, through the ravages of time, it has possibly eroded beyond recognition—as the nostalgic little stream rolls on and on.

Joinery Masterpieces

Skigersta's innovative *sgoth* builder and village joiner Donald Mackay of No. 17 *Lathamor by the sea* was so neat and dexterous that many old-timers were absolutely sold on his meticulous method of getting things done. In fact, other craftsmen's work was to them mere mediocrity. The *bodaich* were like that, loyal to an uncommon degree in matters concerning their own. If, for example, one of the joinery artists of the famed Taj Mahal, a magnificent monument of elegant craftsmanship, offered the Skigersta *bodaich* to repair their three-legged stools, they'd turn him down cold if *Dòmhnall MacFhionnlaigh* was available.

Many of Donald's progeny were outstanding creative figures, especially Malcolm's sons—Donald, William, and John. Another grandson, the gallant Murdo, laid down his life for the king and country in World War I. His father *Calum* was also a gifted man, handy with tools and an able *sgoth* skipper all his adult life.

Dòmhnall MacFhionnlaigh was a warm friend of my *Baile Shuas* grandmother and of my next-door neighbor, the Bard's mother—two widows of the tragic Great Drowning of December 1862. The beautiful four-tiered dish cupboard—*dreasair*—which *Dòmhnall* especially built for my grandmother, along with a small stool, finger holed in the center, clearly revealed the singular skill of the gifted old-timer. Mother proudly pointed them out to visitors as *Dòmhnall MacFhionnlaigh's* joinery masterpieces, which indeed they were.

A Skigersta Salty

Malcolm Mackay, our village joiner of long ago, who also skippered *sgothan* nearly all his adult life, besides working his trade, was one of Skigersta's many sharp-eyed stalwarts. Also Malcolm's sons, with the possible exception of the gallant Murdo, were superbly creative to a man—Donald, William, and John. Their skills, manifest in the elegant exhibits of cunning work left behind, speak of their singular talents and delicate eye-catching works of art.

Skipper Malcolm, short and stubborn, could ruffle feathers when aroused and as a no-nonsense skipper was a rigid disciplinarian, but as a counterbalance, when it came to evaluate the good points and potential of fellow fishermen, he was fair, fearless, and downright honest.

Back in those days with fish and fishermen on everybody's mind, crew members often discussed among themselves who was the best buoy builder of the many skillful buoy makers in the sprawling Ness fishing community. There is much more to designing and constructing a perfect buoy, which can flawlessly sit in water without tilting ever so slightly, than landlubbers realize. Malcolm's own buoys were things of beauty, and of course, the Bard's buoys always carried the stamp of his wonderful pair of hands. One day, while on this topic, Malcolm cleared the air as to who was first in this field with the following emphatic declaration for all and sundry: "There's none like the Bard's buoys bobbing up and down anywhere on the high seas, because their contour and balance are unique in their perfection" affirmed the colorful *Calum* of long ago.

My father died in 1990 nine days before his eighty-seventh birthday. In the last year and possibly two of his life, he was in very bad health. It is poignant for me to see the date on the following sketch, 1987, probably the last year in which he enjoyed a modicum of mental and physical strength. So in 1987, he was busy doing what he had been doing for forty years, writing about the worthies, saints, bards, and *bodaich* of his lost world. What follows, then, may well be one of the very last segments of his "letter to the world" that never wrote to him.

The "other" Skigersta Bard was a man of multiple talents: a poet of course, wit and storyteller but also a businessman, building a house and grocery shop "combine" as my father calls it. He apparently built the house himself and so had no one but himself to blame when he discovered an error. How he remedied the situation clearly highlights his intelligence and daring while giving Skigerstonian witnesses a genuine, bona fide, unforgettable spectacle.

The Other Skigersta Bard

Alex Nicholson, the famous bard whose romantic verses still sparkle Lewis lore, was better known for his literary achievements than for his other innumerable faculties. Nonetheless, Alex's versatile capabilities were amazing, as Skigersta's inhabitants, who watched him produce and create, can readily attest to.

It was rare indeed to see Alex stroking whiskers or scratching hairs pondering perplexities because he instinctively knew the right approach and appropriate solving of nearly all complex problems that cropped up in his daily tasks, such was the man's higher than average intelligence quotient. Like all mortals, however, able Alex misjudged a matter or two in his day, one of which is recalled in this brief sketch of a truly great man.

Reared in a creative Lionel family, Alex's adolescent years were indicative of forcefulness and initiative, besides displaying the natural wit of the born poet in casual conversations since a wee lad. No sooner had *Alasdair* finished his attractive two-story shop and home combine, which stil stands on the *Baile Àird's* intersection, than, to his horror and chagrin, he discovered that his completed handiwork was much too far off the road for the convenience of customers. One can easily visualize his crestfallen mood on becoming aware of so glaring an error on his part, of all people, noted for his multiple talents throughout the land.

However, when the *bodaich* learned that dexterous Alex was feverishly preparing to move the whole house, intact, closer to the highway, they were the ones that were crestfallen, even astounded.

Some of them were utterly unaware that a project of such magnitude was ever before attempted. Their first reactions were that every able-bodied stalwart from Cross to *Cnoc a' Choilich*, the Butt to the *Baile Àird*, would have to be recruited for what subsequently turned out to be the only spectacle ever seen in Skigersta, before or since.

When Alex accumulated the necessary paraphernalia for the big move, he only asked a handful of the current strong men to assist in pushing the project along. When we youngsters arrived on the scene that unforgettable afternoon, some of the doubting *bodaich* were already there, watching in awe that finished home solidly mounted on log-sized rollers ready to move. Moreover, their wide-eyed expressions when it did finally start to move smoothly toward the highway is an equally unforgettable recollection. Some stood speechless, incredulously gazing at Alex's latest miracle. To this day, that handsome home, removed some forty paces from its original foundation, still stands, a fitting monument to our other Skigersta bard, the gifted *Alasdair MacNeacaill.*

Norman Murray, Sheep Expert

In Skigersta of long ago tall, wiry Norman Murray on the southern slope of the beautiful *Baile Shuas* was in many aspects of his busy, brief life in a class by himself. For example, his keen eye for recognizing sheep, stray or otherwise, was phenomenal. On more than one occasion, his sharp, discerning faculties in spotting the valuable fleecy hide of a disappearing stray clandestinely showing up in unexpected quarters, three miles from Skigersta, stirred the community.

Norman sounded the alarm that mischief was afoot and the legal apparatus of those days went into high gear concerning one particular case. His scholarly younger brother John, *Iain Bàn*, well versed in many points of law, was his counselor and won his case "hands down," as lawyers put it.

Norman, widely known as the *Sasannach*, had long cheekbones, a thin nose of Roman contour and a prominent-looking forehead. His big blue eyes sparkled like an alert bird about to soar.

In streaking across the moorland, Norman surpassed by far his contemporary men of the moors. No one in our day could compete with those wiry, long legs vaulting across gullies with the ease of a giant bird. His brother John, a powerfully built six-foot fisherman, frequently commented on the one and only time he foolishly attempted to race his fleet-footed brother across the moor. "He sure humbled me," *Iain* used to admit candidly.

Norman Murray fathered a large family of seven boys and one girl. Just a little beyond his prime, Norman succumbed to appendicitis, a tragedy keenly felt by all the boys for the rest of their days. He was closer to the boys than any Skigersta father was to their sons in my time.

Murdo Macpharquer, Miller

When Murdo Macpharquer, North Dell, Ness, noted farmer and mill owner, first ordered his huge steel pocketed waterwheel (mill's sole power drive), he faced an unexpected dilemma: how to install the monstrous-looking thing? This was long before the turn of the century when expert engineers and skillful millwrights were few and far between. There wasn't a single journeyman engineer in all of Ness at that time. The closest to a millwright were the Glasgow shipyards where the world's best millwrights were employed.

As Murdo retired that night with a colossal steel drum laying on flat ground, as incongruous looking as a ship stuck in the water tossing about in his mind, he resolved to have all the strong men of the Ness community invited to push the mammoth wheel in place the following morning.

Murdo's worries were all for naught because when he got up very early next morning he saw, to his astonishment, that the big wheel was securely affixed in its proper housing as if a miracle from above had taken place. It was a foregone conclusion that Murdo, a devout man and much respected throughout the district, thanked the Most High for what transpired while pondering matters in his heart.

It seems that the manufacturers sent an engineer and a millwright, who arrived late to do the job and who worked all night rolling the big wheel into place—just the two of them. Without any fuss, noise or confusion, the two trained men installed the monster wheel while *Niseachs* slumbered, a feat which Murdo thought would take a multitude to accomplish. It was also a feat for which the pious Murdo was eternally grateful.

Gordon MacLeod, Postmaster

It is very doubtful if there ever was a more respected personality in all of Ness, except men of God and ministers of the Gospel, than Gordon MacLeod, our postmaster of long ago. He was postmaster long before I started school in 1908 and was ably running things when I left on the *Marloch* in 1924.

Skigersta is two miles south of Port-of-Ness, Gordon's home town, where he conscientiously served the community for a whole generation. By way of shortening our distance to reach Port, we Skigersta youngsters used to cut through the *Slugaid* at *Taigh Thorcuil*—reducing the distance to almost a mile.

Gordon, named in honor of the great general Gordon, was looked up to by old and young. It could be truly said of him that he was the epitome of everything that is noble and decent in a human being. Soft-spoken and pleasant to approach at all times, he was always immaculately dressed, sporting a neatly trimmed, narrow, waxed moustache highlighting his handsome, slender features to perfection.

There was that unmistakable scholarly, refined look about him which made him conspicuous in a crowd, besides exuding warmth and goodwill which unlearned men like me cannot properly define. He was an exemplar of the manner in which human beings are supposed to conduct themselves. Gordon MacLeod was a light in our community somewhat akin to the manner that Christians are a light in the world.

Kenneth and Donald, Postal Officers

Ness postal officers, brothers Kenneth and Donald, were in our young days, as Gordon MacLeod was, highly respected and looked up to in our Ness community. For years, they transported the mail between Stornoway and Ness for six days a week without fail. They also had the distinction of being the first in Ness to own an automobile, but some suspected that the Post Office was the real owner. Others assumed that Bard Alex Nicholson, our "other" able Skigersta poet, was the first real owner of an auto in the Ness district.

When the First World War broke out on August 4, 1914, a disturbing incident occurred in Ness which shook our Christian community like an unexpected seismic tremor. For generations, our community was noted for its towering spiritual lights of godly men and women, with special regard for the sanctity of the Sabbath day. In the Hebrides of our day, it was always the "Sabbath," never called Sunday.

Amidst all this calm, devoted climate, *Dòmhnall a' Phost*, like a bolt from the blue, commenced to haul the mail on the Sabbath day. Our Ness God-fearing colony, especially the elderly, was terribly hurt at this grave matter, sending many to their knees in prayer.

It took one fearless woman, however, who had just emerged unscathed and triumphant from the Declaratory Act wars to face the mischief head on. She walked three miles to Donald's home and took it upon herself to personally remind him of his blatant desecration of the Lord's day. Her lecture was brief, poignant, and sharp as a two-edged sword. Donald, always the gentleman, never uttered a word of protest.

Louis MacIver, Stone Mason

Angus Mackay, High Street, and Louis MacIver, brother of grocery store owner *Iain*, were neighbors for several years. Louis made his home in John's house, just across the street from Angus, who insisted that there never was a stone mason as skillful as Louis since the geniuses who built Solomon's temple. Angus was by nature like that, loyal to a fanatical degree.

Louis, on the other hand, was a skillful craftsman, of the same caliber as the Nicholson brothers of Lionel, considered the best in the business in our corner of the world. When old Angus started to build his fancy stone chimney, Louis, of course, was constantly around for advice and assistance.

We youngsters stood around quite often waiting for Louis to walk across the street with that fancy little hammer in his hand, ready to slice away at the most ungainly looking clunk of stone in the pile. It was absolutely unbelievable what that able mason could do to a shapeless stone by just chipping away in the right places. It was as if he understood the creative nature of the stone in front of him. Watching old Angus's happy expression, however, was our greatest joy of all. We liked Angus, and to watch him watching Louis in action made our day.

Doctor Mackinnon

There are three references in my father's memoirs to doctors. In two cases, the doctor refused to live up to his professional responsibilities because the sick were Free Presbyterians. One victim was, I believe, my grandmother. The doctor in her case never came to see her. A second sick woman was seen, very reluctantly, after the man of the house reached out and grabbed the horse's reins as the doctor was galloping away. The doctor then saw the patient, scribbled a prescription, and was off as rapidly as his horse and fancy gig could take him.

The third vignette about a doctor is a positive one—and a bit of a chuckle.

When I left Skigersta, our doctor was the respected Dr. Mackinnon. He examined all of us and appeared to be very efficient, soft-spoken, and kind. In his own quiet way, the doctor was not averse to pull some legs and though allegedly an alcoholic, had a way with people and a low-pitched sense of humor which the bulk of the populace admired.

When it was determined by the medical powers that be that he was designated to be our Ness community doctor, he drove around the district in his shiny, beautiful car. He talked to many people by way of "testing" the waters in dipping in the toe. While driving through Eoropie, he stopped to chat with an elderly lady who had no inkling of who he was.

The canny doctor kept first inquiring about schoolteachers, children, and ministers—just to keep her off guard. Finally, the topic of doctors had to come up, and Mr. Mackinnon gingerly inquired about the previous doctors serving the community. "Oh," she said, "there were complaints, but the rumors of getting a new one are now making the rounds. However," she added ruefully, "the rumors also have it that the expected newcomer, although a skillful doctor, can drink the shirt off his back."

No one was more amused at the old lady's gruff evaluation than the doctor himself, who gleefully related that story to many of his close cronies throughout the years of able service to our Ness community of long ago.

It would be an understatement to describe D. B. Mackay, my adoptive grandfather, as an eccentric. By all accounts, he was a thoroughly outlandish human being who lived life on his own terms, regardless of consequences, and saw the world only through his own spectacles—regardless of the myopic view that gave him. He founded and ran a successful shoe tree factory in New York City. My father appears to have been quite fond of him as well as proud of a fellow Skigerstonian who made it big in the Big Apple.

D. B. Mackay of *Lathamor*

In all the history of Skigersta's existence, reaching back to the 1820s, no one was ever reared within its modest borders that could even come close to match the inordinate career of one Donald Buchanan Mackay of *Lathamor*. Even as a mere boy, his own father, a respected village joiner, despaired of the youngster's unbridled obstinacy to the point where he used to utter in sheer helplessness: "The more I discipline him, the more of a devil emerges."

This quote was repeated to those of us that were in close contact with D. B. in New York City for many years, so repetitiously that we at last dreaded the sound of it. D. B. always quoted his father's complaint in triumphal laughter, clearly importing the defiance and dauntlessness which characterized his approach to all matters, great or small, throughout a successful business career.

Strangely enough, however, and in harmony with many other contradictory aspects of his complex personality, D. B. deeply respected his father, a gifted craftsman, and was so loyal to his memory that he constantly and admiringly talked about his skill and achievements. As for his mother, whose enlarged picture in beautiful oval frame he always displayed in the most conspicuous panel of his home, it is doubtful if any son ever adored his mother with more tender and warm compassion than D. B. On many occasions I've seen him in deep, solemn reflections gazing at her picture, obviously straining to hold back the tears. Within the time element of mere seconds following such grand emotions, something irksome would either cross his mind or block his path, and before one could say D. B., he'd become meaner than a cobra in a chicken coop.

Therefore, it appears that D. B. Mackay was two contrasting personalities, good and bad, mysteriously alloyed into one, in which immediate circumstances instantly decided who for the moment was enthroned within, the saint or the sinner. In his case, the sinner invariably held sway.

However, regardless of an outlandish lifestyle, in which his rebellious stance and excessive behavior became a legend of New York's social circle, he was the only Skigerstonian who, by rising from obscurity solely on his own innovations and hard work, made it big in the business world.

When one considers that this mercurial figure had no formal education, his achievements in competitive New York must be characterized as phenomenal. Only two of our Skigersta residents, both privileged with grammar school education, realized the ownership of a going business, but they were only partners in already established enterprises. I refer to my cousin Alick Murray, "Sandy," who married into a prosperous South African department store and *Dòmhnall Anna*, D. B.'s nephew, who found himself upon arriving in old Gotham sitting on a veritable gold mine—staked out, fenced, dug, and promoted by an irrepressible uncle who founded a factory singlehanded around the time his nephew was born.

Colorful Cobbler

In Skigersta of long ago, a village of close to three hundred population, there was only one bona fide journeyman who served full apprenticeship at his chosen trade until after the First World War. That same person was also the sole Skigersta resident to this day who made a fortune entirely on his own initiative and hard work, though utterly lacking formal education.

The background of this amazing episode started long before the turn of the century, when an equally amazing youngster, burning with ambition and defiance, left his humble thatched home on No. 17 *Lathamor* to learn a trade. He was the well-known Donald Buchanan Mackay, who, to his dying day, insisted that he was a relative of America's fifteenth president, James Buchanan.

Known as D. B., his success stemmed from the production of a specialty which he created while pursuing the lowly trade of cobbler—apprenticed in Stornoway, of all places. In his particular case, the whole matter turned out to be an epic in itself, because of the colorful character involved, who, even in his late teens, showed every sign of rising above cobwebbed normal methods of getting things done, with consummate contempt for the status quo.

D. B.'s fertile brain appeared to function in some mysterious way in complete reversal to ordinary mortals, and as a New York crony of many years acquaintance, putting things in perspective regarding him, he said "his inverted, cart-before-the-horse approach to all problems, great and small, brought him a fortune."

My father and the Bard, along with many of the local *bodaich*, ever since I can remember, never ceased to recall the various exciting incidents in which they all got involved during the feisty apprenticeship of the D. B. years in Stornoway. There never could be a dull moment within a stone's throw of D. B. because dullish normalcy drove him to the wall, and equated a total abstinent state to that of the damned.

So it was that the village fathers created such an aura of adventure and good times about D. B. that we youngsters visualized him as a knight in shining armor. Compounding our fantasies regarding him was the fact that our hero was well established in a successful business of his own creation in the heart of New York City, which, to us at that age, was a mammoth metropolis with golden pavements and silver skyscrapers.

There were grand pictures of D. B. constantly arriving on *Lathamor* along with his luxurious yacht. He was then in his early forties, all decked out in marine officers' uniform, looking every bit as impressive as the old-timers described him. The broad Hudson River, which they told us was hundreds of miles long and a mile wide, showed in the background, with our hero posing in rakish white cap crowning as interesting a countenance as nature ever devised, exuding determination and defiance.

Further perspectives on D. B. are provided below from Angus's sketches or as indicated.

> *On Effie*: He adopted Effie, of Back parentage, when she was nine months old; went all the way to Canada to fetch her. The same warm affection that was meant for his own only child, a girl who died in infancy, was showered on Effie in genuine love and admiration. She lacked nothing, including a stepmother's affection, which was perhaps unsurpassed in tenderness and loving care anywhere on this earth.
>
> *On the law*: He just loved to live outside the law. To D. B., most of manmade laws were sheer humbug, a nuisance and a challenge, something

to be torn to shreds, tossed into the nearest garbage can and forgotten.

On the British Army: He spent his whole life hating the British army because they refused him admission into the Stornoway drill contingent of long ago due to his short stature. When war broke out on the British in 1939, D. B. would shake his head and mumble, "Ah, the bumbling British, they'll probably get beat as usual." His ego was such that he was absolutely convinced of the fact that their refusing him military service would eventually bring them disaster.

On abstinence: He was against it.

On whisky as Christmas presents: One year as he was listing the people he would be giving whisky to as Christmas presents, someone in the room said, with respect to a specific person, "What if he doesn't drink?" D. B. said, "Oh, everybody drinks."

On honoring standard right of way regulations while on the water: He was against it. My father provided the following story to illustrate.

In that same yacht, he refused to give way to a passenger ferry loaded with New Jersey commuters and came within four or five feet of colliding. He still would not slow down. The ferry skipper panicked and reversed his engines with his whistle in nonstop scream but could not get his craft on the move, with old engines malfunctioning from severe reversals. The ferry was stuck in the middle of the Hudson for hours.

On Rudolph Valentino (1895–1926): He didn't know who he was.

This is a story from my mother. At the very height of Rudolph Valentino's fame as a silent film star, he had his chauffeur drive him to D.

B.'s factory. Though he obviously could have sent someone into the shop on this errand, Valentino elected to do it himself. My mother worked for her father at this time and saw Valentino come in with a pair of his dancing shoes and request assistance. D. B. barely glanced up from what he was doing and shoved a piece of paper in front of him with the words: "Put your name here, boy." Valentino complied and left the shoes with him. What happened to that pair of shoes and that scrap of paper is a mystery. I seem to recall my mother saying that the shoes themselves were in our basement in Bayside while I was growing up, though what happened to the paper is unknown.

On Dolly: See the sketch below.

D. B.'s Dolly

D. B. Mackay's tiny dog Dolly was as popular in New York's Chelsea district as was D. B. himself, who, in his many years of residing on Twenty-First Street off Eighth Avenue was, more or less, overlord of Chelsea's sidewalks for many years. On normal days, a rare event in D. B.'s career, tiny pet Dolly trailed right at his heels, a no mean role, even for an agile dog. When sidewalk traffic thickened, however, he'd shove Dolly right into his coat pocket, where the faithful animal warned all and sundry to keep their distance. A clumsy collision meant an instant sidewalk scene.

Everybody in D. B.'s bank, from the porter to the president, sat up and took notice the moment D. B. pushed through the front door—such was the power of his strident personality on old and young, rich and poor.

One day, while standing at the teller's window with Dolly tucked under his arm, a gentle, well-dressed elderly lady stroked Dolly's head and said, admiringly, "Oh, how I wish you were mine." D. B. bristled to attention, as was his wont when startled, and said, smilingly. "Lady, you haven't got enough money to buy this precious creature."

The teller, who had known D. B. for years, was grinning broadly when the old-timer reached him and said, "Mr. Mackay, I couldn't help but hear your brief exchange with the lady. She happens to be one of the wealthiest women in New York City, if not the whole world. We have her accounts."

10

Of Fish and Fowl: *Cudaig*, Ling, *Guga*, and Skylarks

My father wrote about his favorite fish and fowl, not an unexpected topic for a man raised on an island. In the process of reading his vignettes, we learn about the only way to properly enjoy eating fish and potatoes, hear a sermon inspired by ling, discover the difference between a beautiful adult bird who delights as a "diver" and its babies who delight as a meal and celebrate the song of a famous bird beloved round the world.

The *Cudaig*

In Skigersta of long ago, the tasty *cudaig* of the cunner species, which in late autumn arrives at our coves and bays in great abundance, were the most welcome visitors to our shores. These dusky, lively fish, about six inches long of light-colored bellies and shapely heads, were true delicacies, fit for the monarch's cuisine.

Much delightful rock fishing took place in late autumn when the *cudaig* were in biting mood and jumped on our cat-gut rigs with abandon. Our fishing crags were known by quaint Gaelic names such as *ileir, Pol-thaigeil*, and the *Pala-dubh*. At night, the *cudaig* are prone to bunch together in a bulky mass, but whether for respite or security reasons against nocturnal predators, littoral experts are not certain. They do affirm, however, as men of great knowledge in their own field that most fish do sleep.

It was not unusual for *Dòmhnall Anna* and his uncle Malcolm, a *sgoth* skipper all his adult life, both living near the quay's crest, to amble down onto the quay on moonlit nights. On one such night they spotted two or three huge dark objects floating underneath the surface in the lee cove of our quay which they first mistook for submerged seaweed.

On closer scrutiny, however, they were startled to discover that it was the *cudaig* by the tens of thousands, perhaps millions, appearing to be in a solid mass and solid slumber. Some neighbors were immediately notified and the old corner of our quay, which mason Donald Weir built for the *bodaich*, was a busy spot that night with *taigh thàbhaidh* (scoop net used for fishing cuddies) scooping up about a bucketful in every haul.

Comely *Cudaig*

As a senior expert and hoary authority on many matters, I find it incumbent on me to lay down certain specific rules regarding the boiling of my all-time favorite fish, the flavorful *cudaig*, a very special treasure of the sea, fit for the monarch's table.

Frying the *cudaig* is unforgivable sacrilege. In order to really capture the genuine flavor of the shapely and tender cudaig, savoring its exquisite taste of gourmet delight, it must be guardedly boiled just a mite above simmer agitation, avoiding excessive cooking with all diligence, not exceeding fourteen minutes. Thus, by so doing, its comely contour, smooth symmetry, shape, and size remain intact, utterly free of the fragmentary bits and pieces resulting from the bubbly boilings of delinquent supervision.

The *cudaig* by all means must be partaken with potatoes boiled in their jackets, a choice commodity which, if cooked in any form sans jackets lose 12 percent of their original taste. Under no circumstances should potatoes be allowed to over boil beyond eighteen seconds. All these imperative measures are of no avail, however, unless the *cudaig* is, as tradition demands, eaten with the fingers, greatly enhancing both flavor and taste and, as a final honor to the most pleasurable repast known to man, should be slowly washed down by its grand, aromatic sauce of incomparable sipping delight.

The Ling and the *Cnàmh*

Many respected Christians of our era were inclined to believe that both momentous events, the ling moving twelve miles out and the dreaded potato blight *cnàmh* occurred simultaneously. Our reliable historian and next-door neighbor, *Iain Pìobaire,* averred on many occasions that many signs indicated such was the case.

The Irish famine due to the *cnàmh* in which tens of thousands of Irishmen emmigrated to America occurred in the middle of the 1840s. Great Ness lights such as MacDonald of Eorodale, Morrison of Fivepenny, and *Seumas* of Skigersta were also inclined to believe that it was a mark of God's displeasure because greedy fishermen commenced to commercialize the share of fish which ordinarily went to the poor of the land. *Seumas* himself was an avid ling fisherman until old age intervened.

Whatever conclusions scholars, scientists, naturalists, or Christians can arrive at, it's gratifying to know that our poor in Skigersta continued to receive their share of the catches as they arrived, generously and willingly distributed by our salty stalwarts with hearts of gold. Up until the time I left on the *Marloch* in 1924, neighbor *Iain* continued to discuss these two phenomena at our *cagailte* from time to time. John, a *sgoth* skipper most of his adult life, was obviously more convinced than ever that the overruling hand of Providence was clearly manifested in both matters, which incidentally was instrumental in changing the economic lives of multitudes.

Additional comments on ling from another sketch:

> Ling was the basic family support in our fathers' and grandfathers' time—sixpence a head, if

memory serves. In the 1860s, ling were caught in copious quantities just three miles off the Skigersta shoreline. Since the turn of the century, it was futile to look for ling within a twelve-mile radius of the Hebridean coastline. Some phenomenal event occurred, which the old folks discussed with awe and wonderment. The ling literally moved into a more remote habitat—puzzling sinners but not the saints.

How regrettable that today the ling's prestige and market price have woefully dwindled to a lower level than the dreaded dogfish of our grandfathers' time. My young seafaring nephew *Alasdair* of Eorodale, a veteran merchant marine mariner and former crew member of the popular fishing craft *Alpha*, is an expert on many matters pertaining to oceanic and littoral waters. He once told me many years ago that the real reason for the ling's undervalue came about when nosey nutritionists discovered that the ling couldn't be sophisticatedly fried to the modern taste. Our forebears, who adored ling and appreciated its worth, considered frying ling—or any fish—almost a sacrilege, tolerated only in sinful places like Paris and Piccadilly.

Solan Geese: *Sùlaire*

The fiery enthusiastic expression of the *Sùlaire* in a keen competitive climb for altitude, exuding fierce determination and defiance, is an unforgettable sight. As youngsters, while fishing in the open *sgoth* on the comely *Camaisear* and elsewhere, over three score years ago, we had ample opportunities to watch this colorful, busy, and beautiful bird in action—now a treasured recollection.

When sufficient diving height is obtained by the *Sùlaire*, which is considerable when the herring, their prime prey, schools deep, there are no set patterns of their behavior prior to the famous grandiose plunge. This spectacular dive by the "Great northern diver" is unmatched in beauty, rhythm, momentum, and aim by any other winged fowl of God's creation.

Always in a preparatory mood while flying aloft, with sharp eyes constantly on prey, jockeying for position, the alert *Sùlaire* gracefully glides to and fro and ascends with equal grace and ease, rapidly flapping wings in glee, followed by an occasional piercing shriek of sheer joy.

Suddenly, in seeking summit advantage for the grand splashdown, the dramatic bank of a smooth rising angle is clearly noticeable, and, presto, the swift downward tumble is executed in almost faster than eye speed. No sooner is the prominent beak pointing seaward than the speedy wings are drawn almost tight against the sides, and the diving champion of them all is now in his element—a glorious, gleaming white steak heading straight for the brine.

The solan geese, inedible in themselves, have babies which are. Capturing them—on *Sùlaisgeir*—has been a way of life for Skigersta folks for generations. This is how Donald MacDonald, in his book *Lewis. A History of the Island* (1978), describes the process.

> Sulisgeir or Gannet Rock lies about eleven miles southwest of Rona. It is about half a mile long by a third of a mile wide with cliffs rising steeply from the sea in most places. The only landing place is at Geodha a' Phuill Bhain, where a ring is fixed in the rock for securing boats.
>
> From time immemorial, the daring men of Ness have gone to Sulisgeir every September to kill gannets. In the [eighteenth] century and long afterward, they travelled the forty miles in an open six-oared boat, without even a compass. Before the ring was fixed in the cliff to secure

a boat, some of the crew had to stay on board sheltering on the lee-side of the island, while the rest were ashore killing the gannets, which were so tame that they could be slain with sticks. Nowadays, the gannet or guga hunters are taken to Sulisgeir by motorboat and fetched back on an appointed date. During their stay, the men live in five stone huts which lie close to each other.

Gorgeous Gannets: The *Guga*

In Skigersta of long ago, exciting flocks of white gannets—northern diver, *Sùlaire*, tireless hefty birds, entertained us youngsters with the most thrilling diving spectacles enjoyed anywhere along the Seven Seas. No bird of creation can match the fierce, speedy, straight dive of the gannet. These handsome birds hatch by the tens of thousands on two craggy forbidding rocks—*Sùlaire* and Stack—jutting out of the windswept north Atlantic.

Sùlaire is about forty miles due north of the Butt of Lewis. Skigersta—a fishing village of twenty full crofts, is three miles south of the Butt. The gannet's tasty offspring, noted *Guga Niseach*, is now gifted from Ness to friends ranging from the USA to Canada and kindred colonies.

The celebrated *Guga Niseach*, top heavy with Epicurean dainties and gourmet delight, of a most enticing aroma, is a rare delicacy, fit for the monarch's table. According to trained naturalists, no other bird of coastal fowl is pampered like the *guga*, the gannet's chick. Their busy doting parents enjoy lugging strange objects and choice luxuries from the deep to their nests, just to amuse an overindulged brood.

When the fledglings who narrowly escape the annual *Niseach's* invasion are sumptuously reared and wing off on their own, the overworked parents are completely dried out but retain their verve, beauty, and comely contour to the very end. Experts claim that their meat at this stage is as dry and tough as birchwood. All their energy is put into the chicks' well-being.

The gannet's fiery enthusiastic expression in a keen competitive climb for altitude, exuding fierce determination and defiance, is a sight impossible to eradicate from memory. I left on the *Marloch* sixty-three years ago next April, and I can still vividly recall their wild capers above the *Camaisear* of long ago.

In his novel *The Blackhouse*, author Peter May describes a modern-day hunt for the *guga* on the island of *Sùlaire*. His description is a tour de force. Recently a documentary of the *guga* hunt was filmed by director Mike Day. One has to be impressed on every level. Fighting fierce Atlantic winds and waves, the whole experience is a tribute to the men of Ness who, over many generations, braved ferocious weather conditions to bring much-needed protein to their families—a tradition that, as I understand it, is a point of pride to this day.

From my personal experience, it is difficult to fathom what monarch would want to sit down to a feast of *guga*. Somehow, I can't see Queen Elizabeth indulging in this strange bird, which was apparently a delicacy for my father and his friends and neighbors. But then, we in New York certainly did not experience the bird in the best light. What was sent to my father were not freshly killed birds but undoubtedly salted and preserved ones with the expected results in terms of flavor, odor, and texture.

I was born in 1944, so I suspect my earliest recollections of the *guga* were somewhere in the fifties and lasted for about five or ten years. What I remember is that one day a postman came to the door looking like something out of a cartoon—holding this smelly, oily package out in front of his nose and trying not to inhale. My father was delirious with delight, and one look at my mother told me it was time to flee.

What we did—mother, Norman, Christine, and I—was to run off to the movies. In those days, you could almost live in the movies. Each movie had as a prelude a series of cartoons, a newsreel and coming attractions of upcoming movies. Then you saw the movie, and, if you wished, you could see the movie again and again without anyone ushering you out of the theater.

But alas, in the end, we had to leave the movies and go home. There we found our father smacking his lips and celebrating the sumptuous repast he had just had. His family sent him two *guga* in the mail. They appear to have packed the birds in a square cookie tin, like the ones holding Belgian Christmas cookies. Around the tin was a thin layer of brown paper and a bit of string holding the whole thing together. The packaging was totally inadequate for the oily substance within.

So we, the prisoners of the *guga*, had to endure the smell for a whole week. On the first day, my father cooked the two birds. That was the day we spent at the movies. Then he ate one half of the first bird. Next day he ate the second half of the first bird. Next day the first half of the second bird and last day the last portion of the last bird.

Lest anyone think that was the end of the story, it was not. The entire week the *guga* was in the icebox, the contents of the box smelled of *guga*. Butter smelled of *guga*. Milk smelled of *guga*. If my mother made me a ham sandwich that week to take to school, I threw it away—it smelled of *guga*. Only after the two birds were consumed could the lengthy cleaning up process begin.

I guess it was inevitable that a confrontation ensued, after many years, in which my mother put her foot down and said, "No more *guga* in this house." And that was the end of the story.

But not exactly. I am now enormously fascinated by the story of the *guga* and the men who pursued them over the years at such personal cost and with such indisputable bravery and skill.

All that was innocent, secure, and achingly beautiful about my father's Shangri-la is summed up in the sound of a bird. But what a bird!

Skigersta's Skylarks

In what appeared to be a relayed pattern from dawn to dusk, our Skigersta skylarks in sweet strain gracefully soared aloft and in perfect singing form encircled for a spell, then, suddenly stayed put—as if affixed in the firmament. In this seemingly attached posture, they sang their sweetest, prior to descending in a glorious glide invariably in the general direction of the nests, outpouring such rapturous melodies as to remind the most hardened worldling of the blissful beyond.

The shapely skylark, adorably crowned with a tiny, fluffy plumage—hence the *Topag* (skylark)—bears a striking resemblance to the common sparrow until closely examined. Its delicate contour is more handsomely outlined than the sparrow, who betrays more ungainly puffiness than the streamlined skylark.

Our Skigersta skylarks, who never seemed to tire of song and praise, provided us four youngsters—two Normans, Angus, and Alick—with a musical aura of such lofty quality that only a Burns or Byron could justifiably define. Looking back on it now from the nostalgic high peak of "three score and ten," the sage's observation in pointing out that "youth is waste and old age a regret" belatedly comes to mind.

It is quite obvious, and regrettably so, that we never did truly grasp the quintessential qualities of our grand surroundings. As inseparable four outdoor *Baile Shuas* cronies, we frequently stretched out on some rural, daisy-covered patch of green, drowsily listening to the *Topag* while happily indulging in the unbridled, unrealistic daydreamings common to innocents since the world began. At that wonderful, uncomplicated phase of our young lives, we four felt as free and secure as the high-soaring skylark, whose limitless domain was the eternal canopy of the blue, from which she so devotedly and sweetly entertained us from day to day.

11

Worthies, Wags, Wits and Oddballs

My father was amazed that in a community of less than three hundred souls, you could have such a variety of personalities—in his words: "worthies, wags, wits, and oddballs." But so it was, as we have already seen in the personalities presented above and those highlighted in the pages below.

Worthies

The dignified Dòmhnallach: Reverend MacDonald. It took many years for ultra conservative *Nìseachs* to fathom the singular wisdom and quiet depth of the reserved and dignified *Dòmhnallach*—Church of Scotland pastor. This despite the fact that the unassuming clergyman enjoyed an active role in all worthwhile causes throughout the community. That the scholarly *Ùigeach* (someone from Uig) was rudely shunned by many, even by sensible Skigersta fathers, has now, in hindsight reflections, become painfully embarrassing.

As time moved on, however, the basic cause for the frosty relationships became clearer to observant Ness men, who subsequently regretted the impasse between them and a leader of such sterling qualities. Right off, it's imperative to recall that the meek *Dòmhnallach* was as immovable as Gibraltar and in many ways just as tough.

In views on any current topic, whether social, religious, or political, Mr. MacDonald was persistently objective. Shocking as it may sound, to be wholly objective in that difficult era wasn't popular—it rubbed zealots the wrong way. Besides these considerations, Mr. MacDonald from time to time set so many whispering tale bearers so far back on their heels that normal and former equilibrium were never again quite restored.

His harsh treatment of flattering fakers, fawning for familiarity, were, for one of his serenity, shockingly piercing, both in dialogue and context. To sidle alongside the *Dòmhnallach* by way of catching his ear with the latest choice tidbit was dangerous business, standing the chance of suffering from psychological scars for many moons. Therefore, being well aware of this stern side of the minister fostered a sharp, estranging attitude in many who otherwise wished to communicate.

Nonetheless, Mr. MacDonald's calm countenance, even when ired, was a study in poise and compassion. His warm blue eyes ceaselessly radiated empathy and goodwill for suffering humanity. Except odious nicknames, which were abhorrent to his soul, nothing riled the clergyman like oppression of minorities and ignoring the downtrodden. It was obvious that the man was endowed with a gallant, uncompromising character from the womb, a syndrome which made him stand out in a crowd wherever he happened to be.

For example, at one time, a shy Skigersta maiden found herself while visiting kindred hopelessly outnumbered by a group of contrasting persuasions, including Mr. MacDonald. Among those present was an acerbating, asocial kindred of the girl, who almost apologized when introducing her to the *Dòmhnallach*, because she belonged to the *Sèudars* (those who had seceded from the Free Church) as he derogatorily called the fledgling FP order. The gallant *Dòmhnallach* immediately turned on him and said pointedly, "Did the thought ever cross your mind that both of us could be in error, and the *Sèudars*, as you call them, on the right road?"—a typical *Dòmhnallach* performance. That's how he lived and that's how he died, a fearless man of God.

The Dòmhnallach and John the Baptist. There was a spell of quietude throughout Ness when the dignified *Dòmhnallach* was finally ordained as Church of Scotland parson, amid much controversy and objections. In a hassle of this kind, ignoramuses—usually the most vocal in deep disputes—have to be overlooked, but the numerous intelligent *Niseachs* who wanted no part of a scholar of such sterling qualities as the quiet *Uigeach* is something to ponder. With the exception of a few families, all of Skigersta's residents failed to support Mr. MacDonald's ordination.

Consequently, the erudite, calm clergyman remained a total stranger to Skigersta's old and young, a social, spiritual, and intellectual impasse which has to be regretted as a personal and local tragedy. In hindsight reflections, it's embarrassing. However, when the dust died down, with the Reverend MacDonald ensconced in Cross, everybody seemed to be satisfied in attending the church of their choice, when, suddenly, a new upheaval (like ominous seismic tremors) shook the community.

Mr. John Nicholson, of a creative Lionel family, but now a forceful Baptist preacher, home from America, with his charming Yankee spouse, both liberal Baptists, was the new formidable concern for fundamentalists. No sooner had John established himself on upper Adabrock, a bleak, stony area which he named "Edgemoor" and which he subsequently developed into a show piece of modern décor and grand landscaping than deep uneasiness filled the land.

Following the completion of his snug, compact chapel, Mr. Nicholson lost no time in attacking what was regarded as sacrosanct doctrines for millennia. One can readily conclude that the fiery preacher wasn't vying for popularity acclaim in pursuing such a disturbing crusade in a citadel of Calvinistic conservatism. Moreover, there were mounting indications in Mr. Nicholson's preachments and attitude that he considered the puzzling questions and answers of the Shorter Catechism misworded, so woefully misinterpreted from Holy Writ that much of its material was detrimental to the salvation of souls.

The quick reactions to these so-called heretical disclosures among the pious community fathers were the nightmarish fears that a spurious new approach to salvation itself was theorized by the irrepressible Baptist, in neologizing the young onto the broad road of which scripture warns about. Throughout all these charges and counter charges, the dignified *Dòmhnallach* remained discretely silent, refusing to be drawn to the support of either side—to the chagrin of conservatives. It is quite possible that Mr. MacDonald was still smarting from the outlandish notion held by many *Niseachs* when he first arrived, to wit, that he also was too liberal. Rightly or wrongly, the rock ribbed Rev. Nicholson stuck to his beliefs to his dying day, neither wavering nor apologizing to a living soul, from the professor to the peddler, the crowned head to the crofter. Meanwhile, the *Dòmhnallach*, accused of being liberal, began to sound (in comparison to Mr. Nicholson's diversified dogma), like an ardent Calvinist.

The Reverend James. Long before the Reverend James MacLeod of Skye and Greenock came and preached in our Free Presbyterian church in Lionel for the first time, we Skigersta youngsters in our teens heard about some of his colorful characteristics. It is regrettable but true that our strong motivation to see *Seumas* was more carnal than spiritual, an attitude that the pious James wouldn't have appreciated.

At that restless phase of our young lives, we loved different things, different people, and even different ministers, and by some sense, hard to define, we just concluded that James was different, which indeed he was.

The Reverend James was as immovable as Gibraltar, but in defiantly defending his stance, he'd come out with such comical remarks that both saints and sinners were amused. He did not intend, or ever made a play for such reactions; he was dead serious in doctrinal debates and the word "compromise" infuriated him. As far as *Seumas* was concerned, it was sheer waste of time and energy to have introduced the miserable word into the common language in the first place, such was his horror of compromising with a single syllable of scripture from Genesis to Revelation. He was a true champion of the infallibility of the Word. It was futile to approach him with any negative ideas; he could verbally clobber a man when aroused.

When we first saw him walking down the aisle toward the pulpit, back in the early twenties, not too far from his prime—he immediately impressed us as a lively, aggressive individual incapable of retreat. When he sat down, he scrutinized every soul in that church as curiously and minutely as if he were seeing human beings for the first time. The disapproving stare of his sharp, round, blue eyes made one already feel condemned.

Wallace Bruce Nicholson. My late Skigersta boyhood pal, Wallace Bruce Nicholson, was probably the most unlikely of the six of our village age bracket to become a minister of the Gospel. Not that Wallace was a whit more mischievous or mundane than the rest of us but because of certain early characteristics which showed, even in his boyhood behavior, indications of directing toward other phases of learning.

For example, secular literature fascinated Wallace since a mere boy, and no one envisaged that most of his adult life would involve solemn, ministerial duties and precise divinity training, embodying deep exegetical exercises. Be that as it may, it just so happened that Wallace and his brilliant cousin Percy of Edgemoor became—by a country mile—the two best scholars of my age crop, born shortly after the turn of the century.

In all fairness to the late Reverend Wallace, however, those remembered traits pale in significance when compared to his basic personal character, of which, regrettably, very little is known among *Niseachs*, especially the young. His gifted father, Bard *Alasdair MacNeacaill*, whose moving lyrics brought tears to the eyes of Lewis exiles for generations, remarked on more than one occasion to contemporary parents, including my own, that Wallace's single mindedness in making a clean breast of any misconduct in which he found himself involved amazed him.

Poet Alex discussed these matters concerning Wallace, his first born, with the mixed emotions of pride, puzzlement, and exuberance. Not one of Wallace's young cronies, including myself, showed his spunk under harsh parental interrogation. On the contrary, we resorted to every sly stratagem devised of demons to circumvent parental punishment. Not so young Wallace, who fearlessly and candidly revealed all, knowing full well that swift and sure corporal correction awaited him, all of which was a crystal clear attestation to both his common honesty and common courage. *Nàbaidh* (neighbor; mate).

Wallace and Percy. My onetime Great Lakes shipmate and Skigersta boyhood pal, Wallace Bruce, besides his rigorous swimming sessions up and down the Detroit River, utilized most of his spare time aboard ship in heavy reading. At that particular point of time, Wallace was a bit of a daredevil in diving off dizzying high decks of the D&C fleet, all of which were highly super structured.

In a brief study for pilotage, while vying for a maritime and pilot's career, his fast progress in pinpointing lake lights, estuaries, rivers, and their various buoys and currents were fantastic. He singled me out for fielding questions out of his lake manual, and it was easy to sense that the man was a born scholar.

To absorb and retain knowledge was second nature to Wallace Bruce Nicholson. This valuable gift was of course enhanced by two poignant factors, namely, his strong urge for learning since childhood and offspring of a creative Lionel family of skilled masons, a minister and talented bard father. His uncle Donald was the best Gaelic singer in Ness, if not in all of Lewis. It is truly sad to relate that the sudden and untimely death of his illustrious father changed Wallace's whole world.

His cousin Percy of Edgemoor, my classroom crony whose advanced knowledge on all subjects seated next to him for a whole year filled me with uneasiness and inferiority complex—went on to even bigger scholastic achievements. The classic telegram received by proud parents upon graduating from college speaks for itself: "Smashed the records to Adam—coming home in triumph." So wired the brightest pupil of the Lionel complex. Wallace never forgot that telegram.

Among the things that my brother-in-law sent me following the death of my sister was my father's Gaelic Bible. In that Bible were about fifteen very yellowed-with-age newspaper clippings—from the *Stornoway Gazette*, I presume. The Reverend Wallace commented on various biblical passages. Below is one example:

Know Your Bible: Philippians

Paul visited Philippi about 52 AD and converted Lydia. He soon came into conflict with the city magistrates, was scourged and imprisoned, and was the means of converting the jailor.

The church in Philippi had a high regard for Paul and sent him generous contributions. In his Epistle, Paul expresses his thankfulness for the courtesy of the Philippian Church and their liberality toward himself, and he dwells on his own imprisonment as leading to the spread of the Gospel.

He exhorts the Philippians to the grace of humility, and he dwells at large on the humility of Christ as the Great Exemplar. He warns against fake leaders and evil workers and exhorts the members of the church to the grace of unity and a holy and consistent life.

Philippi was the first place in Europe where the Gospel was preached and this invests it with a peculiar interest.

From the solemn tone of the Epistle, it seems that Paul envisaged his own departure as being near, although he encouraged the Philippians with some hope of regaining his liberty.

The Epistle to the Philippians breathes the warm spirit of a ripe Christian whose piety was mellowing for the harvest, and of one who felt that he was not far from heaven, and might soon be with Christ.

The Epistle was written from Rome when Paul was in prison, about 61–63 AD.

Margaret Morrison

In Skigerta of long ago, we all had the privilege of knowing old Margaret Morrison, a pious woman known all over Ness as *Màiread 'n Alasdair*. There were also *Màiri NicLeòid*, Mary Mackenzie of the

Àird and *Màiread Donn*, Margaret Thomson of the *Baile Shuas*—three elderly women of exceptional piety who stood out as spiritual beacons of light throughout the land.

This brief sketch concerns *Màiread 'n Alasdair* because of a certain single incident bearing on my own person which occurred in our lowly *taigh dubh* on the *Baile Shuas* facing the *cladach*, enjoyed a clear view of Margaret's home on *Lathamor*, which faced south.

My mother, who loved Margaret dearly, could spot her whenever she opened her front door. One drizzly, windy Thursday, *la na coinneimh ùrnaigh* (prayer meeting), my mother, while peering through our window, saw old Margaret battling the elements on her way to the house of prayer at an age when she could scarcely drag one foot after the other.

After watching her in awe for a few moments, my mother excitedly called me to the window with the following request, word for word: *Aonghais, thig a seo is seallaidh mise dhut cùis farmaid.* (Angus, come here and I will show you an object to be envied.) It is now well over sixty years since this solemn scene unfolded before my eyes but is as clear in my mind's eye as if it happened a mere fortnight ago.

And Ye Shall See the Difference

Back in Skigersta of long ago, I knew a woman whose eagerness for attending the means of grace far surpassed all her other desires and commitments, no matter how demanding, attractive, or urgent. She performed her daily chores as if the midweek prayer meetings, Sabbaths, and especially communion seasons were constantly uppermost in her mind.

The closer the Sabbath got, the more mellow she became, and when it did arrive at the stroke of 11:00 p.m., her comely countenance exuded strange warmth which worldlings are unable to understand. Her delight in merely anticipating the biannual five-day Communion services, celebrating the Lord's Supper, clearly showed in her buoyant conversations and attitude prior to that happy Thursday.

This divine day was to her the beginning of a sacred five-day furlough from the world, the devil, and the flesh. To her Monday—blue Monday for worldlings—was the last joyous day of one sermon concluding her spiritual festival of sheer joy. Tuesday morning was her blue day in which returning into worldly attire and facing duty head on was an ordeal of the deepest dye. She candidly admitted it was her hardest task of all, but remembering the words "Do this and leave not that undone" clearly settled the matter.

The Other Skigersta Bard Mystery

To be in possession of a keen reflective mind in the twilight of life is a priceless blessing and stimulating pastime. For example, while in my early eighties, my mind's eye is active monitoring childhood scenes in Skigersta of long ago. I can, for instance, visualize a clear picture of Bard Alex Nicholson, dexterous craftsman, merchant, and skillful joiner, building one of the two beautiful homes which still stand on the *Baile Àird*.

As children, we watched him sawing and nailing rafters, placing shelves and fitting doors with the expertise of a trained journeyman, though never serving one hour of apprenticeship. Amazing Alex was the gifted author of the immortal and nostalgic line: *An tèid thu leum a rìbhinn mhaisich?* (Will you go with me beautiful maiden?)

No one who ever read or sang these Gaelic romantic verses ceased from wondering who was the comely lass that really inspired poet Alex to compile one of the loveliest lyrics in Lewis lore, a secret he took to his untimely grave. As curious Skigersta youngsters, who proudly claimed Alex as our own—despite being reared in Lionel—we had a go at the riddle on many occasions while cozily sitting around *teine meadhan an làir* of long ago.

However, we were never able to come up with a concrete conclusion as to who was the real *Rìbhean mhaiseach* in Alex's famous *òran*. His attractive wife Marion was in her young days one of the foremost beauties of the large Lochs community, but where and when Alex first laid eyes on the comely Marion was obscure then and is to this day.

It is reasonable enough to assume, however, that her late son, the well-educated Reverend Wallace, a scholar since childhood, made careful research into the background of his illustrious parents prior to his death in *Àird Dhail*—just a day's journey from the spot where his famous father perished.

Presumably Bard Alex was a hardworking young man in Vancouver, British Columbia, plagued with homesickness when the famous song was composed and therein hangs the puzzle. We centered our so-called conclusions and probabilities on two poignant aspects of the baffling matter in which we all participated.

First, that it was quite possible Alex met and dated Marion prior to his immigrating to Canada and in visualizing a day when she would join him until sufficient savings were realized, at which time both could happily head for home where he again could see *Am muir gun sgìos ri bualadh creagan ruadha gruamach àrd* (the sea continually pounding).

Our other conjecture was that some fair Canadian lass caught his fancy, and being acutely perturbed by the three potent forces of homesickness, love, and loneliness, which have moved poets of all ages, he was inspired to pour out his feelings in tender verse, picturing himself and his lady fair on a sweet stroll to *Lional ann an Eilean Leòdhais*.

Of all the young group who discussed these matters at *Cèilidhean* in the long, long ago, of which I'm the only survivor, I was the only one to obtain a golden opportunity of finding out for myself, once and for all, who was that adored damsel in Alex's background, but failed to do so.

At one time, back in the middle twenties, I enjoyed the privilege of living with the Nicholson family in Windsor, Ontario, where the fair Marion made her home. On several occasions, I had the opportunity of inquiring Marion concerning the elusive and romantic *Rìbhinn mhaisich* but refrained in fear of reviving unpleasant memories of the talented, ill-fated author who died suddenly, just a little past his prime of life, in which a great literary light was lost to Lewis forevermore.

Child Prodigy

My uncle Murdo, *Murchadh Buidhe*, and my next-door neighbor, John MacKenzie, *Iain Pìobaire*, were great and truthful storytellers in my young days of long ago. The following enigmatic but true tale was told by my uncle and one on which *Iain Pìobaire* corroborated.

There were in one of our Lewis villages two youngsters, male and female, of the same age crop who were mentally retarded from birth. Both were harmless and the residents just let them be. As they matured, however, intimacy between the two became common place, and the girl gave birth to a male child who turned out to be a child prodigy.

From the age of five, he was giving clear evidences in class of higher than average intellect and keen grasp of elementary learning. Needless to say, he held the lead in grammar school, college, and finally university. Eventually he became a professor of theology in one of America's most prestigious seats of learning.

Right off, one may ask what is so extraordinary about all this? The following analysis of an expert is rather astounding. One of the great medical scientists, upon learning of the boy's background, recorded an amazing deduction, in which he confirmed that nature compassionately endowed the boy with the exact same amount of intellect and brains which both parents lacked and emerged a genius.

Marion Nicholson: Widow of Gifted Bard *Alasdair MacNeacaill*

Back at the beginning of World War II found me again on the Great Lakes after an absence of eleven years. In 1928, when I left the Lakes, Marion Nicholson, subject of this sketch and widow of the other able Skigersta Bard, lived in Windsor, where I enjoyed the privilege of boarding with the family during the winter of 1925 and into 1926.

I arrived on the Lakes when Hitler was about to lead his hordes across the English Channel—allegedly so at least—as the British army found themselves entrapped at waterline. The impact of this dreadful news crushed me to the point where it affected my whole behavior—such as it was—and came as close to crumbling into a mental and physical heap as any human could possibly come. It clearly proved to me, once and for all, that whatever else I was (or pretended to be), a hero I was not.

Amid all this gloom and despair, I happened to run into an old shipmate, Finlay MacLean, Habost, who told me (while nursing his own woes about the defeat of the British army) that he dropped in for a brief *cèilidh* on the Nicholson family in Buffalo where Marion had settled down.

Listen to what Marion Nicholson, a deeply religious woman, told us at *cèilidh* the other night, Finlay said, in that loud matter-of-fact manner of speech that we all came to know so well. She emphatically told us all while discussing the crisis that no German soldier would ever set foot on British soil, whether hostilities were brief or prolonged. Needless to say, I was astonished, Finlay remarked, but it sure made me feel good.

He wasn't the only one. Marion's prophecy, which proved to be so true, rendered my own shattered soul its first glimmer of hope.

For my father "worthies" were not, of course, only those men and women close to his time frame, they were also the great figures of the past, especially the MacDonald past. And what MacDonald does not have an interest in that most extraordinary woman who ferried the prince, in time of great danger and personal risk—"over the sea to Skye."

Flora MacDonald's life (1722–1790) would seem to have had more than its fair share of drama, melodrama, tragedy, triumph, and sheer excitement. Her father died when she was a child and her mother was abducted and married to Hugh MacDonald of Armadale, Skye. What kind of woman (mother of nine) could have survived the Tower of London, the Americas as an enemy, her husband's imprisonment—except a very sturdy, courageous Scottish lady? More than survive she did and is now buried in the north of Skye in Kilmuir churchyard, wrapped, they say, in the sheet on which both Bonnie Prince Charlie and Dr. Samuel Johnson had slept.

MacDonald Worthies of Yesteryear: Flora MacDonald and Hector MacDonald

As a MacDonald Hebridean Gael, and no hero, I was always fascinated by two of our brave MacDonald Gaels of long ago. There was, of course, Flora of South Uist, not too far from my own birthplace near the Butt, who skillfully disguised Bonnie Prince Charles as an Irish female maid—Betty Burke—and ferried him clear across the Minch to Portree under the very noses of redcoats.

Flora was no ordinary female. She had spunk, gumption, and savvy. Subsequently, she did get caught and was sent to the Tower of London. She was freed and married another MacDonald of her own small island, Benbecula.

She and husband Allan emigrated to America two years before the war of independence exploded all around them. Allan joined the British cause and was taken prisoner. Flora came home and died in 1790 at the age of sixty-eight years. Flora was a MacDonald to be proud of.

My other favorite MacDonald Gael was Sir Hector MacDonald of Ross-shire who distinguished himself in the Boer war and others. He was promoted to colonel for his gallant leadership in the hot battle Omdurman. Subsequently, he became an aide-de-camp to the great Queen Victoria herself, who adored the handsome Gael.

At the close of the century, Sir Hector, now known as "Fighting Mac," became major general with a high office in Indian Affairs. At the turn of the century, he became a KCB and was in charge of the British troops in Ceylon. In 1903, Sir Hector, somehow, some way, showed up in a Paris hotel where he allegedly took his own life. People of Sir Hector's sterling character don't commit suicide. He was fifty-one years of age.

What my father meant by the word *wag* I am not quite sure. The dictionary definition speaks of wags as jokers or of "young men" or "chaps." Following are sketches of young men playing pranks on others, some of which seem innocent enough, others not so much. My father's narrative has already told of ruffians who added to the unhappiness of a Skigersta wedding gone wrong by destroying a wedding carriage on the wedding night. All the more tragic a scene because this groom never came home.

Wags

Smùid na bèist dhuibh: Intoxication of the otter. Many years prior to the turn of the century, a hapless otter, locally known in Gaelic as a *Bheast dhubh*, was ensnared on our Skigersta *cladach* by three village youngsters, then in their late teens. The identity of the three, who spent their entire lifespan abhorring the sound of these four words, shall remain obscure—for obvious reasons.

Knowing the value of the otter's fur, the cornered animal was quickly slain, but the amusing aftermath of the matter evoked gales of laughter among old and young for several subsequent generations. Today, it's very doubtful if there are more than two (my next-door neighbor *Tarmod a' Bhàird* and Donald Mackay) surviving in Skigersta who recall even the rudiments of the hilarious episode. Furthermore, it appears that distorted versions of the event were invented and disseminated for extra merriment to all and sundry.

The youngsters, on the threshold of manhood, were still unaware of life's pitfalls, as they eagerly rushed to Stornoway with the precious pelt in a *poc* (bag). A village *sgoth* just ready to leave for town was happy to have them aboard on their first venture toward fame and success.

Upon arriving in Stornoway, a certain well-known tradesman was approached, and sensing the lads burning eagerness for sale, he magnanimously handed the youngsters a goodly price for their pelt, the amount of which was never divulged—also for obvious reasons.

With a fistful of pounds, the three bigwigs made a beeline for the swankiest saloon in town and got "juiced to the eyeballs"—as they say in Texas. From this famous spree which turned out to be loud, boisterous, and comical, *Smùid na bèist dhuibh* was coined.

BLACKHOUSE GOD'S HOUSE

The Eleventh Commandment

There once lived in one of our Hebridean villages two elderly Christian gentlemen whose adherence to the New Commandment was known far and wide. The village youngsters, like all village youngsters, were not averse to contrive local mischief and schemed up a sinister practical prank by way of testing the beautiful bond existing between the two godly men.

It was the custom in our part of the world to kill a sheep occasionally during the scanty winter months, strip it clean, and hang the animal up on its hind legs in the cold barn until the meat settled—ready for consumption.

The sly culprits, knowing that one of the pious men did not kill that winter, went and took the other man's sheep (while the village slumbered) and hung it in his friend's barn—quickly scattering to await developments.

In the morning light, when the so-called thievery stirred the neighbors, the boys, as prearranged, volunteered for the search, and of course found the missing animal. Their devious ploy backfired, however, as they watched the other Christian fervently imploring them not to divulge the matter to a living soul.

He begged and begged, almost in tears to keep everything to themselves until the truth was known. The fact that he didn't fly into a rage against his friend spoiled everything for the pranksters, who forlornly dispersed, probably concluding that these Christians are undoubtedly peculiar people.

To this day can be seen on a small grassy eminence, known in Gaelic as *Helistuder*, the shieling (a mountain hut used as a shelter by shepherds) foundations of my Eoropie forbears of ages past. It is southwest of our *Baile Shuas* and directly south of the *Baile Àird*—not too far from *Allt a' Mhaide*. Eoropie's elderly loved *Helistuder* in summer shielings, overlooking the beautiful *Baile Shuas* and lovely *Lathamor by the sea*.

So deeply revered were those shieling *bothan* (small hut) by Skigersta's old-timers that up until around 1915, their crude roofs, walls, and makeshift interiors were left untouched—venerated like things of antiquity. This respect stemmed from the tender memory of Eoropie's worhies, who enjoyed tending to their cows atop the tranquil little hillock of long, long ago.

Alas, in one dismal evening of unbridled disorder, the silent much loved shieling *bothan* fell on evil times—a cold callousness for which my guilty conscience pursues me as relentless as my shadow to this day—seventy-one years later.

One late evening, a group of us young misfits, while examining the lowly *bothan*, tugged on a spar here and a slat there in quest of excitement—to the devil's delight. Suddenly, a rebel crony yanked loose the main supporting rafter of one shieling and the entire roof crashed to the floor with a resounding plop. To our warped minds, this noisy collapse was sheer play, and within minutes, all shielings were leveled to the ground.

On the following morning, the village elderly were angry and appalled: a nostalgic landmark was no more. My mother's sharp eyes, instinctively sensing that I was one of the culprits, having no faith whatsoever in my stability—so searingly penetrated through my guilty soul that I felt stark naked before her.

Wits

We have been introduced above to some individuals who brought merriment to their friends and family, some because they were naturally witty and others because they were who they were, and quite naturally aroused amusement. Below are some further sketches of these two types of wits—some intentional, others not.

Contrasting Rivals

Until poet Alex Nicholson's sudden, untimely death in an auto accident, our village of Skigersta enjoyed the services of two busy grocery shops managed and owned by two of the most dissimilar personalities that ever breathed. Neither Alex nor John, the owners, were born in Skigersta but loved the residents in general and the *bodaich* in particular.

John MacIver was born in Swainbost, and of course, Alex was from Lionel, as he so ably put it in one of his classical lines: *Lional ann an Eilean Leòdhais* (Lionel in the Isle of Lewis). The keen competitive rivalry between these two men, both respected by the village folks, was a riot of comedy, especially for the *bodaich*, most of whom enjoyed an occasional lusty laugh.

The two were poles apart in conduct, conversation, and attitudes—enhancing comical climate between them from day to day. John was easygoing, slow gaited, and mumbled to a maddening degree. Customers were frustrated trying to grasp his low-toned nasal mutterings. Annie Morrison, *Anna a' Bhàrd*, our next-door neighbor, a jolly, witty girl who was John's shop attendant for many years, kept us in stitches explaining how she lip-read her boss' orders from time to time. Alex, on the other hand, was wiry and always on the go. When engaged in common conversation, his words were as emphatic and clear as a campaigning politician seeking office.

One day, Alex attentively watched his easygoing rival serenely and slowly walking by in the painful, measured gait of one who appeared to care less whether he lived or died. "There indeed goes a most extraordinary individual," Alex commented wryly, "slowish since childhood but is the only creature in captivity who refuses to die—and also refuses to live."

Contrasting Christians

Reverend John Nicholson, the vigorous Edgemoor Baptist preacher of my young days, was always the first to get anxiously involved in distressing local problems. His personal courage, especially in cliff scaling, was proven beyond doubt on many occasions. Mr. Nicholson, of a creative Lionel family, was a svelte, wiry individual with sharp piercing eyes, and so energetic that he seemed to arrive at widely separated points with the swiftness of Phillip the evangelist.

However, when he set out to build a seaside summer home atop a menacing-looking cliff of forbidding coastal rocks of dizzying heights, miles from the beaten path, many wondered if his noted courage wasn't slipping into something more sinister. Yet, despite the fact that his house's foundation was only a mere few feet from disaster, the finished home was truly a work of art. Adorable landscaping scrupulously planned and planted by the gifted Mrs. Nicholson, a grand, well-educated American woman, was of exotic textbook design.

Weekend guests, however, entrapped within Mr. Nicholson's bird cage during southwestern gales had both harrowing and amusing tales to tell, as if precariously tilting on the edge of doom. One of these was Donald MacLeod, noted Eoropie merchant and friend of the Nicholsons, both devoted church people of different denominations, who reluctantly acquiesced to a weekend invite to the bird cage, one to be remembered by the merchant to his dying day.

There were no weather reports back in those days when Donald MacLeod took off on a temperate afternoon for a weekend visit to Mr. Nicholson's summer home atop the cliffs. As Donald proceeded through the moorelands on foot, an ominous precipitation reared its ugly head above Tolsta—a gloomy-looking blackness spearheaded by a stiff southwesterly breeze, auguring distress, if not disaster.

Perhaps for the first time in his illustrious career, the merchant felt a mite wobbly around the knees but courageously entered the bird cage where Mr. and Mrs. Nicholson awaited with open arms. As the evening progressed, so did the wind, and likewise the merchant's concern, with every weather sign known to mariners indicating that gale force winds were roaring across the heathery moor in calamitous rapidity.

An alarming gust now and then clearly convinced Donald that a ruined weekend was already in progress. Sometime in late evening, as Donald silently and unmercifully upraided his own gullibility in jeopardizing his life which a simple "no" could have averted, a noisy gust wafted out of the atmosphere, shaking the cliff domicile to its very foundation.

At this point, Mr. Nicholson, calm as Camelot, suddenly became aware of his friend's panic and quietly assured the merchant that only strong faith and solid Christian confidence were the obvious qualities one must possess in order to really enjoy a place of this grandeur—as he and Mrs. Nicholson busied themselves with household trifles like it was a becalmed summer afternoon.

Murdo and Norman

There were only two men, outsiders, married to Skigersta girls during my young days on the beautiful *Baile Shuas* of long ago. As time moved on, however, there were several men from the northern outlying villages who took Skigersta brides—three from Lionel alone. The two in our day were Murdo MacDonald, Knockaird, and Norman MacLean, Swainbost.

These two men, Murdo and Norman, frequently came under a barrage of good natured teasing from some of the Skigersta *bodaich*, who slyly hinted that pilferage was unheard of in the village until northern aliens moved in. This suspicious and explosive type of banter occasionally aroused the dander of these two upright men who felt hopelessly outnumbered and who never dreamed of perpetrating anything shady to soil their good name.

On becoming aware of putting these fine men on the defensive the *bodaich* ceased the matter, except *Cròaic* my good neighbor Angus MacDonald, a chronic tease. With four simple sounding words, "strangers in our midst," *Cròaic* brought on the fireworks, especially from Murdo.

Whenever Angus engaged in any casual conversation within Murdo's hearing, these four exacerbating words without fail found their way into his nonstop, inverted chatter—just to get Murdo riled. It worked every time and Murdo, in command of awesome Gaelic adjectives when aroused, recoiled in savage sarcasm—to the amusement of the *bodaich*, who wished, but to no avail, that Angus would once and for all give up his ludicrous, outlandish innuendoes.

MURDINA D. MACDONALD

More about Murdo

Murdo married Johanna Morrison, *Lathamor*, a witty, beautiful woman whose sense of humor and comical, earthy observations cheered that corner of *Lathamor* for a whole generation. Norman MacLean married Margaret MacKenzie, *Àird, Màiread Dhòmhnaill Tàilleir*, another comely lass and sister to Donald MacKenzie, the well-liked *Toel* into whose house on the beautiful *Baile Àird* she moved with her family when her popular brother, to the grief of all Skigersta's residents, moved to Quebec.

Murdo MacDonald was slender and wiry, about five feet ten inches in height, and never accumulated any fat on his straight frame, probably because of his disciplined ways in never yielding to excesses. Moderation was Murdo's credo. *Seonag*, Murdo's wife, actually teased him throughout their married life for his straight-laced posture and rigid regard for prudent behavior. At one time, she told her nephew, *Aonghas Alasdair*, the village wit and comedian of our day, that her husband didn't even have the common frailties of other ordinary men. "He is so perfect that he sometimes bores me," *Seonag* concluded with a lusty laugh.

The Cow That Loved Flour

My friend Norman MacKenzie, "Broxy," Habost and New York City, a Christian gentleman who never disseminated telltales, told me the following funny story. There were two witty first cousins from *Rudha* boarding together in Buffalo, New York, and the exchange of wit and teasing between the two were a riot of comedy.

One day, in reflecting on home life in *Rudha*, one said to the other, "You know, your home was always swankier in common amenities than ours was." "You people always enjoyed *min fhlù.r* [white flour], *silidh* [jam], *Lofaichean* [loaves], and other fancy morsels. All we ever had was barley bread, barley porridge, and barley brose [broth]."

"*Oh, mo chreach! Cluinn air an fhear tha bruidhinn! Thubhairt am fear eile 's gun do bhàsaich a' bhò agaibh leis 'an spaideireachd.*" ("Oh my goodness! Listen to the one who is talking," said the other fellow. "And your cow died because of how posh you were!")

It seems there was more to the funny remark than meets the eye. They did have a cow who was afflicted with some unidentified malady which old *Seonaidh an ceàrd*, the so-called expert of those days (see his biography under "oddballs") recommended trying *min fhlùr* in the animal's diet.

That they did, and the creature got so sophisticated that she wouldn't touch anything else—until too late. She just perished, obviously for lack of solid fare which other cows were happy to live on, which she disdained: dying as a toff.

The comical cliché made the rounds, however, according to Norman's report: *Gun do bhàsaich bò Dhòmhnaill leis a' spaideireachd* (That Donald's cow died because of how posh they were!)

So-Called Comical Christians

True Christians do not wish to appear comical as worldlings consider comedy, because no less an authority than the apostle Paul warns against giddy, shallow behavior in his converts. Nonetheless, an occasional pious funny man can be found among the redeemed who inadvertently makes both saints and sinners laugh out loud.

For example, a devout old worthy of our church religiously warmed his pocket watch by the fire on cold mornings prior to inserting it into the small pocket by the belt line. This weird little harmless ceremony invariably evoked giggles from all and sundry.

He owned one cow, and the comical situations arising out of his eccentric relationship with that confused animal kept everybody in stitches. Since old age caught up with him he was deathly afraid of lingering long in wet clothes. At one time during Communion while living with friends who loved him, a sudden shower drenched him just a mere few yards from shelter. He rushed to the front door and bolted through yelling, "Trousers! Trousers!"

At another time during communion season in his own home town, with several guests under his roof, they were held indoors by another sudden shower which poured out of the atmosphere close to the opening of church service, leaving everybody on edge.

The old-timer fervently kept watch for a lull. It came, and upon opening the door and seeing the blue sky once again, he just closed the door behind him and made a beeline for the church without saying hi to the anxious guests nervously awaiting on the *cagailte*. When one of the men opened the door and saw the old fellow hastily making for the church, he said, "Folks, the flood has receded. Noah's dove shall not return."

Uncle Murdo

Since any of our family could recall, my uncle Murdo wore a thin, spade-shaped grey beard which he always trimmed neatly. With his tall frame and prominent features, this particular style of beard suited him well. When all dressed up for special services, he looked like a stern, ramrod-backed Prussian general deploying troops for battle.

All his life, he exuded a commanding, stern look and a fast flash of the eyes when aroused. Throughout the years, none of us had any inkling of what his chin looked like, and no one cared. We just took my uncle's beard for granted from day to day, and so did the rest of the village residents.

Then, one memorable night something startling occurred on *Cnoc a' Choilich* which amused many, saddened some and astonished the rest. While Skigersta slumbered, Uncle Murdo went to work and cut off the whole beard, leaving only a narrow Ronald Coleman moustache to ornament the upper lip.

When he surfaced on *Cnoc a' Choilich* the following morning, the only feature that neighbors recognized concerning him was his booming voice. The facial arrangement was unbelievable—amid furtive giggles and strange stares. My own reaction when he walked into our house was sheer panic. It appeared to me that his entire chin had literally vanished, while mother said sadly, "*Oh, bhrònain bhochd chan eil agad air!*" (You poor soul. You can't help it!)

He was not senile, lived many years afterward without showing any symptoms of senility. He could describe minutely nearly every character in *Pilgrim's Progress*. A brilliant man.

More about Uncle Murdo

My uncle Murdo, *Murchadh Buidhe* of *Cnoc a' Choilich* in Skigersta of long ago, was an expert in naming the characters in *Pilgrim's Progress*. He made a lifelong study of John Bunyan's masterpiece. Murdo also was frequently accused of being a mite too fond of a dram. He spoke a lot about "Talkative," a character in *Pilgrim's Progress* who seemed to be never at a loss for words and always found in or near the town's watering hole.

My mother respected Murdo's gifts and vast knowledge of scripture besides *Pilgrim's Progress*. She often spoke of the danger of one with his knowledge in spiritual matters missing the real significance of the pilgrim's journey and his narrow escape from the City of Destruction.

One day, as Murdo talked on and on of characters in *Pilgrim's Progress* sitting at our *Teine meadhan an làir* of other days, mother pointedly asked him, "Murdo, did you ever find yourself amongst the many characters of *Pilgrim's Progress*?" "Oh, yes, indeed, I did," Murdo answered candidly. "I'm Talkative at the saloon."

Talkative Murdo

In our day, a tiny, interesting colony of versatile mechanics, brilliant boat builders, a merchant, a minister, and even a World War hero, snuggled on the southeastern corner of Port—officially known in the United Kingdom as "Port of Ness." Now, if one included the respected Gordon MacLeod and his thriving post office, just a stone's throw from our subject matter, *Niseachs* of our era were tempted to conclude that this compact corner was indeed the brain center and prime cynosure spot of the big Ness community. I refer to the illustrious MacLeods, Macfarlanes and merchant *Dòmhnall* Gearr, who plays an important role in the following true tale.

The virtual autocrat over this successful corner of Port was headstrong, white-haired Murdo MacLeod, *Maurdo*, not to be confused with his neighbor *Meurdi*, also a gifted gentleman. In the conversational sphere of human society, Murdo MacLeod was the world's undisputed champion, mostly because he perfected a sinister technique of communicating on several decibel levels and was heard.

He mumbled, groaned and whispered, shouted and snarled, as everybody respectfully listened, simply because there was no alternative whatsoever—he just wouldn't stop. By way of refueling, he occasionally got off the sound track and into painful seconds of mute silence, but his lips, moving rapidly, kept forming words as if still in the thick of conversation and thus maintaining a running chatter, even in dead silence.

Lest the reader doubt that old Murdo was a chronic talker, consider the true yarn told by his son John, the hero of the *Iolaire*, within my hearing over half a century ago. John, a quiet, stable man, and adroit *sgoth* builder of note, frequently felt frustrated at meal hours with the old gaffer blabbering nonstop but remembering the fifth commandment, kept his peace.

On one occasion, however, John, obviously a mite overwrought, wagered his father half a crown that he couldn't keep silent during an anticipated big family dinner which he wished to enjoy in peace for a change. Old Murdo quickly accepted the wager in gleeful mood, apparently assuming it was the easiest half crown that ever came his way.

Prior to this friendly family bet, however, a most unusual event occurred in the immediate neighborhood. It seems that merchant Donald, out of compassion, brought his sick bossi into his swanky kitchen, nourishing the ailing creature like a tender babe, to the amusement of all the neighbors, who just couldn't get over the incongruity of it all.

Meanwhile, at the *Maurdo* household, everybody was happy around the dinner table, with Murdo savoring the last morsel or two of the big meal in tomb-like silence when suddenly, the thought of a sick calf in a kitchen crossed his mind and abruptly declared loud and clear his astonishment at *Dòmhnall Geàrr* rearing a calf in a kitchen. Immediately John demanded his coin, which the old-timer reluctantly handed over—sadly shaking his gray head.

Four MacDonald families occupied *Cnoc a' Cholich*, our favorite *Baile Shuas'* vantage point in Skigersta of long ago. I can vividly recall fourteen lively human beings working that colorful *Cnoc*, with whom I mingled from day to day. One was neighbor Angus, *Cròaig*, two doors from ours, a most unusual individual and a good neighbor.

Of all our village *bodaich*, Angus, with the exception of *Seòris*, was the most comical, though utterly unaware of it, and cared less either way because charging Cossacks couldn't contain *Cròaig* from being himself and doing what came natural.

For example, it was impossible for Angus to hold his peace when another *sgoth* approached on the high seas. He was always ready to hurl some crude remark across the waters at some touchy fellow in the other *sgoth* whose dander was bound to explode, to the amusement of the crew, especially his brother Malcolm, who always said to him when another boat was passing, "*Chròaig, cùm do bheul na thàmh. Leig modh a' chuain mhòir dha na daoine.*" (Chròaig, keep your mouth shut. Let the people have the courtesy of the deep sea.)

One day, out at sea, a Port *sgoth* came close with quick-tempered Angus MacBride, Adabrock, a victim of *Cròaig's* teasing over the years, leisurely standing back aft enjoying the scenery and at peace with the world. MacBride in later years became quite bald, a fact he didn't relish being persistently reminded of, and when *Cròaig* spotted the shiny, bare pate of his old sparring partner, he shouted through cupped fingers over the calm waters, "*A dhaoine, cò às a fhuair sibh an rùda maol tha na sheasamh anns an deireadh?*" (O people, where did you get the hornless ram that is standing in the back?). MacBride exploded.

MURDINA D. MACDONALD

Malcolm MacDonald

My good-natured neighbor Malcolm MacDonald, known all over Ness as *Calum Maag*, was perhaps the jolliest of the thirty-four bona fide *bodaich* in Skigersta of my day, where I spent twenty years. This commendable disposition on Malcolm's part does not by any means signify inferior intellect. On the contrary, Calum was quite versatile and shrewd as they come in business matters, going about his affairs with rare buoyancy and a hearty laugh—a refreshing sound to us youngsters.

One of our happiest diversions growing up with Malcolm on the beautiful *Baile Shuas* was his occasional lively sparring match with our Lionel policeman, known as *Mac an Portair*, a strapping, well-liked constable who related to Malcolm through their similarity of temperament. They went together like *Buntàta is sgadan* (potato and herring).

The folksy constable, wasting away with boredom in a staid community where wrongdoing was unheard of, occasionally surfaced on our *Cnoc a' Choilich* just to say hello to the *bodaich* and perhaps wishing that some Skigersta native would get a mite out of hand now and then for the sheer pleasure of reminding himself of the happy fact that he still possessed a vestige of power and prestige.

No sooner had the policeman set foot on the *Cnoc* than a flailing, sparring exercise between the two jolly men ensued in earnest. To us youngsters, this open skirmish was the height of play, especially on one certain day when Calum in a wild swing knocked the constable's uniform hat off right into the dusty street, as everybody gasped. I can still recall Malcolm holding his sides in spasms of laughter.

Malcolm swiftly took off in the opposite direction, wobbly from laughing, as only Malcolm knew how, and that brass-buttoned policeman, calmly retrieving and dusting off his beautiful blue uniform hat, benignly grinning from ear to ear, is to me, even to this day, an unforgettable recollection.

BLACKHOUSE GOD'S HOUSE

More about Malcolm MacDonald

Calum made up the third of the three early risers on the *Baile Shuas*, the others being my Uncle *Murchadh Buidhe* and that lively man of the moors, Norman Murray, who bounced out of bed at dawn. Malcolm owned and toiled over one of these huge *lioseans* (gardens) whose *ceap* (sod) constructed dyke entailed untold drudgery in upkeep. It was nothing uncommon to see Calum at dawn, somewhere around that *Lios* either chasing a sheep or mending the *gàrradh* (garden wall; dyke), as even tempered at that hour as other mortals feel at high noon.

Iain Deilidh Adabrock

At one time during *Iain's* distressful wilderness journey in this world, he was torn between his love for the parson and some annoying aspect of the minister's behavior. He knew that a great big beautiful church like the *Eaglais Mhòr* could not function without money. What was getting *Iain* down in the dumps, however, was the constant Sabbath clamor for more and more. It got to the point where poor *Iain* went frequently down on his knees on account of the matter, irksome to his soul like Paul's thorn in the flesh.

One Sabbath morning, with a considerable crowd in attendance, *Iain* stood by the collection plate at the door when some unsteady clod of faulty equilibrium lurched heavily against the plate and spilt the coins noisily all over the floor. In a hushed, silent church, a noise of that nature carries far. As disciplined Christians, however, they all behaved circumspectly and sat in silence during the service.

It wasn't recorded whether the sound of money sufficed to blunt the minister's yen for cash on that particular Sabbath, but coincidence or no, monetary matters were not even mentioned from the pulpit that day.

On the way out, at the closing of service, a woman acquaintance of *Iain* sidled up to him and said softly, "My goodness, John, that money sure made an awful lot of noise." "Not nearly the noise that would have erupted if there was no money at all," John retorted sadly as he pensively walked out through the front door and out of sight.

More about *Iain Deilidh* Adabrock

It was going on forty years before I again saw *Iain Deilidh* since I used to pass by his home going back and fore to the Lionel school complex from Skigersta of long ago. On my second trip home since the *Marloch* (1979), I went to Stornoway alone just to browse around.

As I sat down for lunch at a restaurant table, this quiet fellow wearing a cap ambled by me and sat right opposite me, immediately removing his cap when he sat down. It struck me right off that it was *Iain*, much younger than our age bracket, but now a noted Christian gentleman. Not yet too sure of myself, I kept thinking that if he says grace, it's him for sure. His lunch arrived and *Iain* folded his fingers and closed his eyes as solemnly as if praying in the hallowed *Eaglais Mhòr*. "And ye shall see the difference." Neither *Iain* nor myself made the slightest attempt at communicating—strange lunch fellows.

In his own quiet way, *Iain's* wit made *Niseachs* quite frequently roar with laughter. In America, he probably would have become rich as a comedian. For example, there was this communion season in some remote part of the island when *Iain*, devoted to the means of grace, arrived on Thursday. He entered a home with which he was a mite familiar, but nobody was in except a talkative tyke who did not know who *Iain* was.

As he listened, sitting quietly by the fireside, the kid said to him, "There is nobody attending Thursdays of Communion services around these parts anymore, except *Iain Deilidh*, and even he didn't show up this time." "Oh," *Iain* said softly, "there is no telling, perhaps he will eventually show up—one never knows," with as somber and straight of face as if conducting family worship in his Adabrock home.

Oddballs

My father's world included people who were considered to be outside of the mainstream of their own community mores. This had nothing to do with theological differences, which were understood to be just that by all the parties involved. These people were viewed as strange, odd—apart. A few of their stories are told below.

Ness Quacks of Long Ago

In Ness of long ago, there was hardly a village without a quack or two meandering among the peasants, looking and feeling important. Our local quacks were weird esoteric mumbling ancients, exerting awesome influence on the naïve and superstitious. Incredible as it may seem, very few *Niseachs* of our generation were entirely liberated from its eerie and powerful grasp, despite the Gospel's free and complete emancipation from all its satanic black magic.

To define the true blue-and-black quack of our dismal days is one who brazenly, unabashed, and unlicensed suggested and concocted mysterious nostrums based on the ambiguous background of a former faker—long gone to where quacks go—or deserve to go. Interesting indeed were the prerequisites necessary to qualify for this simulacrum underhanded profession, which the following disclosures might shed some light on.

First, it was absolutely imperative for the quack in line to outlive all predecessors without qualms, quivery, or bat of an eye. Longevity was its own reward, enhancing prestige, and that shadowy peculiar aura hovering around those who tenaciously refuse to die. Like choice vintage, their mystique improved with age.

Secondly, indulging in tolerable eccentricities, supposedly the mark of genius in some immortals, helped our quacks quite a bit, along with outpouring of far out folksy colloquial chatter and occasional flights of fancy around the bend—launched our quacks into business.

Seonaidh an Ceàrd (Tinker John)

Overshadowing our own Ness cult of quacks was the High Grand Hippocrates of the lot—old John—a Barvas peddler, so ancient that local historians amusingly insisted calendars weren't invented when he first saw the light of day. John, widely known all over Lewis as *Seonaidh an Ceàrd*—Tinker John, was presumably capable of accurately diagnosing all ailments affecting everything that breathed, including the traditional expendables, human beings.

Ailing horses ambling onto the glue factory were his prime specialty, after which came the cows, followed by dogs, cats, sheep, lambs, and dying calves, all of which received *Seonaidh's* immediate attention and loving care. His so-called expertise was such that all our local quacks looked up to him in awe as the head healer capable of diagnosing all maladies, especially those bedeviling the animal world. Also, his so-called knowledge was such that he considered highly trained medical experts of seven and eight years college background quacks.

Seonaidh an Ceàrd was only a mite over five feet tall, svelte and stooped, with dark brownish, mummified wrinkly skin, reminiscent of some antiquated object preserved for posterity. *Seonaidh* talked a blue streak and for a man of no schooling whatsoever was exceptionally gifted in Gaelic dialogue. It is something to ponder, nevertheless, that with all of old *Seonaidh's* outlandish mores, many *Niseachs* consulted him as regards sickly animals, and so did some Skigersta folks, a people noted for native intelligence and common sense.

Angus of the Hills: *Aonghas nam Beann*

He was called Angus of the hills because most of his life was spent roaming and praying among the Scottish Highland hills of his immediate surroundings. I once heard one of our FP ministers say of Angus: "He could scarcely count the fingers of one hand." Yet this phenomenal individual was so versed in scripture and so articulate in divine discourses that learned ministers of the Gospel envied his gift of words, befitting trained theologians.

Strangers listening to Angus's spoken words in public on *Là na Ceist* were never aware of the fact that he was utterly unable to count to ten. His beautiful explanation of saving grace, quoting scripture after scripture as he articulated, astounded even true born-again Christians. Angus was never at a loss to minutely explain hard questions frequently asked him concerning salvation, which, according to reports, occasionally embarrassed godly men.

Nevertheless, it was quite evident that Angus never matured above the mentality of a mere child. He lived in that wholesome childish world all the days of his pious existence on earth and died that way, as the following anecdotes shall reveal.

At one time two ministers, one who knew Angus well and the other who just heard of his talents, were walking a country road when Angus unexpectedly loomed in the distance. The unfamiliar parson thought this would be a propitious moment to ask Angus about a certain verse of Holy Writ which puzzled him, but, being a mite shy, asked his brother minister if he would do it for him. "Oh, no," was the polite retort, "I would much rather that you do that bit of delicate inquiry on your own"—obviously still either envious or embarrassed of the in-depth explanation Angus rendered the minister concerning some scripture text he wished to define in the past.

In another incident, Angus's minister was down in the dumps. Strange as it might seem to worldlings, this sort of setback occasionally assailed many great men of the past. This preacher was so low that he was almost despairing of his soul's status between himself and his Maker. One day in sheer desperation, he blurted out to Angus, "Angus, I'm afraid that God has forsaken me," to which Angus unhesitatingly replied, "Well, at one time He forsook one much more worthy than both of us."

Everybody who knew Angus, including his minister, had great faith in the power of his prayers. On one occasion, the minister was bedridden with some malady, and when Angus approached the bed, the minister pointedly asked him, "Angus, are you praying for me?" "Oh, no, I'm not. I haven't got enough for myself," Angus candidly replied.

When Angus's time came to part from this world, which to him appeared to be chaff, dross, and mire at best, he was stricken with a fatal illness while on his way to celebrate the Lord's Supper at communion season. It became quite evident to all and to himself that the appointed time was at hand.

He did some complaining to the Lord in the manner a simple child would plead to an earthly father under dire duress. He was heard to say on his death bed: "Oh Lord, weren't you rather hard on me, when thou well knew that it was on the way to celebrate thine own Supper, I was laid low?" In that childish manner, the pious Angus of the hills closed his eyes in death and went to heaven, where in all likelihood he was warmly welcomed by a host of angels.

Murderous *Mac an t-Srònaich*

In a village like Skigersta and in all of Ness, there cannot have been much crime. How unbelievable therefore to know that there was, in fact, a murderer in their midst—a serial killer, in fact.

When my sister Margaret, born 1893, went to the herring slave labor toil of long ago in a three-girl crew, she had interesting tales to tell upon returning home. At one time, she really startled us by relating that she travelled past the home of monster *Mac an t-Srònaich*, homicidal maniac, a mental malady so utterly vicious that those afflicted can dispose of their best friend with the same satanic satisfaction as destroying their mortal enemy.

The mere name sent shivers through our young souls because of his murders on our moors, long before we were born. Such a creature was *Mac an t-Srònaich*, the only man of his ilk to emerge in our corner of the world. We never did get the real background of the man or whence his origin. I had completely forgotten the location on *Tìr Mòr* where Margaret was shown the birthplace of this fiend, having exiled myself for close to sixty years.

In 1979, I paid a short visit to Ullapool to see my ailing nephew, Norman MacDonald, Eorodale, Margaret's son, known and loved by multitudes. Norman, an excellent truthful storyteller, related to me some interesting material concerning *Mac an t-Srònaich* which were never revealed to us youngsters during our twenty-one years at home.

"As you came up to my home on train or bus, you passed the home, or at least the site of the home, where the notorious *Mac an t-Srònaich* was born," Norman said as calm as Camelot, while I almost slithered out of my chair with excitement.

"Did you ever hear the true story of how, when, and why he became a homicidal maniac?" Norman asked. I readily admitted that I never did, but was burning with curiosity regarding the background of the awful man who gave us nightmares as children of long ago.

"Well, his first murder took place right in his own home," Norman said, "the victim being none other than his own sister." "It happened in the following manner, and possibly quite true, because his first gruesome crime, perhaps accidental, would suffice to unhinge the strongest minds and bring madness to most men."

It seems that his father ran a small roadside rooming house, accommodating not more than three or four guests, and out of which the old-timer eked out a meager existence. Back in those days, dire poverty was rife throughout the Scottish Highlands, with most mortals unable to realize a pound sterling.

Upon noticing an affluent-looking lady with some jewels visible on her person checking into his father's place, young *Mac an t-Srònaich*, like Judas of old, allowed Satan to enter into his heart and purposed to relieve the so-called wealthy lady of her jewels that night while in deep slumber. However, it so happened that while arranging and rearranging sleeping quarters his sister ended up in the very same bed that the jeweled lady was supposed to occupy.

In the wee small hours while busily poking around for treasure, the young would-be robber sensed some stirring in the bed and in sheer panic, furiously seized upon the occupant's throat, choking her instantly.

In no time at all, the horrible crime came to light and the young murderer took flight and wandered as a wanted fugitive throughout the Highlands until landing on the Lewis moors where he murdered some, but Norman didn't know how many.

It is regrettable that the most interesting part of this sad tale is obscure: how and where was he apprehended and execution. Our elders used to tell us that he regretted bitterly drowning a small boy somewhere in Lewis—but details were obscure.

(Note from Donald MacDonald's *Lewis, A History of the Island*; 1978, p 194)

> One of his victims was said to be a young boy from Ness whom he drowned in a pool near Muirneag, a murder which lay on his conscience for the rest of his life. He is reputed to have made the following statement:
> The look the child gave me from the deep pool; I would rather than anything that he were on my knee.
> On the scaffold he was reported to have said:
> Seven years you kept me safely, O brown moors of Lewis, and as long as I kept to you, you preserved me.

12

Dying

We have already seen in my father's writings depictions of death and dying: death by war, by shipwreck and drowning, by appendicitis (Angus Mackenzie) and auto accident (Alex Nicholson). In this chapter, we explore other means of expiration: exposure to the elements, flu epidemic, heart attack, unknown illness affecting both old and young and freak accidents. But it is not the means of death but the manner of death that marks these recollections. My father was at pains to highlight the enduring faith that carried the terminally ill to their graves, a faith he shared and honored. And in doing so, he celebrated the communal solidarity that treated each death as the death of a family member.

Càrnan Balach a' Bhac

On the outer fringes of Skigersta's *Gàrradh a' Bhaile*, a few paces from the cliff, was in our day a crude-looking *Càrnan* (memorial) commemorating the death from exposure of a young Back lad whose death on that spot brought tears to the eyes of many. It was small and roughly bunched together as if hastily formed, with a couple of oblong stones leaning toward the sea.

This *Càrnan* meant something to me because the youngster's remains were brought to our house where they reposed overnight.

From thereon, No. 7 on Skigersta's *Baile Shuas* meant a lot to the people of Back, especially the lad's kindred.

It all happened long before I was born. This youthful, devoted Back lad was one of many young men who followed Communion services all over the island. Crossing the moor on foot in those days was a mere delightful exercise, especially for the young. However, so late in season was the Ness Communion at that time that the lad failed to find a travelling companion to venture the bleak stretch of heathery moorland between Back and Ness—via North Tolsta.

His thirst for the Gospel message was such, however, that he took off alone underneath a frowning, precipitative sky. According to handed down reports, his ill-fated journey was initially plagued by a tardy beginning, not clearing Tolsta until about 2:00 p.m. This was the first ominous omen.

As if the very elements were bent on his destruction, the wind abruptly and wrathfully swerved to northeast, directly contrary to his general goal and in blizzard roar swept the Hebrides from the Butt to Barra.

His fierce struggle to stay alive from thereon must be left to the speculative, analytical imaginations of current seasoned old men of the day. They reasoned that following a night of terror, in which he often crawled on hands and knees, feeling for gullies and ravines, with an overriding fear of drifting onto coastal cliffs, he finally stumbled into Skigersta's *Gàrradh a' Bhaile*, somewhere east of old *Cafann Lathamor*.

At this point, he made the error of turning east toward the cliff of sheer drop while blindly groping along the wall, desperately hoping it would lead into Skigersta proper. Meanwhile, great sheets of snow wafted out of the angry atmosphere in near gale force, in which the blurry outline of the wall was impossible to follow.

By now, the drowsiness of death from indescribable suffering, strongly urging to lie down and sleep it off was rapidly gaining the upper hand. Nevertheless, he bravely struggled on fighting the twin monsters—sleep and snow—until within a few paces from the precipice, he crumbled in a heap—exactly where that lowly and sad *Càrnan* is heaped to this day.

Death of *Doilidh Mhurchaidh*

In a small village of less than three hundred souls such as Skigersta of long ago, the passing away of one villager was almost as keenly felt as death in one's own family. Our cohesion was such that we acted and reacted toward one another as if we literally were members of one mammoth household. Death's sobering effect on all was evident from the *Baile Àird* to *Lathamor*, the Murrays to Macfarlanes on the *Baile Shuas*—as all outside pursuits were abandoned for three solid days.

Skigersta's First World War fatalities were six: three from *Lathamor* and three from the *Baile Shuas*; luckily the *Baile Àird* was spared. While cold statistics were no comfort to those whose kindred were slain, nevertheless, per capita wise, Skigersta's loss in view of the fact that forty were involved, including the militia, army, navy, and the merchant marine, all of whom were engaged in the common struggle, was indeed minimal.

Two died at the height of the flu epidemic, one in Canada and the much loved youngster *Doilidh Mhurchadh*, the subject of our sad story. So popular and greatly admired was the handsome *Doilidh* that his sudden demise cast such a dismal pall over old and young throughout the community as to surpass the grievous bereavement previously endured at the news of our gallant men falling in battle.

No death in our time affected such genuine, far-reaching sorrow, in chain reaction gloom from Swainbost to Skigersta and beyond, as the passing away of this unusual lad. It is safe to assume that nearly all of *Lathamor's* residents were in tears on that mournful afternoon when *Doilidh's* remains, in that somber slow procession, passed their doors on the way to his final resting place.

Doilidh Mhurchaidh, affectionately known as *Doilidh*, came into this world in command of such an attractive, exuberant personality that Skigersta's elderly became so attached to him they themselves couldn't quite define their fondness for the ill-fated youngster. One of our more observing village fathers in all likelihood voiced the opinions of all when he explained that *Doilidh* was the embodiment of every endearing quality a parent wished in a boy.

For example, at fifteen, his shapely straight frame was equal to that of many twenty-year-old males. Snapshots of *Doilidh* are still extant but woefully misrepresent his comely face and form. When combed and shined on evening strolls, with his high crown of dark-brown hair, snuggly fitting navy-blue jersey and trousers to match, only the biblical figure of "no spots or blemish" could compare with his tall, outstanding physique. Small wonder that one of our fairest village maidens who adored him with singular passion since childhood still tenderly cherishes his memory in bruising nostalgia and silent tears.

Malcolm and Margaret

There were many devoted couples to one another among the *bodaich* and spouses in Skigersta. Of course, there was also a scattering of harsh relationships, as is bound to occur everywhere, in which a crude *bodach* or two treated his wife as something to be utilized in the rough manner one handles a battered wheelbarrow.

One particularly devoted couple stood out in our village as a pair whose pure love for one another remained undiminished from the honeymoon to the grave. They were Malcolm and Margaret MacKay, *Lathamor*, who, after raising a family of four boys and two girls—all of whom died quite young except one—were still communicating when approaching ripe old age in the tender vein of lovers in their twenties. It was a happy fact that their honeymoon never ended or waned until death intervened.

Margaret, from Swainbost, was so sold on her man that if a shopworn cliché is excused, worshipped the ground he walked on. In turn *Calum*, our village joiner and rugged *sgoth* skipper who, when aroused, could verbally clobber a man, talked with and treated Margaret throughout their long married life with the same sensitive approach which he obviously applied when first dating his lady fair. They were genuinely enamored with one another all their domestic lives in a clear demonstration of what a marriage made in heaven is all about—an epitome of loveliness.

One can imagine the stunned reaction of our village, and even the whole community, when one midmorning, Malcolm MacKay and devoted spouse Margaret died within minutes of one another, perhaps seconds, because no one was near to verify the time element. Which of the neighbors or kindred first came upon the tragedy is now obscure, but they speculated that Margaret was attending Malcolm, who was ailing at the time, and upon discovering that he had suddenly died, succumbed to heart failure—as if Providence had decreed not to part them, even in death.

In considering Margaret's great love for her husband, such conjectures made a lot of sense, because she wasn't young and family tragedies in which three sons and a daughter perished were bound to damage the heart. Skigersta's residents were shocked in silence, some quoting Psalm 46:10: "Be still and know that I am God: I will be exalted among the heathen; I will be exalted in the earth."

Even though I'm now absent from Skigersta for over sixty years, I can still vividly recall that morning on our own *cagailte* when the news reached us that Calum and Margaret died perhaps within seconds of one another. We all stepped outside to gaze down toward *Lathamor*, and a gray, low ceiling canopied the village, as if in mourning for the grand devoted couple who "were lovely and pleasant in their lives, and in their death they were not divided."

Mary Morrison's Last Moments

Back in the early twenties, an amazing episode occurred on Skigersta's *Baile Shuas* which was recalled by surviving residents in awe and veneration. It concerns the unequalled last hours of our dying next-door neighbor, the young and beautiful Mary Morrison, the Bard's third daughter. Mary's whole personality was literally uplifted to her future heavenly abode in glorious visualizations of that prepared place as she calmly awaited her appointed time. In this peaceful state of bliss, she uttered wondrous words, worthy of recording, to pious parents who listened with the strange mixed emotions of joy and sadness.

It appears that Mary was mercifully removed from the tumultuous earthly scene prior to entering into that perilous, sophisticated phase of life so irresistible to the young, in which the deadly dainties of "Vanity Fair" are so fatal to multitudes. One day while convalescing, Mary hailed me as I passed by to exchange a few words from her upper story window. While her former glowing smile had somewhat waned, her full face showed no pallid traces of mental or physical anguish, buoyantly anticipating complete recovery.

Shortly thereafter, however, the same Mary no longer harbored any affection for the world. On the contrary, she sincerely wished to be swiftly removed from it all, as if literally accepting that the very ground was accursed as God declared to Adam and the whole world lying in wickedness as affirmed by John, while longing to be delivered from its present evil influences, as craved by Paul. Her whole being was completely swallowed up in the heavenly visions that immediately accompanied her sudden conversion, which, like Saul, appeared to have occurred in a single revelation.

One evening, as the end came near, Mary stirred in a spurt of renewed exertion to assure her mother that she wouldn't stay past her appointed time for "a thousand worlds." Quite near the end, the distressed mother in a desperate urge to ease her dying moments offered her a sip of wine which she sternly refused with the following words: "Do you wish me to appear before my Lord smelling of drink?" Shortly afterward, she closed her eyes in death, looking like a serene, contented child in deep slumber.

The Pious *Iain Beag*

Not in our time, or perhaps rarely in any other, was there a personage just quite like *Iain Beag*, John Morrison, my devoted neighbor of two doors away and brother of the Bard, whose last days in this world are still remembered in awe and veneration. So detached from mundane matters was this godly man for about a year prior to his demise that he considered everything under the sun, except spiritual matters, a maze of materialistic dross. It was as if his daily conduct and conversation were shouting from the housetops to all and sundry: love not the world, nor the things that are in the world.

That *Iain* was neither senile nor mentally disturbed was utterly ruled out because of his obvious disciplined and alert mind and seasoned-with-salt discourses on Christian experiences, along with a keen grasp of current church vicissitudes, for which he prayed without ceasing. Moreover, John was an avid reader of former divines, well versed in the writings of Thomas Boston, Richard Baxter, John Bunyan, and R.M. MacCheyne—spiritual giants of other days.

As illness gained the upper hand, *Iain's* whole personality appeared to have been transported to that "Celestial City" toward which Bunyan's famous pilgrim made the most interesting journey of all time. On his brief visits to our *cagailte*, he used to tell mother that the words in Micah: "Arise ye and depart, for this is not your rest" clearly spoke to him out of scripture. At this phase of his illness—"ripening for the harvest"—as the Reverend Wallace Bruce puts it, there was no point of launching on any worldly topic, as he sat by our peat fire pouring out praises to the Lord in raptured eloquence befitting the learned sages.

Scottish Giant (1825–1863)

Giant Angus MacAskill, 7'9" tall, weighing over 425 pounds, and who measured near four feet across the shoulders, was born about fifty miles south of my home—in Harris.

None of the other twelve of Angus's large family were out of ordinary size. His father was a mere 5'9" tall. After attending class for about one year, his parents emigrated to Cape Breton Island, where they purchased a small farm and settled down.

At the age of twenty-four, a vaudeville scout, impressed by Angus's enormous size, meek manners, and brute strength, signed him for a vaudeville tour, which he accepted with glee and was off to perform throughout the United States. On this tour, good-natured Angus obliged everybody by lifting everything in sight of curious onlookers who sometimes used little or no judgment. The fact that he did not know his own strength was his downfall. This tour eventually brought him face-to-face with the great "Victoria Regina" herself, who at that particular point of time was adored by the whole civilized world. Angus was proud of that meeting but silently—never given to visible emotion or anything distasteful.

As was bound to happen, however, that fatal day finally caught up with easygoing Angus on the Boston waterfront, when a cluster of senseless, inebriated sailors talked him into lifting a 2,200-pound anchor. This caused instant internal damage to some vital organs, a wound from which he never recuperated. He did survive in ill health for five years but was gradually wasting away until at last the big, harmless Scottish giant was no more. Dead at age thirty-eight.

13

Emigration

When Lord Leverhulme's schemes failed, so did the economic prospects of the island of Lewis. My father was part of a Lewis diaspora in 1923–1924 that consisted of about nine hundred persons. The historic context of this human dispersal is outlined in the recent study by T. M. Devine entitled *To the Ends of the Earth. Scotland's Global Diaspora 1750–2010*.

My father was twenty-one years old when he boarded the *Marloch* in 1924. Little did he know that he would be forever separated from the only world he ever knew, the only world he loved, and the only world to which he would ever be truly connected.

Migrations of Long Ago

While growing up on the beautiful *Baile Shuas* in Skigersta of long ago, shortly after the turn of the century, when at the impressionable age of five or six, our street's population was in the neighborhood of ninety souls.

Then commenced the nostalgic migrations to Canada and the USA, depriving our small street of fourteen youngsters, six of which lived almost within a stone's throw of my door: the two Donald Morrisons, *balaich Iain Phìobaire*, and *Iain Chròaig* along with four maidens: Kate Morrison, cousin Johanna MacDonald, and the Buchanan sisters Christina and Robina. The other three were the Murray brothers, Murdo and Norman, along with *Aonghas a' Chaoidhich*, who perished in France serving in the Canadian army.

Back in those days, emigrating to Canada or the USA was tantamount to journeying to some inaccessible, remote region of the world. Their shattering departures were as traumatic as watching a loved one disappear over a demarcation line of no return.

In a sad sense, that's exactly what it turned out to be for most of the migrants. Only three came back on a permanent basis and were buried with their fathers: my neighbor *Dòmhnall Iain*, Donald Morrison, and Norman Murray of No. 11 and my cousin Johanna MacDonald. The other eleven are buried in cities ranging from Vancouver to Fort William, Edmonton to Saskatoon, Chicago to Detroit and Flanders Field.

Mellowed *Giagan*: 1924

Before leaving on the *Marloch*, my father and his friends visited Lionel for one last time and were treated to a surprising farewell from an old enemy.

Neither the class nor I will ever forget the *Giagan*'s startled expression as he warmed up toward me following a severe cold hand thrashing one winter morning of long ago. His cold blue eyes humanely softened in wide, compassionate glow as he sat me by the fire when my face looked like that of a corpse—according to classroom cronies. To see the *Giagan* exuding humane emotions shocked the whole class—they stared open mouthed in disbelief, refusing to accept the impossible.

They were utterly unprepared to see the *Giagan* behaving in fatherly fashion to anyone, even his own brother Malcolm, whom he thrashed with abandon. So accustomed had we become to the constant snarls and scowls of our teacher that it was just weird watching him behave the opposite—humanely—that is. It was even embarrassing. We even came close to feeling sorry for the gangling galoot, who was roundly hated by all and sundry.

About eleven years thereafter, John Gunn emotionally shook hands with a van load of former pupils, including four Anguses from Skigersta, on the way to the *Marloch* in 1924. We stopped at *Còrnair Taigh Loudan* in Lionel, and there was our former nemesis, meek as a lamb.

It was obvious that he was keenly cognizant of the nostalgic farewell to former students, most of whom he was never going to see again. The drastic change in the *Giagan's* personality was unbelievable. He looked, talked, and behaved like a soft-spoken, dignified country squire. The old *Giagan* was no more—vanished forever.

The Second Highland Clearing 1923–1924

During the brief period of one year and some days 1923–1924, three oceangoing liners removed the bulk of Lewis youngsters to Canada, 95 percent of whom never returned on a permanent basis to their native land. To make the one way of no return more alluring and romantic, the big ships dropped anchor in the placid Stornoway bay: an enticing epic and master plan subtly offered in three attractive packages to commence and complete the Second Highland Clearing—this time in style.

Only during the *Iolaire* disaster were the Stornoway piers subjected to such heartbreaking weeping as when a whole generation of eighteen- to twenty-two-year-old males were lost to Lewis forevermore. We were now paying a bitter price for our supine, cowardly behavior in allowing corrupt bureaucrats to harass the munificent mogul Baron Leverhulme right out of our economic lives.

Confounding our embarrassment and shame was the awful fact that our island malcontents—bums—were ruthlessly utilized by these zealous men to do their dirty work, encouraged by the Irish, our mortal enemies. Naïve and green as we all were, as miserable migrants, however, we quickly learned that when disposing of human beings in surplus multitudes, British legendary know-how is unmatched in displaying efficiency and thoroughness as regards castaways in the familiar area where they excelled long before the first infamous Highland Clearing.

The three attractive enticements offered us were a sponsored fare, promise of a farm job, and an eight-day leisurely luxurious cruise across the north Atlantic, all the way to Montreal. Thanks for nothing.

Crossing the North Atlantic on the old *Marloch* took many days. All passenger ships are alive with rumors. Our own current gossip aboard concerned the captain, who, amazingly enough, we hadn't laid eyes on in eight days at sea despite our gazing from stem to stern for a glance at the braided buccaneer who brazenly pirated us from *Steòrnabhagh Mòr a' Chaisteil*. It seems that on a previous run, somewhere in the Clyde estuary, a collision was so narrowly averted that the "Old Man" spent most of our voyage on the bridge—hence the absence, according to deck hands and stewards, most astute combination of gossip mongers on the high seas.

During the slow but uneventful crossing—best eight days we ever enjoyed—many new acquaintances were made throughout the various Lewis districts and some Harrismen. The trauma of sad good-byes on the Stornoway piers brought us closer together. It became commonplace for small groups to huddle in all corners of the deck discussing the various Canadian provinces to which we were assigned.

Most of us were optimistic regarding the farming commitments, unaware of what lay in store. *Cha chreid Mac Leòdhasach a' chreach gus an ruig' 'n doras aige* (a Lewisman doesn't know what difficulties are until they come to his own door). One exasperating aspect which irked us was the shadowy presence of government watch dogs (agents) appointed to check our daily routine, solely on account of our sponsored fare (the famed fiasco) instrumental in the thorough accomplishment of the sweeping second Highland Clearings of 1923–1924. These starch collared toadies were our first real brush with beastly British bureaucracy in action, in which its subtle, clandestine influence was keenly felt, like one being stalked by a monster.

They made certain in typical British maritime "Captain Bligh" exactitude that none of us would silently slip over the side in mid-Atlantic and escape on a mattress. Therefore, it's a cold fact of life that as naïve, shy lads, unaccustomed to beg or borrow, and on our first venture into a harsh, competitive world, they put us woefully on the defensive—a shabby, vulnerable posture heading straight for the St. Lawrence.

The thought of that unpaid fare engendering a guilt complex, frequently crossed our young minds, stupidly ignoring how gleefully the "powers that be" disposed of us with the cold callousness of one ejecting accumulated garbage. During the subsequent sufferings of many Lewismen entrapped in peonage/servitude within the greedy fangs of exploiting Canuck farmers, many escapees often wondered if the great and good God would ever forgive the transgression of even pondering paying a pittance in return for that fare fiasco.

In their wildest dreams, Canadian farmers failed to visualize a day when youthful, able-bodied Scots wouldn't fulfill all of their ambitious whims in dawn-to-dusk toil in return for room and board. Yet, this was their euphoric posture when in 1923–1924, multitudes of strapping Lewismen came knocking at their doors in the sad wake of our mass stupidity of long ago.

There were many advantageous deals afoot in favor of the Canadian farmer while quickly grasping the green Lewis migrants of that traumatic transplanting era. It was a time when the fierce, inherent pride of many Lewismen was humbled into dust while traipsing—hat in hand—all over Western Canada like common indigents, struggling for survival. Anyone in such a desperate state can be easily manipulated, a cruel fact of life not lost on the canny Canucks. It has been established without the shadow of doubt that the Canadian farmers of that unhappy era succeeded in exploiting the miseries of migrants to an uncommon degree.

However, as was bound to happen, the Gael's innate insistence on liberty propelled many into action, and some crestfallen farmers found themselves staring wide-eyed into an empty, unmade bed at the first gray glimmer of dawn. Others beat the system in avoiding servitude by boldly disappearing in Quebec and Montreal.

On our brief stopover in Quebec, for example, several familiar faces vanished into thin air and were seen no more. In Montreal, the disappearing continued in earnest as three Skigersta Anguses performed a vanishing act of their own, worthy of magicians and prowling pussycats. We just vanished—and were seen by agents no more.

Escape from the *Marloch*

When the three Skigersta Anguses decided to elude our farm agent in Montreal and escape from the *Marloch*, we made certain needless, precautionary measures. The bounder was nowhere in sight when we furtively walked off that gangway with bags in hand making for the nearest cab. We hastily piled into it feeling like thugs with something to hide.

However, the boldness, adventure, and danger of the matter appealed to us somehow, ala the three Musketeers. It was fun, but at the same time, we were shaking with emotion. It was ridiculous. We were almost as much on the defensive as common criminals, too dumb to realize that the government's overall plans were now complete in getting us into Canada. From thereon, as far as the government was concerned, it was: you're on your own—get lost. And many of us did.

We only had two addresses, one in Toronto, miles into the interior, and one in Scotstown, Quebec, a small lumbering town, not too far from Montreal. Angus MacFarlane's brother Alick was employed in Toronto, and we were absolutely depending on him for help in finding a job.

When we arrived at Alick's boarding house, we discovered that Alick had just flown the coop and was in Buffalo celebrating his brand-new American visa, and that he intended to stay. And there we were without money, friends, or job, exuding helplessness, hopelessness, and despair.

An t-amadan Blàr: 1924

The winters of Scotstown, Quebec, where the three Skigersta Anguses toiled in 1924 upon escaping from the *Marloch*, were so severe that ice and snow seemed to cover and dominate every single inch of the whole town, including human beings. While peering out through a spot here and there of our ice-covered windows, we took particular notice of this tiny bird about the size of our own *Topag* busily pecking away at something in the ice amidst that fierce, forbidding frozen Antarctic environment.

We kept wondering what on earth was a bird with able wings to escape doing in a veritable glacier like Scotstown? We even envied the foolish little critter, wishing, like the Psalmist, to have wings so as to fly right back across the Atlantic and enjoy the cozy flame of *teine meadhan an làir*—whence we came.

My relative, D. L. MacRitchie, a born naturalist because of his forest upbringing, explained that the Gaelic speaking people of Quebec, offsprings of the Highland Clearings victims, named the so-called foolish bird *An t-amadan Blàr* (the plain fool) because of a spot or spots between the eyes.

However, I regret that I've completely forgotten Donald's explanation of how that rugged little feathered *amadan* eked a living out of Scotstown's ice and snow—but he did. It's ironic that I forget what is probably the most important point of the whole enigma—but I do.

My father spent 1925 boarding with Marion Nicholson, the widow of the Bard Alex Nicholson, in Windsor, Canada. In the summer of 1926, he worked on a gravel sucking scow on the lakes and gives us a glimpse of what that world was like in his sketch "Lake Sandboat."

Lake Sandboat

My long summer season of 1926 as a deckhand on a lake gravel ship is impossible to eradicate from memory. Ten Lewismen, including Wallace B. Nicholson, signed in Windsor for deck service on this sand ship, actually a glorified scow. When Wallace saw the cramped quarters, he couldn't get off the tub fast enough to join his D&C fleet across the river where he enjoyed a uniformed brass buttoned job and quarters fit for the Duke of Edinburgh. This is where the difference between brains and brawn is clearly manifested.

These cumbrous ships sucked the gravel from the lake bottom by means of lengthy, elongated, fat pipes whose toothy maws reached down onto the Lake Erie bed where choice gravel abounded in copious quantities. The machine which supplied the sucking power was affixed on top deck above the pipes, was about four feet high and two feet wide, and so noisy, right in front of our bunks that it was near season's end before any of us got used to the racket and finally enjoyed a good night's rest.

We operated the machine in two-hour turns, and the poor guy who didn't have any luck in sucking gravel on his watch during the night was considered a dolt by the skipper, whose first duty every morning was to peer into the gravel hold.

Our bunks were no ordinary bunks as common seamen are accustomed to. They were makeshift boxes hastily thrown together like one would speedily assemble for a stray dog. I had a lower bunk and Donald Gillies, Shabost, above me. When we retired, Donald seemed to be a comfortable space between us, but as the night progressed, he kept slithering downward and was almost on top of me by morning light.

Embarrassing Summer Season

Back in the summer of 1926, a group of us young Lewis migrants, mostly escapees from the *Marloch* and SS *Canada* of 1924, ended up in Windsor, Ontario, after some Canadian wanderings hither and yon. Right off, I met Angus Graham, Back, my dining room crony on the *Marloch* for eight days. The drift toward Windsor was of course the Great Lakes—our main objective.

That particular summer a strange thing occurred, however. Eight Lewismen shipped out on one sand and gravel boat from Windsor, including Angus and myself and a lone Scot from Glasgow; two from Shabost, Donald and Malcolm Gillies, cousins; two from Ness, Donald Mackenzie, Port, and myself of Skigersta; two from *An Rubha*; and one from Lochs. Angus was our other craneman—we had two aboard.

As a proud young Lewis crew, we had reached that so-called sophisticated phase where we assumed that we knew a thing or two. Our chef for that season was a middle-aged Windsorite, whose extensive knowledge of the world around him was phenomenal.

Eight months of close contact with our brilliant cook, lecturer, and naturalist should have broadened our characters a degree or two. Instead, he infuriated us by pointing out how little we really knew about our own native land, a country which he never even visited.

We didn't even know the square mileage of Lewis or the population of Stornoway—never gave it a thought. Neither did our teachers, preoccupied with thrashing. The lengths of the rivers Clyde and Thames were to us a blank. My own greatest fear for eight solid months with the chef aboard was that someday, somewhere, he'd inquire about Skigersta's population, of which I knew no more about than about how many aborigines lived in Australia.

Connecting the dots in my father's biography is difficult to do, but in the following two sketches, he provides some clues. He worked on the D&C line of ships carrying passengers throughout the Great Lakes until 1928. In the fall of 1928, he arrived in New York City. In 1936, he married my mother in Reno, Nevada, and they settled into their first apartment in Oakland, California. On the declaration of war in 1939, according to my brother in law, he went back to service on the Great Lakes and was therefore part of the war effort transporting important material to Europe. Apparently this service during wartime was one of the things he was most proud of in his life.

Another thing we see in the sketches below is his love of Gaelic song, a love for the beautiful ladies who sang it and a love for the land they celebrated.

Songstress Mary Catherine

In Skigersta of long ago were reared many lovely lassies, some of whom would be considered by today's beauty experts ravishingly attractive. Outstanding in appearance as these were, however, none showed any promising signs of extraordinary singing talents until about a score of years after the turn of the century. In the early twenties, as if to brighten the void, two young and beautiful rising singing stars on which Skigersta laid claims burst forth on the scene like luminous meteors in a darkened sky.

One was the gorgeous Mary Catherine Nicholson, gifted daughter of the gifted Gaelic poet Alex Nicholson, author of the immortal lines *An tèid thu leam a rìbhinn mhaisich?* (Will you go with me lovely maiden?) The other, of course, was the renowned and beautiful songstress Kitty MacLeod, also of Skigersta. While Kate MacLeod's star as a super songstress rose high in the Gaelic-speaking communities of her day, Mary Catherine's, on the other hand, due to a series of unfortunate circumstances, commencing from her father's sudden and untimely death, never soared into the limelight—a tragic loss to multitudes of exiled Gaels throughout the globe.

It is interesting to realize that when objectively evaluating the voice qualities of Mary and Kate, as many of us who admired both have had the opportunity of doing, one is at a loss to distinguish the superiority, if any, of one over the other—such was the closeness of their singing ability and degree of excellence. In all fairness, however, Kate's clear advantage in receiving some professional training, a privilege of which Mary Catherine was deprived, must be taken into consideration.

By a cruel twist of fate, Mary Catherine never sang to a Skigersta audience, despite a burning desire to be heard by the residents who loved her dearly and throughout the years warmly inquired after her welfare and whereabouts in nostalgic reflections. No other girl in our time made the impression on the contemporary male colony within her wide social circle as Mary did, when, at the peak of her popularity and singing prowess, she settled in Windsor and Detroit back in the middle twenties.

Without any doubt, she was at that buoyant point of her time the undisputed "belle of the ball." Those were the happy years that so many Gaelic-speaking seamen from Mull to Melness, Caithness to Cromarty, Skye to Sutherlandshire, and the Butt to Barra sailed the Great Lakes, many of whom knew Mary personally.

Yet, while in clear command of a charming, outgoing personality, wit and sparkling vivacity, she nevertheless kept both feet solidly on the ground and was never carried away by gaudy influences so potent in leading millions into mischief. The late and lamented *Màiri Alasdair MhicNeacail* strictly maintained an unsoiled reputation and rigid regard for Christian conduct until graciously ushered into that Divine Domain where her song and praise shall never end.

Songstress Mary Catherine—Continued

In 1939, over two score years ago, on my way back from California to New York by Greyhound, I stopped in Detroit, eager to see the Great Lakes once more. Eleven years had come and gone since I reluctantly finished my last season of service on the attractive D&C passenger fleet of six magnificent side-wheelers. Those fast and convenient ships served in overnight runs the cities of Buffalo, Cleveland and Chicago, loaded with happy humans in holiday mood. Looking back on it now, it strikes me that those six ships surpassed in sheer pleasure, romance, excitement, and general entertainment any cruising consortium known to man until this day.

It was on this stopover that I met one of the most interesting *Niseachs* encountered in my many acquaintances throughout the numerous points I touched on as an incurable wanderlust. He was John Graham from Dell, known on Detroit's waterfront as *Iain Thuathain*, older than our age category, who emigrated to Canada around the time twenty-three Skigersta youngsters took off to faraway places.

Finlay MacLean, Habost, another Lake sailor known as the *Bran*, introduced me to John, who right off impressed me as one more *Niseach* sorely afflicted with the identical malady I myself endured for years—homesickness. Like birds of a feather, John and I saw much of each other for the next three seasons.

Iain picked up a considerable amount of education on his numerous lake assignments as an able shipping consultant between seamen and powerful owners, whom lake sailors mistrusted. His tiny, lake front office was a cozy *cèilidh* corner for Gaelic-speaking exiles from all over the Highlands. It was pointless to talk of shipping in John's office if one Gael was present to reminisce of home, especially Dell. He could literally talk nonstop about the twin Dells.

Then, as was bound to happen in Detroit of those days, something momentous occurred in John's life that uplifted his spirit right into cloud nine. He met the foremost Gaelic songstress of that era, Mary Catherine Nicholson, at a *cèilidh* in which he, for the first time, heard her sing

An tèid thu leam a rìbhinn mhaisich
Am falbh thu leam a rìbhinn òg

(Will you go with me lovely maiden?
Will you go away with me young maiden?)

After that, the attractive Mary Catherine, gorgeous lass on which Skigersta proudly laid claims, and still does—became, to *Iain Thuathain*, the ready panacea for all life's ills. There was a problem, however. John found it impossible to hold back the tears from the moment Mary's clear soprano voice rent the air.

Tarmod Geal: Whitey

In the early twentieth century the people of Skigersta were living in blackhouses, thatched roof dwellings of three compartments, including one compartment for animals—without electricity, indoor plumbing, hot and cold water. So hygiene, in the way we are accustomed to it today, did not exist.

Unpalatable as it may sound to our socially conscious selves, some humans are intrinsically of cleaner propensities than many of their fellow mortals, a crystal clear distinction which daily shows in their hygiene habits, inclinations never derived from disciplinary measures. Therefore, the inherently clean individuals can never escape their commendable but burdensome syndrome from the cradle to the grave: its spit and polish for life.

The clear proof of this fact was daily displayed and exemplified in the spotless person of my cousin Whitey—Norman Murray—born and brought up on Skigersta's beautiful *Baile Shuas* of long ago. Besides being a youngster of rare magnetic personality and reckless derring-do urgings, Whitey was also in his brief span of life a living legend in support of the point this sketch wishes to convey.

To begin with, such was the drastic difference in Whitey's general appearance to the rest of us while knocking about town as boys, that we all looked begrimed in comparison. This was entirely due to his extraordinary clean physical appearance, in which he actually arrested everybody's attention from the babe to the *bodach* as someone whose credo was that cleanliness is next to godliness. In long white moleskin trousers, white shirt, and a high crown of almost jet-white hair, set off by pinkish white skin and large blue eyes sparkling with merriment, Whitey looked like a good will visitor from some unsoiled other world.

Upon leaving for Canada in 1923 and eventually landing in the US, he, like a duck takes to water, shipped out of Detroit and immediately became known all over the Great Lakes as *Tarmod Geal* (White Norman or Whitey) by the many Gaelic-speaking Highlanders who sailed the lakes back in those colorful days.

As a Lookout on the old *Eastern States*, Norman was warmly favored by the first mate, who took a fatherly interest in him and who jokingly bragged to other mates that "he hired the cleanest looking sailor on the lakes." The mate was a fellow Lewisman, *Aonghas an Rubha*, Angus MacKenzie, an old salty who at one time was heard to remark on watching in horror Whitey's high diving exploits off D&C boat decks: "Someday, Whitey, someday," as if clearly visualizing his ultimate destruction which subsequently came all too soon in a reckless, fatal dive.

Whitey's roommates on the *Eastern States* also had problems with *Tarmod Geal*, but of a different nature. One roommate with whom he sailed for a season never ceased to comment on Whitey's compulsive craze to keep clean. "His scrubbing, scraping, combing, and rinsing with no respect for clocks, hours, time, or tides almost compelled me to join the French Foreign Legion," the shipmate groaned in desperation.

While living with his married sister Annie in Detroit, it was the same story. She once told me that during his stay with her, most of his spare time was taken up in washing and ironing every strip he owned, as if soiled garments were the spawning grounds of deadly diseases.

As an American, I celebrate every pilgrim who made it to these shores, whether Canada or the US—places they hoped would bring them a new life. For many, those hopes were realized in the New World, but for others, the journey did not end well, but tragically. My father grieved for them.

Carloways's Murdo MacLeod

In Windsor Ontario over half a century ago, the following deplorable incident occurred in which the arrogance and cruelty of those in high places destroyed the promising career of a strapping young Lewisman of Carloway. Murdo MacLeod, known as *Murchadh Mòr*, was suitably equipped, mentally and physically, for rising to the pinnacle of success in any chosen field.

This raw item of injustice involving the handsome *Murchadh Mòr*, newly over from Lewis and just joined to the Windsor Police force, took place in 1926 when I lived in Windsor with the Nicholson family.

No sooner had Murdo felt his way around the precinct as a raw rookie than, figuratively put, the whole roof came crashing down on his handsome head. This bit of infamy came about because Murdo, as a young, upright patrolman, issued a ticket to a lordly bureaucratic politician, high in the city government, for illegal parking.

The furor this unconscionable tyrant created over the affront to his so-called lofty status in city affairs was such that the full force of his evil, potent, political influences assaulted Murdo—a foreigner, no less. Even the fabled champions of the underdog, the press, scampered ashore when Murdo became the sinking barge at dockside—among whom an occasional "Iscariot" can be bought for less than thirty pieces of silver.

Big Murdo learned a bitter lesson the bitter way. In no time at all, *Murchadh* received his official walking papers—a disillusioned, broken young man. For years thereafter, this outstanding-looking, six-foot-tall Lewisman wandered from pillar to post until finally joining the vast army of forgotten men. The fact that he probably perished on skid row haunts me to this day.

In the fall of 1928, my father made it to New York City and was employed by D. B. Mackay in his shoetree factory. There were so many exiled Scots in the city that each area appears to have had its own society, i.e., the Lewis Society, the Skye Society, the Barra Society, and many others. My mother was raised in this social environment and apparently, as a good dancer, enjoyed the jigs, reels, and other dances of the day that were a part of this social life.

My father, at this time frame, was running around with a bunch of single Scots in the city. In due course, he would connect with the social settings that included my mother, but the following sketch describes one event that he and his buddies attended as Lewismen who were always fascinated with clergymen, the "rock stars" of their generation.

Professor Mackenzie

More than half a century ago in New York City when the Lewis and Skye organizations were having good relationships, our joint annual concerts were grand evenings for all Gaels, far and wide. One particular year, something special was offered as the stellar attraction of that night which we all looked forward to, a Lewis theological professor of Princeton University, no less, and a *Rubhach* to boot.

Back in those days, as single, carefree exile hordes, we moved around in packs, and a goodly crowd of us attended a packed hall that night in old Gotham of long ago. We spotted the professor right off as he sat between two speakers on the rostrum. He looked so Lewis and so *Rubhach* (person from An Rubha), there was no mistaken of either. Besides, we didn't really believe what they taught us in Ness, that all *Rubhachs* look alike.

The men sitting next to him spoke before the professor's turn came. Then came the big moment, when Professor Mackenzie of Princeton was introduced. He looked to be in his middle fifties, immaculately dressed in navy blue, with black, shiny hair and clear expressive eyes. He appeared to be about 5'10" tall and solidly built in a rugged *Rubhach* frame.

No sooner had the professor launched on his topic than all and sundry were convinced that the scholarly *Rubhach* was a born orator. He pleased the Skyemen with his keen knowledge of their island home, not forgetting his native Lewis, our favorite topic—a perfect evening for exiled, homesick Lewis and Skye Gaels of long ago.

14

Angus on Angus

My father wrote these sketches, in my view, (1) to honor and celebrate the people he loved in Skigersta and the wider community of which he was a part; (2) to keep alive his connection with this lost world of his; (3) to confess actions as a young boy and young man—some innocent pranks and others not—for which he felt great remorse; (4) as an exercise in self-reflection, i.e., an attempt to understand who he was and who he had become, and why; and (5) because he craved this exercise in self-expression. Where else was he free, except in these pages, to express himself as an artist, both visual and verbal, a naturalist, a historian, a theologian, a humorist, a humanitarian, a patriot, and a journalist. There *was* nowhere else, I believe.

Below are some of my father's reflections on himself.

Small Stone Ledge

At the height of Skigersta's fishing activities of yesteryear, with the harbor and environs constantly permeated with a strong fishy aroma, our seagull population appeared to canopy the bay when catches arrived. Early recollections, especially scenes pertaining to boats, fish, coastal wildlife, rocks, mounting billows and placid waters, along with stiff breezes and serene skies, all of which were the stories of our young lives in Skigersta, are seldom, if ever, eradicated from memory.

One of my most cherished recollections of youthful years is peering out through our old *taigh dubh* window on the *Baile Shuas* to enjoy the erratic antics of our *cladach* seagulls in their mad slapdash whirl around the quay when the *sgothan* touched on shore. I was about four and the whole world looked lovely.

Our blackhouse window structure was elevated about four feet from the floor, but so scrubbily built was our interior wall that a whole inch of one stone protruded beyond the facing about halfway between sill and floor. On this small step, my tiny toes found sufficient leverage to heave my fragile frame onto the sill to scan the *cladach* commotion, in which wildly fluttering gulls avoided collision by mere split seconds of time.

That small stone ledge remained in our wall, though concealed behind some makeshift repairs, until our house was leveled off twenty-two years later (1929). By this time, having removed myself thousands of miles from the *Baile Shuas* and upon learning that the old domicile was torn down, my small stone step which became so much of a part of my happy childhood days constantly crossed my mind in strange, nostalgic vividness.

First Suit of Clothes

My tall, handsome cousin *Calum Mhurchadh Bhuidhe* was a most unusual personality with a phenomenal memory. For example, at one time of his young life, he could remember every single surname in the entire District of Ness, consisting of thirteen villages in his day. Moreover, he could recall the blood relationships of nearly every family in Ness, and whence their offspring, besides relating how sisters and brothers got married into the various villages ranging from Dell to Port, Eoropie to Skigersta.

However, *Calum* wasn't the easiest man to live within our corner of the world simply because of a deep-rooted ego which he managed to subdue, except when I was around. I, as an overindulged youngest of the family, with oodles of ludicrous conceit of my own, came in handy for Malcolm's frustrations. I was always there for *Calum's* release of tension—the belittling was devastating and the insults overbearing.

With my very first suit of clothes, a blue double-breasted beauty, and first church attendance on a Thursday Communion service, I was absolutely on cloud nine when *Calum* walked in to look me over. He wouldn't have missed it for a king's ransom, being as nosey as he was ornery. After calmly scrutinizing me from top to toe, standing in *doras a' stìl*, he said softly, almost inaudibly, " *'S e,' arsa esan. 'treallaich de dhuine eireachdail tha annad am a broinn na deise ùir.*" ("Indeed," said he, "you are rather a fine-looking fellow in that new suit.")

Edgemoor 1915

Besides being an incurable theorist, the vigorous Reverend John Nicholson of Edgemoor (in gaelic Am Blàr Beag) was remarkably innovative, highly intelligent and forever on the move. As an aggressive Baptist liberal, he seemed to appear ubiquitously at too many different places at the same time to suit fundamentalists—for obvious reasons.

I was about twelve years of age when, both shy and a mite scared, I tensely knocked on Mr. Nicholson's front door for my very first visit to a real elaborate home of modern décor. Frankly, I was overawed at the imposing-looking place and nervous as a kitten upon reaching the threshold. There were some intricately worded forms involving our croft which Mr. Nicholson was familiar with that brought me to seek his advice.

Suddenly and unexpectedly, I found myself face-to-face with the gracious lady of the house, Mrs. Nicholson, radiating both charm and congeniality. Immediately, upon sensing my tense predicament, she warmly offered her white, bookish hand and said, smilingly, "I will announce you to Mr. Nicholson," half turning on her heels and nodding in the delicate manner one greets a royal personage. Having never been previously treated with such respect or greeted so cordially, I turned into a bigger emotional and embarrassed mess than before, standing there as a timorous, confused *amadan* (fool).

Right off, the Reverend John stepped into the lobby and briskly headed my way flashing the famous penetrating blue eyes; his outstretched hand and disarming smile instantly put me at ease. *Thig a steach* (come in), he said warmly. I can still recall walking behind him on a soft, red hall carpet leading to his study, which deeply impressed me. The feel of that soft red carpet underneath my rugged shoes filled me with the "bull in the china shop" complex—my first brush with luxury, which deftly dodges my lot to this day.

Hearing Things in the Scottish Hebrides

In our corner of the world, second sights, ghosts, omens, etc., were usually pooh-poohed, especially by the devoted of our day at the turn of the century. They strongly contended that the glorious, all powerful Gospel message as a final and perfect panacea for all maladies, including sin, forever freed mankind from such satanic imaginings as plagued humanity prior to the Gospel era.

For example, they did not believe that the spirit of Samuel ever spoke to King Saul at Endor. They were convinced that the whole sordid episode was the devil's device from the moment the ill-fated misguided monarch yielded to witchcraft. Therefore, in view of these weighty matters, one can imagine our family's reaction when one morning I told them that my Uncle Murdo's voice clearly spoke to me at early dawn while in deep slumber as audibly as if literally standing at my bedside. Reactions around our *cagailte*, or utter lack of any, clearly indicated to me that my morning mutterings went for naught. Nevertheless, this strange episode did occur in the following manner.

My bed in the old-fashioned *cùlaist* of long ago was in the middle facing the window. One early autumn, when crops were in constant danger of invasion by the dreaded *Caoraich an taobh thall* (Eoropie's sheep), my uncle's voice as clearly registered in my ears, while fast asleep, urging me to get up immediately, as if his tall, six-foot frame stood over my bed. My uncle's house was four doors away, and he assured one and all that he was in sound sleep at that time.

It was our family's turn to keep close watch on this particular night. Every village croft owner did likewise in turn, with no margins allowed for sleepy heads. Our old dilapidated *Gàrradh a' Bhaile* (village dyke) just couldn't hold those beasts at bay.

To this day, well over sixty years later, I can still recall Murdo's exact words and Gaelic warning, to wit: *Aonghais èirich, tha caoraich an taobh thall a' leum gàrradh a' bhaile.* (Angus arise, Eoropie's sheep are leaping the village dike.) I bounced out of bed and was outdoors in a flash, just in time to see about twenty of the roaming rascals heading straight for the tender crops, just showing above the soil (Texas, 1983).

Death Wish of Long Ago

On a particularly warm, stuffy day with an agitated, sickening sea in progress, our *Baile Shuas sgoth* settled about two miles off the Skigersta shoreline to fish for cod. All the monstrous-looking *Borgs*—ugly enough to scare any fish—were enthusiastically hurled over the side, except one, mine. I was in my early teens, out in my father's stead, who was ailing.

The close, tepid day and irksome, long running swells made me deathly seasick and as useless as warts on a turtle. Most of the *bodaich* had little sympathy for seasick victims, especially my uncle Murdo, the booming voiced *Gille Tòisich*, with the restraining patience of a rogue elephant, caring less—outwardly at least—if I was buried at sea. He was visibly annoyed at his nephew's incapacity to withstand the rigors of boats and brine, which explains why experts in human behavior have been for generations utterly unable to define whether Gael pride is madness, manliness, or sheer stupidity.

For hours I crouched in that bow like a dead fish, embarrassed, sick, and wishing to die—already looking like a three-day corpse. In my dire distress, the truth of what seafaring men averred from bitter experiences for generations of going down to the sea in ships, that extreme seasick sufferings engender a desperate death wish reaction—dawned on me in shuddering clarity. It is absolutely valid.

By evening, the ultimate in despair and pain had now been reached in my own body and soul. I am convinced that I wouldn't have cared a Scotchman's hoot if that fish-smelling *sgoth* had made a nose dive straight into Davy Jones's locker.

Hero?

It will be hard to believe, but in all honesty, and no modesty whatsoever intended, because modesty and humility are the last refuges of the bonafide scoundrel, I once played the hero's role and saved a life back in my boyhood days in Skigersta of long ago. It was the life of young Donald MacKay, known in those days as *Dòmhnall Beag Mhurchaidh* that I gallantly snatched from the jaws of death.

I use these noble words because my feat sounds more heroic. Donald still survives, a grandfather, settled on my own beautiful *Baile Shuas* and is quite capable of minutely detailing the matter to all and sundry. He was also gracious enough to remind me of my so-called valiant deed on all of the five trips I made home since the *Marloch*.

Donald was not a cripple from birth as was sometimes assumed. On the contrary, he was a robust, lively lad when injured in a high jump, not too far from his own door. It was a great pity because he was physically strong and wiry and, like his father before him, in command of a powerful pair of arms.

One day while frolicking around *Geòla Tharmoid Sheoc* at high tide inside the cove of our quay, Donald just silently slithered over the side unnoticed. I happened to look toward the right direction just when the last tuft of his hair was disappearing outside the gunnel. He could not swim at that early age. I made one wild leap for the fistful of hair rapidly submerging and luckily made contact. I dragged his head up onto the gunnel, and together we pulled him aboard, actually half drowned.

On my first trip home in 1952, I proudly reminded Anna Chalum of the fact that I saved her husband from an early drowning—expecting the accolades and praises due deserving heroes. *Oh mo chreach* (Oh, my goodness!) Annie loudly exclaimed, "*Cha chluinn mi dheireadh.*" (I won't hear the end of it.) And they both roared with laughter.

Tolsta Road

During the happy construction of the Ness-Tolsta Road in the prosperous Leverhulme days, three of the road gaffers were from Skigersta. They were Alick Morrison, *Lathamor*, and my cousin Angus Murray, later of the Glasgow police force and my next-door neighbor Donald Mackenzie, *Pòil*, husband of Margaret Morrison, the Bard's daughter.

After a spell of sloshing about, pushing a wheelbarrow, which wasn't too rigorous by any means, my neighbor *Tarmod a' Bhàird* took me into his shed as a handyman in assisting around the hauling engine he operated with great skill while the work was in progress.

It was a fairly sized winch (mach), which hauled gravel wagons from downhill by means of steel cable, with Duke Bherri, Port, as sprag man. The Duke was a born comedian and kept everybody in stitches. I felt grand while working with Norman, who, even then, was in command of higher than average IQ.

Suddenly, like a bolt from the blue, and almost without any warning whatsoever, everything came to a swift and sad ending, as the mighty and munificent baron was both rudely harassed and double crossed right out of our economic lives.

This frightful black skullduggery, perpetrated by evil, local, and jealous mischief makers in high places paved the way for the "Second Highland Clearing" of 1923–1924, in which all of Lewis was deprived of a whole generation of youngsters forevermore.

Off to Glasgow

"Your growth shall be stunted as of the moment you leave this house," bluntly blurted my protective father on being told that I and a boyhood pal, Angus Thomson, were off to try our luck in the Glasgow shipyards.

For many years following his gloomy prognostication, I desperately strived hard with a sneaky, vengeful urge to prove him dead wrong, but failed. He was absolutely on the mark. Without question, our first bone-crushing job, a toil which my perceptive old man envisioned would be our lot, in which twelve-foot-long-by-thirteen-inch-wide planks were lugged on tender shoulders as slaving stage hands for a whole hectic year, evoked such a loud "I told you so" from my old man as to be clearly heard from our *Toer* to the *cùlaist*.

Dire negative reports of the First World War's effect on post national economics were to us young mavericks merely old wives' tales. Still in our teens, we were prepared to enter upon a collision course with the whole world. Mother, like all mothers, concerned about our first venture into the secular, sophisticated Glasgow jungles, warmly advised us to seek out a childhood crony who, upon reaching manhood, had made it big on the famous Clyde.

This popular gentleman, *Dòmhnall Beag Dhòmhnaill Ghuirm*, was probably the most widely known and respected individual of the multitude of Hebrideans in and around Glasgow. We quietly and respectfully listened, jotted down her friend's name without the slightest notion of ever approaching the industrious fellow, doggedly determined to shift for ourselves, come famine or fish and chips.

Immediately upon leaving home, however, the psychological and physical pummeling we received in the splashing *Sheila* caught in the severest southeastern gale on record until that time—fourteen hours—so pulverized our ludicrously inflated ego to a point where King Rehoboam's famous folly so vividly struck home, we humbly conceded between ourselves that perhaps paying heed to our elders wouldn't be such a bad idea after all.

It took fourteen hours of roaring waves and mounting billows, one dead passenger, and many injured cows to puncture our horrendous Hebridean pride, an innate seething syndrome, which for generations of painstaking research, the most erudite psychiatrists are still utterly unable to define whether our haughtiness is a malady, manliness, or sheer madness.

Smelly SS *Sheila* of Yesteryear

Back in the early twenties, Angus Thomson and I on our first venture away from home boarded in Stornoway the most notorious, if not the most infamous and certainly the most hated vessel ever plated together in maritime designs. She was the soulless and bungling SS *Sheila*, more suitable for manure hauling, dog catchers' conventions, and witches wakes than transporting humans to Kyle.

The rumor that she was denied a maiden voyage due to erratic rolling in calm waters when tied to the dock was probably without foundation. However, allegedly incurable Stornoway drunks actually sobered up forever while observing the ancient *Sheila* incongruously pitching in the calm, glassy waters of the south pier, convinced that alcoholic madness had indeed inundated body and soul.

It was said of the *Sheila* that if placed in a placid pond, she'd still nauseate travelers into myriads of maladies, ranging from seasickness to sneezes, cramps to coronary, bends to bellyaches, from the sheer negative psychological impact of her bumbling background, ugliness, and smell.

John MacGregor, Carloway Foreman

Now that I can look back from the lofty peak of four score years, I'm as convinced as ever that when Angus Thomson and I arrived in Glasgow in the autumn of 1920 in search of a job and still in our teens, we were probably the greenest pair of Heeland men in captivity. We carried a note from *Dòmhnall Beag Dhòmhnaill Ghuirm*, Eoropie, a childhood acquaintance of my mother but now a respected foreman carpenter on the Clyde, to his friend John MacGregor in a Renfrew shipyard.

The note earnestly requested John to give us a job because his own shipyard was in a sorry state of postwar recession. Renfrew is a few miles downstream from Glasgow, opposite Clyde Bank and Brown's shipyard. John's shipyard was Simon and Lobintz, specializing in dredges.

When we first laid eyes on foreman carpenter John MacGregor that unforgettable, nervous, shaky morning, we thought that he was either the yard's president or the mayor of Renfrew. He was dressed so neat and expensively in a beautiful, blue serge suit, stiff high collar, black tie and bowler that he was clearly a fitting subject for the opening speech in the House of Lords. We later learned that all important yard personnel dressed in like fashion.

He searchingly scrutinized both of us with the curiosity of one seeing freaks in a circus for the first time. He didn't say yes, no, how do you do, or drop dead. He just coolly asked his stagehand gaffer who stood by to put us to work, as he regally walked off in the manner a monarch struts the palace. John was offish by nature and cool as a glacier, quite in contrast to the average friendly Carloweigian. Strange man and two strange Heelandmen.

Reverend Neil Cameron, Glasgow

Away back in the late fall of 1920, Angus Thomson and myself, amid much family opposition, took off for Glasgow, with specific instructions from our parents to attend the Sabbath services of the rock-ribbed Reverend Cameron, then at the zenith of his popularity. Having heard so much about the uncompromising clergyman since coming of age, both of us, who never before laid eyes on him, were eager to see and hear the troublesome figure who for the previous twenty-seven years and before was turning the world upside down.

Whether the legendary minister (bad luck omen) trailed us for our deep desire to see the embattled warrior, we know not, but it so happened that we immediately ran into the worst S. E. Minch gale in the *Sheila*'s history until then—fourteen hours to Kyle of Lochalsh—it's in the records.

We settled in the Cowcaddens, a hefty walk to Blythswood square, where the hallowed St. Jude welcomed strangers from Caithness to Cornwall, Uig to Ulster, back in those days. They came from all corners to hear him; many just curious to see an individual who withstood such verbal onslaught and abuse from year to year and survive. Mr. Cameron could have been appropriately called by church historians the "cast-iron Cameron."

Our approach to St. Jude's on the first morning was rather apprehensive. The usual small groups gathered outside instantly became aware of our presence, as newly arrived "Heelandmen," straight from the "boon docks." One smiling, middle-aged man fussed over us and said, "I'm *Dòmhnall Aonghais Shiadair* from Dell—perhaps you heard of me? We did.

Another congenial, short, and stocky gentleman with a *Sgiatheanoch* accent volunteered to find seats for us, and off we trailed after him down the aisle of a packed church, conspicuous and shy, right behind him, as if bent on seating us in the pulpit—and he almost did. Just a mere few rows from the extreme front, the good man beckoned us into a private pew with fancy names carved on both corners, adding to our mortification. Both of us uneasily visualized that someone would literally storm into these prestigious-looking pews demanding their seats. Kindness almost killed us.

The silence of that big, almost crowded church immediately impressed us, as we quietly sat there, almost cowering. It was as if we were the only two sitting within its huge confines. We later discovered that hardly a limb or lip ever moves in Mr. Cameron's church for two solid hours. The plain looking, unadorned door to the left of the pulpit's steps had to be Mr. Cameron's entry and egress we reckoned, because garnish and gaudy trappings of a church's interior drove him to the wall, reminded him of papal paraphernalia.

At this particular moment, the whole congregation affixed their gaze on that door, and so did we. A certain mystique had gradually built up around Mr. Cameron over the years which attracted multitudes. Nearly everybody wanted to see him, and within seconds, we found out why. The door opened and in walked the gray-haired distinguished-looking Cameron, exuding the most somber, no-nonsense expression ever to project from a human face. An arched left eyebrow, like a thespian emphasizing deep drama, along with the celebrated piercing stare, were the first two facial features to catch the eye. An elderly, small, and gentle-looking lady, dressed completely in black, followed behind him, obviously happy with her role as mother to the foremost valiant for truth of our generation.

She sat two rows in front of us as Mr. Cameron climbed the steps leading to the pulpit, which at that point of time was the hub of the struggling FP order. While ascending the steps, Angus and myself immediately took notice of the least publicized feature concerning the clergyman, which no one even mentioned—his shapely and flawless physical frame.

His black clerical coat fitted him as snugly as if literally tailored and ironed on his form. The straight back of his head, harmoniously lined with his equally straight back, as he impressively climbed on with the same deliberate and determined step, which symbolized his whole stormy career.

That unmistakable mystique hovering around the man's person did indeed arrest attention, even ours, and still in our teens. On stepping into the pulpit, his gaze made a swift sweep across the entire congregation while reaching for some leaflets on the lectern. So far in front were we seated that Angus and myself saw no more of him until he rose above us to commence the morning service.

If a choice were given, neither of us would have had selected any other spot on earth to be in at that particular time except exactly where we were, on that Sabbath morning in St. Jude's of yesteryear. Even at that age, we were quite aware of being in the presence of "greatness in our time."

Rueful Reflections

Of all the childhood upbringings on official record by trained and erudite psychiatrists in medical archives here and there, I've come to the shattering conclusion that my own was perhaps the most disastrous. As the youngest of a family of five, three sisters and a brother nine years my senior, and a father toiling in Canada during some of my childhood years, I fell victim to such a stark situation which in itself spelled calamity. I became vulnerable to the excessive affections of four foolish females who appeared to insist, inadvertently perhaps, on having a blue-eyed bouncy baby boy permanently around the *cagailte*—and regrettably succeeded in so doing.

Now, as I scrupulously scrutinize matters pertaining to human behavior in hindsight reflections, from the high vantage point of old age, and bone up on early backgrounds, the rueful result of this outlandish imbalanced pattern of upbringing was that when I left Skigersta at twenty-one years of age I could scarcely exercise the mentality of a normal nine-year-old but the emotions of a man of ninety.

This rather sad but very complex situation has to be minutely explained away by trained experts, because only those with solid psychiatric and psychoanalytic knowledge of sensitive childhood years are capable of understanding the awesome and weird effect that misguided myopic early environment have not only on our first few years but on our entire lifespan as well. We can no more shake off the syndromes and forms into which we are molded as children—sans concrete counseling of experts—than part with our shadows.

Overindulgence

Countless human beings exist in our society from day to day who are ruined victims of their overindulgent backgrounds in one respect or another, hopelessly handicapped from their first blurry glimpse at a cold, competitive world. From the cradle to the grave, their dependency on others in every phase of human endeavor constitutes a weighty drag not only on themselves but on society as well and is more severely felt by immediate kindred and associates.

It is utterly impossible for the overindulged to independently function rationally on their own, even in the most miniscule of matters. The stark reality of finding themselves alone in any serious situation demanding decision only increases inner chaos, as confusion takes over. When emotional pressure mounts and confronted with crucial problems, they, in total helplessness, with no one to look up to, lean on or lend an ear, become so panic stricken that wrong and outlandish conclusions are hastily forged and speedily implemented, with disastrous results.

Under such extreme circumstances emerges the obvious and conclusive contrast between the overindulgent unfortunates and their stable, well adjusted, rigidly reared fellow mortals, who invariably become the head instead of the tail. Only by the rare coincidence of an exceptionally high intelligence quotient in pinpointing the basic flaw in the enfeebled personality and improving on same can those boxed within such a syndrome ever hope to be salvaged.

Hence, the bleak prospect for the overindulged is one of darkness and despair—the crowning irony of good intentions. However, those afflicted with these disadvantages are not necessarily mediocre, bereft of skill or potential. On the contrary, many in this category are gifted, even brilliant in some aspects of the common pursuit of success and security, but in the drive for the top, talent is invariably stagnated in the absence of common confidence, common maturity, and most deplorable of all, common courage—the exact opposite pattern initially intended by myopic loved ones, who spared the rod and spoiled the child.

Homesickness

In the following sketch, my father talks about homesickness. The date on this writing suggests that this was among the last he wrote, if not the last indeed, before his terminal illness made it impossible to write anymore. If this was, indeed, the last letter he wrote to the world that never wrote to him—how fitting that it was a love poem to the land of his birth.

It seems that deep-rooted homesickness is more acutely felt among Scottish Gaels—especially with Hebrideans—than with any other breed of humans on the face of the globe. I have made this startling discovery the hard way, by mingling with nearly every nationality in existence, including ten years with Orientals, in my sixty years of wanderings throughout the USA and Canada.

I have also my own three children, grown up in Long Island, New York, who are now scattered throughout the States as proof positive that American children are free from the pangs of homesickness that lingers with me for over sixty years. The two comfortable homes in which my children were reared are almost forgotten, while their old man, brought up in a scrubbily structured thatched *taigh dubh*—blackhouse—and middle of the floor peat fire, with no hygienic facilities whatsoever, not even running water, is groaning with nostalgia from year to year.

Our beautiful bay and comely *cladach*, about one eighth of a mile downhill from my door, is as clear in my mind's eye as if I were standing on *Bàrr a' Chladaich* watching lovely *Lathamor by the sea* come alive on balmy mornings of long ago.

The little *Seòlas*, our favorite frolicking lagoon, where we splashed barefooted, chasing stray *cudaig* and digging for porstans, is vividly recalled, along with some boulders and rock formation showing at low tide.

The *Gormisgean* is probably still there—bare, blue, and beautiful as of yore. That murmuring little stream flowing down through the gulch which divides *Lathamor* from the *Baile Shuas*, passing the *Fuaran* and expending into the beach, is very clear in my mind's eye—as I write this in Texas, sixty-four years after the *Marloch* (1988).

Folly Is Joy to Those Destitute of Wisdom (Prov. 15:21)

I was thirty-three years old when I made my first Social Security payment. I still have my original number and little yellow card dated 12-21-36. How well do I remember the play we had among ourselves when first we learned of this tiny tax being mandatory—reduced from our weekly checks.

We made a big deal of the age sixty-five. To us myopic misfits, sixty-five—thirty-two years away from where we had our fun—was eternity. Who the heck was going to worry about what thirty-two years from now was going to be like? "Sixty-five before I draw a measly three or four dollars a month?" some wise guy would grumble into his beer, and everybody roared with laughter. "What next will the politicians think of to skin the taxpayer alive?" another smart aleck would ask.

I am now in my early eighties, eleven years retired, and feel a sense of shame at our blatant stupidity regarding what turned out to be the life saver of millions of American elderly. I live alone solely on Social Security checks, which I call the "Lord's lifeline."

There were many earls and dukes, descendants of royalty, throughout Europe in the olden days, who didn't realize the freedom, liberty, independence, and even pocket money that I now enjoy in the United States of America.

Beautiful and Bountiful America

Despite the fact that he was clearly a homesick Gael, my father was also a great admirer of the United States of America, his home for over sixty years. Below he celebrates that home, a place of great physical beauty, which he clearly knew how to appreciate—as well as its compassionate heart.

It is quite possible that there is no other country in the world—with the exception of the promised land which God chose for his own people—as magnificent in natural beauty and bountiful yielding as the United States of America. One can hardly wade through an ordinary stream in America that does not abound with fish, besides its two-thousand-mile rivers, bays, estuaries, coves, creeks, inlets, and extensive gulf coastline from Florida to Texas. In Texas, where I now live, in a sense a country within a country, larger than any in Europe, there are lakes so huge and deep that schools of fish are encountered by divers, just like we have in the North sea, on whose rugged coastline I was brought up. The North Sea—famed fishing grounds—is the open Atlantic Ocean where schools of fish are commonplace, but a deep lake, in the heart of Texas with schools of fish—that is a true fish story.

It is almost certain that the Creator purposed to design this wonderful land, ranging from Canada to the Rio Grande, Maine to

California, for a very special reason which mortal men are not given to understand. Able geologists, experts in their field, claim there is enough untouched pure coal substance under the ground in America to keep this land in energy for a thousand years.

It was in America that human beings first learned and felt what real freedom and liberty was all about. Would the fact that compassionate America fed a large portion of the world after two world wars have anything to do with God's Divine blueprint?

15

Epilogue: Home at Last

In the summer of 2012, I traveled to Scotland with the basic purpose of scattering Dad's ashes on the Minch, or as close to the Minch as I could come. Happily, my friend Catherine Hewlette consented to come with me on this pilgrimage and was willing to drive the rental car. This was something I could not have done on my own, given shoulderless roads in Skye, Lewis and Harris and my own driving skills. If I had been so foolhardy as to have tried it myself, I would surely have had many auto adventures of the most negative kind. She drove well and kept us both safe.

We stayed four days on Skye at Lady MacDonald's Kinloch Lodge, a culinary experience beyond words. We arrived on a Saturday from Iona after a full day of travel. I immediately called the skipper of the small ferry boat that I had rented to assist in the scattering of Dad's ashes. He said Sunday was not good weather. Called on Sunday and was told Monday was not good weather. Ditto for Tuesday. Finally, on Tuesday night, our last night at Kinloch Lodge, the captain said it looked okay to go out the next day.

We had an abbreviated breakfast Wednesday morning at the lodge, checked out, and raced off to Elgol on the southwestern side of Skye. There we boarded the "Bella Jane" and met the captain, Alex and his mate Pam. Turned out to be a beautiful, calm, somewhat sunny day. We took off for Loch Scavaig. In due course, the captain turned off the engines and explained that he could not hover without power for very long for fear of drifting onto reefs, so our ceremony needed to be brief.

Good grief, hadn't planned for that. Had planned for a twenty-minute service, reading from the Westminster Confession of Faith, the King James Version of the Bible, the Larger and Shorter Catechism, and some personal comments. So much for that. I went immediately to the personal comments and talked about my father's great love for Lewis, particularly Skigersta, where he was born and raised, about his perennial homesickness and how appropriate it seemed that his remains would now be surrendered to the place he most loved. I read Dad's sketch entitled "Skigersta's skylarks" in which he celebrated the innocence of youth as well as the majestic beauty of the skylarks' song. I recited from the scripture: "I am the Resurrection and the Life. He that liveth and believeth in me shall never die."

With that, I opened the rosewood urn in which I had carried his remains from North Carolina and hence to Skye. I deposited them in the waters. Catherine took pictures of this, for which I was grateful. Captain Alex asked if Angus was a whisky drinking man. I said that he was known to take a dram or two. With that, the captain came out and handed each of us a dram of whisky to salute Angus. Then he filled a dram and hoisted it over the side with the words: "To Angus."

According to Captain Alex, the ashes in the water would, in about thirty minutes, make their way to the Minch. That was very gratifying to know.

Our next journey, after a night in Harris at *Ceòl na Mara*, a lovely B&B, and a look at the magnificent St. Clement's Church in Rodel, was to Galson Farm in Lewis, where we spent two nights in a wonderful and welcoming place. Here we had a confusion of messages. The proprietor called us to say that an elderly woman had been calling and wanted to speak to me, that she was the only living relative of mine. This was, apparently, Catherine Margaret. Then, somehow, we also received a message that some man had called to say that I was coming to Lewis from Honolulu on July 17. That was the correct date we left the states but clearly not from Honolulu. Since the only person who knew of my departure date of July 17 was my cousin Bella in Canada, I can only assume she passed this on to her brother John Murdo in Lewis.

On Thursday, July 26, I called the only number I had for a Lewis person, John Murdo MacAulay, my cousin. After we spoke a few minutes, he said that he wanted to come and visit me. And so, gratefully, we did not have to trek our way to him in unfamiliar territory in Lewis. He and his "party" came to us at Galson Farm.

And what a night it was. They arrived at 8:00 p.m. and stayed until 11:00 p.m. The group consisted of John Murdo, first cousin, and his wife Mary and Isabel MacDonald and her brother Donald MacLeod, my second cousins. This was so much "over the top" of my expectations. Had not expected to meet *any* of my living relatives, and here they were. I had brought a packet of family pictures and we studied them as we talked. These folks were relatives on my mother's side and apparently have no connection to my father's people in Skigersta, a mere eight or so miles north—as the crow flies.

As if this family event were not enough of an emotional moment, the following day brought another connection, this time to my father's people in Skigersta. Catherine and I went off to the Ness Historical Society in Lewis. Seems the road sign is misleading and that the Society has moved to a school several miles away. As we were wandering about, Catherine walked into a store and made some inquiries. The ladies of this shop apparently called the folks at the Ness Historical Society and spoke about some American ladies who were looking for relatives.

I think the CIA should try recruiting on Lewis, because these folks are good.

When we arrived at the Ness Historical Society, someone asked me who I was researching. I said Angus and Effie MacDonald and her father D. B. Mackay. This lady said, "Do you mean the Mackay of the shoe trees Mackay?" I said yes and was immediately escorted into a room where they had all kinds of memorabilia of Lewis people. On a shelf was a set of D. B.'s shoe trees and attached was a short biography of his life.

The folks at the Ness Historical Society then put in a call to Anne Thomson, a local expert on genealogical history, and she was gracious enough to come out to the center to meet us. She brought her laptop, and she and I looked over materials for quite a while. In due course, she volunteered to take us to Skigersta and to point out the site of my father's house at No. 7 Skigersta.

It was a drizzly, gray day. Not the best for picture taking. I was thrilled to be in front of No. 7 Skigersta. So this was the site of my father's old *taigh dubh*, blackhouse. The modern house that now was on this site, complete with an attractive stone wall, was not, apparently, in the hands of the family, so there was no thought of knocking on the door and asking to be let in.

Anne then led us to her own home at No. 17 Skigersta. This was D. B.'s old site. Her husband inherited this place, which includes the old shed that D. B.'s father used as a shop.

When we went back to the Ness Historical Society, we met my father's relatives. The occasion at the Society was brought on by the death of a member of the community. A social was being held in her honor. Here I met Catherine Margaret MacDonald, the widow of my cousin Alex, son of dad's sister Margaret. When I was a child in New York City, Alex had come to visit us. His brother Murdo came first. Both boys to us girls were like bronzed Greek gods. Both had spent their young lives in the merchant marine, out in the open all day, and their skin was like sparkling copper.

It was an emotional event to meet Catherine Margaret on that day in the Ness Historical Society. We sat down to share a bowl of soup. She asked if she could call others of her family to come join us, and of course, I said yes. In due course her daughter, Margaret Anne MacLeod and others who happened to be in town, joined us, notably, Sandra Getty and Isabel MacDonald, both daughters of Dolena, Dad's niece.

So all the family assembled and we took a family photograph. They honored me by placing the baby, Margaret Anne's son Ross, in my arms. In the photo were Catherine Margaret, Margaret Anne, Isabel MacDonald, myself, and Sandra Getty.

This did not prove to be the last of my connections with either my father's or my mother's family. I returned to Lewis in 2013 and again in 2015. I was able to meet both of Catherine Margaret's daughters and their children as well as extended family members on my mother's side of the family. In May 2016, I visited Canada and connected with two first cousins: Donald Graham and his wife Ann (Donald the son of Margaret, one of my mother's oldest sisters) and Bella and Angus MacLeod, Bella being the sister of John Murdo MacAulay of Back and the child of my mother's sister Isabella. I feel blessed to have such an extended feeling of family that includes all of these loved ones.

Regarding his last days, I flew to Texas from North Carolina in 1988 because my sister said that he was not doing well. When I walked into his hospital room, I saw that he was looking at me with anger in his eyes. He was not in a position to speak. I attributed that angry stare to the fact that I had not gone to visit him in the past two years. Every year previously that I had visited him had been an enormous cleaning exercise for me. His apartment needed help in every way: the bathroom, the kitchen, the carpet, all the linens, his clothes. If I stayed for seven or eight days, I cleaned nonstop for seven or eight days. So I had decided, in the last two years, that I wanted a vacation that didn't include cleaning my dad's apartment and had acted accordingly.

I stayed a number of days visiting Christine and him in the hospital. When it came time to go away, I visited Dad for the last time. He was not able to talk any more than he was at the first day of my visit, but he did have the power to control his eyes. I said, "Dad, you be good and do what your doctors say you should do. Be a good patient. Take care. I'm going back to North Carolina now." And his eyes softened. I like to think they bid me a gentle "good-bye."

On hearing of his death, I prepared a memorial service for him in my house in Wilson, North Carolina, on February 3, 1990. My seminary friend, Lillian Galphin, conducted the service and delivered the eulogy. Mother was present, as she had moved to Wilson three years earlier. Several neighbors attended as did my other seminary friend Phyllis Thomas and friend Beth Stone. The service lasted about thirty minutes, had multiple readings from the scriptures (Isa. 61:1–3; Ps. 23; Rev. 21:2–7) and music on tape—"Scotland the Brave," "Amazing Grace," and "Going Home." It was a good service and a satisfying one.

In thinking back on my relationship to Dad, there are some moments that are special to me and that were unique to the two of us. In Hawaii, I was a driven, round-the-clock kind of student. What was normal was about four hours of sleep a night, if that, the rest of the day spent in going to school, using the library, working after school, and doing homework after school. I would tell Dad when I needed to get up in the morning, times varying depending on how much I had to finish before going to school—4:30, 5:00, or 5:30 a.m.

He had always been an early riser, apparently all his life, even as a child. At the designated hour, he would wake me up with the usual phrase: "Here's your eye opener." With that, he handed me a cup of coffee, a teaspoon of Nescafe in a small cup with milk and sugar. I was grateful for that welcome, warm drink. No one else in the house was awake. We shared a few whispered comments as I sipped the coffee. I think those moments were the most intimate I ever spent with my father.

From time to time, he said to me, "No one who has sacrificed so much for her education will fail to be rewarded." I'd smile and pass that off as a nice thought. He was right, though, on multiple levels. I *did* sacrifice a lot for my education, and I *have* been richly rewarded. Those rewards are not of the monetary kind, but then again, he wasn't thinking about monetary rewards. He was making one of those insightful predictions that could have come right out of his memoirs, right out of the village life he had enjoyed so much remembering.

Whether my father intended these sketches for a wider audience than his family, I cannot know, but I doubt it. He certainly meant them to be like a trail of breadcrumbs for his children, leading us back to Skigersta and to all that he loved in that place, and, I think, leading us back to himself, that silent ghost-like figure of my childhood. While, I believe, he had multiple reasons for these sketches, at bottom he wrote, like one of his heroes, John Bunyan, explained regarding his own composition: *"nor did I undertake thereby to please my neighbor, no, not I, I did it mine own self to gratify"* (*Pilgrim's Progress*, the author's apology for his book, 1678.)

Appendix 1

Residents of *Baile Shuas*

In Skigersta of long ago, some of the original crofts were divided among succeeding offspring, in some cases into three equal parts. Some were halved in two equal parts, while others, such as our own of No. 7, remained intact to this day.

However, most of the *Baile Shuas*' crofts are now lying dormant in large, nostalgic patches of grass. Memories, memories. This division of crofts brought on the asymmetrical layout of Skigersta's beautiful *Baile Shuas*, where, until the *Marloch*, I spent so many happy, youthful years.

There were nearly as many houses situated on our street's roadside, six all told, as were facing the *cladach*. Both Norman Murray (*Sasannach*) and his brother *Iain Bàn's* homes were roadside: one facing south and *Iain's* facing north.

Iain Beag's home, on No. 8 faced south, and so did Angus MacDonald's *Cròaig*, along with his brother Malcolm's *Calum Maag*. Malcolm MacFarlane's home on the extreme north of the *Baile Shuas* faced north. All these homes, except Norman Murray's, were the old-fashioned *taighean dubha* three compartments: *Teine*, *Cùlaist*, and *Teor*.

Eight of our *Baile Shuas*' homes faced the beautiful bay and picturesque coastlines, with a commanding view all the way from MacKenzie's *Àrd* to the *Cladichean geala*. They were as follows: John MacDonald, *Iain Dhoiligean* on No. 10 next to the Murray croft—

now abandoned; Donald Morrison, *Dòmhnall Tharmoid* of No. 9—occupied; the Bard's home on No. 8 occupied by Norman, only surviving of family.

Norman MacDonald, *Tarmod Dòmhnaill Bhuide* of No. 7—abandoned. John MacKenzie, *Iain Pìobaire* of No. 6—abandoned. Annie MacDonald of No. 5, old maid whose home occupied *Cnoc a' Choilich's* summit—abandoned.

Murdo MacDonald, *Murchadh Buidhe* of No. 4 who occupied the northern slope of the *Cnoc* for a whole generation, is now abandoned for almost half a century. Donald Thomson, *Dòmhnall Donn* on the extreme slope of the *Cnoc*, leveled off by offspring and built across the street for old widow Margaret, affectionately known as *Màiread Dhonn*.

There are only a handful of the original *Baile Shuas* residents now surviving. Reflections. 1987.

Appendix 2

Drownings 1862–1900

The origin of the following list of drownings, 1862–1900, found in my father's papers, is a mystery. All of my father's papers were in manuscript. These pages are typed, and all in caps. He made corrections to the seventh boat in the 1862 list, where the fifth seaman was identified as Murdo MacDonald. He crossed through this name and wrote "Donald MacDonald, grandfather" and then added his Gaelic name, "Dòmhnull Buidhe," No. 7 Skigersta.

The Great Drowning, December 18, 1862

1. Neil Morrison	Cross	(Niall)	Skipper
Angus Murray	Cross	(Aonghas MacFhionnlaigh Dhuinn)	
Donald Gunn	Swainbost	(Dòmhnall mac Uilleam)	
John Murray	Swainbost	(Iain Ruadh)	
Murdo MacDonald	Swainbost	(Murchadh Òg)	
Kenneth MacAuley	Swainbost	(Coinneach Alastair)	
2. Colin MacKenzie	11 Habost	(Cailean mac Tharmoid)	Skipper
Murdo MacFarlane	Cross	(Craig's Father)	
Murdo MacKenzie	Cross	(Cailean's brother)	
John MacKenzie	40 Habost	(Iain mac Aonghais)	
Angus Morrison	Swainbost	(Aonghas Bàn)	
Donald MacLean	Swainbost	(Dòmhnall Riabhach)	

MURDINA D. MACDONALD

3. Donald Murray	39 Habost	(Dòmhnall Donn)	Skipper
Alexander MacLean	4 Habost	(Alasdair Dhòmhnaill Ruaidh Bhig)	
Norman Murray	9 Habost	(Tarmod Tharmoid Ruaidh)	
John MacLeod	9 Habost	(Iain Beag's Father)	
Finlay MacKenzie	21 Habost	(Fionnlagh Mòr)	
Murdo MacDonald	23 Habost	(Murchadh Beag)	
4. John Thompson	29 Habost	(Iain mac Sheumais)	Skipper
Donald MacRitchie	26 Habost	(Dòmhnall Chailean)	
Alexender MacLeod	28 Habost	(Alastair Beag)	
Donald MacLean	31 Habost	(Dòmhnall Choinnich)	
John MacDonald	34 Habost	(Iain 'An 'Ic Cuill)	
Kenneth MacLeod	3 Lionel	(Coinneach 'An 'Ic Leòid)	
5. Donald MacDonald	3 Lionel	(Dòmhnall mac 'An 'Ic Cuill)	Skipper
Finlay MacKenzie	North Dell	(Fionnlagh Beag's Father)	
Allan MacKenzie	Cross	(Ailean Bàn)	
John Campbell	1 Habost	(Iain mhic Iain)	
John MacRitchie	25 Habost	(Iain Chailean)	
Donald MacLeod	Port	(Dòmhnall Ruadh mac Fhionnlaigh)	
6. Donald MacDonald	Knockaird	(Dòmhnall Bàn 'An 'Ic Aonghais)	Skipper
Donald Morrison	Habost	(Dòmhnall Buachaill)	
Alexander Morrison	Lionel	(Alasdair Mhurchaidh Bhàn)	
Donald MacKay	Port	(Dòmhnall mac Dhòmhnaill)	
Alexander Morrison	Knockaird	(Alastair Mac 'An 'Ic Alastair)	
Murdo MacDonald	Knockaird	(Murchadh Dhòmhnaill Bhreacair)	
7. Donald Morrison Bard's father)	Skigersta	(Dòmhnall mac Tharmoid	Skipper
Murdo Murray	Skigersta	(The Muig's father)	
Alexander Murray	Skigersta	(The Muig's brother)	
Angus MacFarlane	Skigersta	(Aonghas mac Chalum)	
Donald MacDonald	7, Skigersta	(Dòmhnall Buidhe-Angus' grandfather)	

Notes: Neil and Callan's boats got ashore on the mainland and came back to Ness.

John Murray, Swainbost, died of exposure.

Five boats lost—thirty-one men.

Drownings of May 9, 1882

Angus Campbell	North Dell	(Aonghas Challum Ruaidh)	Skipper
Donald Morrison	North Dell	(Dòmhnall mac Aonghais Fhionnlaigh)	
John Smith	South Dell	(Iain mac Aonghais Chailein)	
Angus Morrison	South Dell	(Aonghais 'An 'Ic Aonghais)	
John Morrison	Aird Dell	(Iain mac Dhòmhnaill 'Ic Dhòmhnaill)	
John Morrison	South Dell	(Iain Alasdair 'Ic Sheumais)	
Angus Morrison	Eoropie	(Aonghas Liath)	Skipper
John Murray	Eoropie	(Iain 'An Mhòir)	
Angus MacLeod	Eoropie	(Aonghas 'An 'Ic Mhurchaidh No. 20)	
John MacLeod	Eoropie	(Iain 'An 'Ic Choinnich No. 26 pòst aig Mòr 'An Mhòir)	
Donald MacLeod	Eoropie	(Dòmhnall Choinnich 'An 'Ic Mhurchaidh No. 23 pòsd aig Anna Iain Òig)	
John MacLeod	Eoropie	(Iain Choinnich 'An 'Ic Mhurchaidh, No. 22 pòsd aig Chalum Mhòir)	
Norman MacDonald	14 Eoropie	(Tarmod Mòr mhic Dhùghaill Sglothaidh's Father)	Skipper
Norman MacDonald	17 Eoropie	(Tarmod Ruadh- Iain Yaa's father Brother of above)	
Angus MacRitchie	28 Eoropie	(Am Balach Dearg)	
Angus Campbell	24 Eoropie	(Dòmhnall Dubh's Father)	
John Campbell	25 Eoropie	(Morag's brother)	
Donald Murray	1 Eoropie	(Dòmhnall Ruairidh Bhig)	

MURDINA D. MACDONALD

Drownings of March 19, 1889

Donald Smith	North Dell	(Dòmhnall Alasdair Bhàin)	Skipper
Alexander Smith	North Dell	(The Skipper's son)	
John MacLeod	North Dell	(Iain 'An 'Ic Dhòmhnaill)	
Allan MacLeod	Cross	(Ailean Chalum A' Ghlinne)	
Donald Morrison	Cross	(Dòmhnall 'An 'Ic Alasdair)	
Norman MacKenzie	Cross	(Tarmod Mhurchaidh 'Ic Tharmoid)	

Donald Morrison	Lionel	(Dòmhnall Sasannach)	Skipper
John Campbell	1 Port	(Iain Ghabhsainn)	
Donald Campbell	Lionel	(Dòmhnall Tharmoid)	
Allan Smith	Lionel	(Ailean Iain)	
Kenneth Murray	Lionel	(Granndach's brother)	
Angus Campbell	Lionel	(Brother of 'An Arcach)	

Latha na Dròbh: 1900—first Tuesday in July

Angus Campbell	3 Port	(Aonghas Iain Bhàin)	Skipper
John MacDonald	19 Port	(Iain Uilleam Mhòir)	
Norman MacDonald	1 Eorodale	(Tarmod Chalum)	
Donald Gillies	15 Lionel	(Dòmhnall Gillies)	
Donald MacDonald	32 Habost	(Am Bostaidh)	
Murdo MacDonald	33 Habost	(Murchdain)	

Appendix 3

Skigersta *Bodaich*

The following are the Gaelic names of the Skigersta *bodaich*, village fathers, current in the twenty-one years that I lived on the beautiful *Baile Shuas* of long ago. We loved them all, looked up to them, considering them all worthies—which indeed they were. However, as regards *Aonghas Beag Dhòmhnaill Tàilleir, Dànaidh*, and *Dòmhnall Ailean*, along with *Tarmod Iain Ruaidh*, we didn't consider them *bodaich*, perhaps because we knew them for years as single men.

Am *Baile Shuas*

Tarmod Alasdair mac Mhurchaidh; Iain Alasdair mac Mhurchaidh "Iain Bàn"; Iain Dhoiligean; Dòmhnall Iain Dhoiligean; Dòmhnall Tharmoid; Iain Beag Dhòmhnaill mhic Tharmoid; Tarmod Dhòmhnaill mhic Tharmoid "Bàrd"; Tarmod Dhòmhnaill Bhuidhe; Iain Aonghais Phìobair; Aonghas Iain Bhreabadair; Calum Iain Bhreabadair; Murchadh Dhòmhnaill Bhuidhe; An Caoidheach; Calum Aonghais Chaluim.

Am *Baile Àrd*

Dòmhnall Mòr; Tarmod Aonghais Phìobaire; Alasdair MacNeacail "Bard"; Tarmod Riabhach; Aonghas Dhòmhnaill 'Ic Fhionnlaigh; Aonghas Iain Dhoiligean; Alasdair Ruadh; Aonghas Dòmhnaill Bhàin.

Lathamor

Aonghas Dhòmhnaill Bhreabadair; Tarmod Beag Bàn; Ailean Bàn; Murchadh Oidheann; Calum Dhòmhnaill 'Ic Fhionnlaigh; Tarmod Sheumais; Seòras Sheumais; Murchadh Chalum Pìobaire; Murchadh Dhòmhnaill Tàilleir; Alasdair Iain Ruaidh; Fionnlagh Dhòmhnaill 'Ic Fhionnlaigh; Murchadh Dhòmhnaill Ruaidh.

Of the thirty-four *bodaich* that I remember, seven had passed away before I left home in 1924. When I returned twenty-eight years later, only two—*Tarmod Riabhach* and *Alasdair Ruadh*—were surviving of a grand group of sturdy men, the *bodaich* of long ago.

Appendix 4

Tribute to the Skigersta Bard

The following tribute to Norman Morrison, the Skigersta Bard, was published in the *Free Presbyterian Magazine*, December 1935, v. 40 no. 8 by Malcolm Gillies. The Bard had passed away three years earlier on November 5, 1932.

The Late Norman Morrison, Skigersta, Ness, Lewis

Though an account of this worthy elder is long overdue, it is not too late to send a notice of him to the magazine. Norman Morrison was born in Ness some time about the year 1859, and he lived without any true hope for eternity till he was about fifty years of age. He was a talented man and composed many secular songs in the days of his ignorance. He even used Scripture themes to exercise his poetic talent and his finished effort would be so conformable to the Word that, as he would say, "the plane could not take a shaving off it."

In the year 1910, it pleased the Lord in His sovereignty to awaken Norman Morrison to a knowledge of himself as a sinner, and he spent that year as one of the doves of the valleys upon the mountains, bemoaning his own iniquity. The means God used to bring home his guilt upon him was his witnessing one very nearly related to him going forward on a Communion Sabbath in Ness to make her first public witness for Christ. The servant sent to loosen our friend's bonds, under the hand of the Holy Spirit, was the late Rev. Donald Graham, Shieldaig. Mr. Graham preached a sermon in Lionel, Ness on John 3:16, "For God so loved the world that He gave His only begotten Son that whosoever believeth in Him should not perish, but have ever-lasting life." God's peace came into the heart of Norman Morrison that day so that he walked in the joy and comfort of it for many days, and it kept his heart and mind to the end of the journey.

It is both unscriptural and dangerous for those who have reason to conclude that Christ has become precious to them as a Savior, to put off making a public profession of their faith in Christ and obedience to Him. Norman Morrison, or the "Bard" as he was commonly styled, found it so to his cost. He had allowed the opportunity to pass and no sooner was it passed than his guilt for neglected duty took possession of him. That awful Scripture—"But ye denied the Holy One and the Just, and desired a murderer to be granted unto you" (Acts 3:14)—brought gall and wormwood into his spirit, and his only relief was to make a solemn vow, that if he were spared to see another Communion season, he would venture on the path of duty.

He was duly elected to the eldership, but it was only after much persuasion and delay that he consented to take office. He adorned the office while he was spared in it and earned the obedience and respect of old and young. We did our best to persuade him to undertake the duties of a missionary, after the decease of our reverend friend, Mr. Malcolm MacLeod, but without success. Though a man of great gifts and of fluent expression, which made him excel in public prayer and speaking, he had a humble view of his own ability and grace, which caused him to court retirement.

He suffered a long illness on his death bed, but the Lord's mercies were abundant during his last days on earth so that he "went through the river singing." He exhorted his family to follow God's truth and to seek a personal interest in the Savior, and continued in prayer for them and for the Redeemer's cause on earth till he fell asleep. He passed away to be with Christ on the fifth of November 1932. May his example and faith be followed by his family at home and abroad who are left to mourn his loss.

—Malcolm Gillies.

An elegy for the late James Finlayson. In an envelope among my father's papers was found a four page typed poem entitled Oran do Sheumas Fiunlaston, nach maireann (An elegy for the late James Finlayson). On the cover of the envelope my father had written; Neighbor Norman's masterpiece. Air chuimhne gu bràth bidh am fìrean. (Psalm 112:6) The righteous shall be in everlasting remembrance.

> On the first Monday of the winter, we heard sad news about the death of our faithful friend who was so upright in his ways, though he had become weak as a result of his age, we did not perceive that the end would come so soon.
>
> He was given length of days on earth—the span promised in the Bible—and a little extra. He diligently laboured for his daily bread. Though he was called out of time very quickly, he was ready to receive the promise which he had faithfully cherished.
>
> You suffered much during your life. First of all, you lost your wife taken from you by fever. That was a huge blow for you. You were often tried by infirmities in your temple of clay and with a sad spirit but you wished to be in accord with your rights in Christ.
>
> O Ness folk, do you hear! James, son of Andrew is in the grave—often his enemies would say that he was a deceiver, that he thrived on discord and hated church members—but even though he is lying in the grave, your misery has not come to an end.
>
> His misery is over and he had a safe speedy journey across the river though many a soul drowned in it. His hope was not deceived though the enemy often threatened him that his pains

would be unspeakable and that his religion was a deception.

It is obvious that some brethren loved you a lot and some godly sisters never doubted you. Some who were members spurned your faith—they were never of the family—illegitimate in a sense.

James was a fruitful branch, the finest cedar tree and though he often experienced difficulties, losing his surety and then finding it—but the secret things belong to the One who rules the universe and when He rewards every creature. He will not wrong anyone.

You ploughed a straight furrow and did not bring disrespect to your profession. You valued the talent you had received as a precious jewel for your soul. Your growth could be seen at times just like a tree growing beside a stream and despite winter frosts there was fruit on each branch.

Though it was obvious that you were taught from on High, often doubts confused and bothered you and though you would go to the Bible where you often found sweet relief, now it was of no use, it was like a sealed book to you.

But when you got your freedom—and the heavenly dew fell on you, your handsome face would be so welcoming and your conversation so friendly. When you were gathering out on the field as was your wont—Booz's field was so rich that you wished tore main there.

The church began to nurture mistakes and you were a member of the session. That made you swiftly leave it though you did not forsake your faith. You kept to the teaching you had received and turned your back on the idol that set the Ness folk on a wrong path.

You did not covet the stone or the lime and you did not like unsound teaching. You followed the holy example of the saints who have gone to glory and you refused the riches of Egypt—they have a putrid smell.

You have now gone home. You have left this wilderness and your visage has changed—that part of you that was destined to die but your soul flew as if on wings to the city of refuge and received an eternal welcome into the land of Canaan.

It is sad for us as a people who listened to you giving us serious warnings—neither young nor old gave heed to what you said, but when you prayed, with your eyes full of tears, it was obvious to all that the dew of heaven was upon you.

We will never again see your face in which we could see sincerity. We will never hear you at prayer and same are very sad about your passing. The tongue that was actively speaking about Christ and the cross is lying still within your jaw, under the strong dominion of death.

Why are we missing you? Though you are not here with us and we will never again hear your voice, your joy has just begun in the company of the saints and the angels. You are freely enjoying it and singing a song of praise which will never end.

But who am I to compose this song. I am foolish to attempt to put words together in ignorance. The carnal mind is so devious but if I could I would like to take my friend's mantle and stand erect in his shoes as long as I lived on the earth.

I will now end though you will not hear a word I have said, but though your mortal remains have slept, there will be a glorious resurrection. The eye that has closed will be opened, the ear that is cold will hear and the silent tongue will speak of the glories of the Lamb that brought you to life.

Printed in Stornoway by Thomas Nicholson

Òran do Sheumas Fionnlasdan nach maireann

Chiad Diluain den gheamhradh, chaidh naidheachd theann tro ar cluasan
Mu bhàs ar caraid bha dìleas, 's a bha cho dìreach na ghluasad
Ged dh'fhàs e lag leis an aois, cha robh ar sùilean cho fuasgailt
'S gu robh sinn idir a' saoilsinn, gum biodh a chaochladh cho luath ann.

Fhuair e ùin air an talamh, an aois a ghealladh san fhìrinn
'S fhuair; e beagan a bharrachd, ri cosnadh arain le dìcheall
'S ma chaidh a ghairm ann an cabhaig, bha esan abaich da-rìribh
A ghabhail seilbh air a' ghealladh, a bha e 'g altram le dìlseachd.

Chaidh thu tro àmhghar san fhreastal, chaill thu an toiseach do chèile
Thugadh uat i le fiabhras, bha buille gheur an sin fèin dhut
Nach tric a bha thu air d' fheuchainn, sa phàillean chrèadha le eucail
'S le spiorad tùrsach ri 'g iarraidh, do chòir an Crìosd a bhith rèidh dhut.

BLACKHOUSE GOD'S HOUSE

A Mhuinntir Nis, bheil sibh cluinntinn - Tha Seumas Anndra san talamh
'S bu tric a theireadh a nàimhdean, gur e bh' ann dheth fear-meallaidh
Gu robh e dèidheil air buaireadh, 's ri 'g altram fuath do luchd-aidich
Ach ged a shìneadh san uaigh e, chan eil bhur truaighe-sa thairis.

Ach chaidh a thruaighe-san thairis, is fhuair e aiseag bha sàbhailt'
A-null gu luath air an abhainn, ach 's iomadh anam a bhàth i
Cha deach a dhòchas a mhealladh, ged is tric a bhagair an nàmhaid
Gum biodh a phiantan do-labhairt, 's nach robh ach mealladh na chràbhadh.

Tha fios gu bheil cuid de na bràithribh, aig an robh gràdh nach robh beag dhut
Is cuid de pheathraichean diadhaidh, nach do chuir a riamh annad teagamh
'S tha cuid ri togail na fianais, bha sealltainn sìos air do chreideamh
Cha b' ann den teaghlach a riamh iad, 's ann bha iad dìolain san t-seadh sin.

'S e fionan torach a bha an Seumas, craobh den t-seudar bu ghrinne
Ged bha e tric ann an èiginn, air call a ghrèim 's e ga shireadh
Ach buinidh na nithean tha dìomhair, don Tì tha riaghladh na cruinne
'S nuair bheir E duais do gach creutair, cha dèan E eucoir air duine.

Rinn thu sgrìob a bha direach, cha do chuir thu mì-thlachd air d' aidmheil
'S ann mheas thu 'n tàlann a fhuair thu, mar neamhnaid luachmhor dod anam
Bha d' fhàs ri fhaicinn air uairibh, mar chraoibh air bruaich nan sruth-chlaisean
'S a dh'aindeoin reòiteachd nan geamhradh, bha toradh trom air gach bagaid.

Is ged a bha e cho soilleir, gun robh an teagasg bho shuas ort
Bu tric a rinn an t-às-creideimh, do chur am breislich le bhuaireadh
'S ged dheigheadh tu dh'ionnsaigh a' Bhìobaill, san d' fhuair thu mìlseachd air uairibh
Cha robh e nis ach gun èifeachd, mar leabhar seulaichte suas dhut.

Ach nuair a thigeadh do shaorsa, 's a bhiodh an drùchd on àird ort
Bhiodh d' aghaidh mhaiseach cho faoilte, do chòmhradh caomh 's e cho càirdeil
'S nuair bhiodh tu dìoghlam, a-muigh san raon mar a b' àbhaist
Bha achadh Bhoais cho fialaidh, 's gum b' e do mhiann a bhith tàmh ann.

Riamh o thòisich an eaglais, ri 'g altram mhearachdan truaillidh
Ged bu bhall thu den t-seisean, thug siud ort teiche gu luath às
Chan e gun do thrèig thu do chreideamh, ach lean thu an teagasg a fhuair thu
Is chuir thu cùl ris an iodhal, rinn muinntir Nis a chur tuathal.

BLACKHOUSE GOD'S HOUSE

Ach cha b' ann ri clach no ri aol, a bha do shùil o chionn fhada
'S cha mhotha na sin thug thu gnùis, don teagaisg ùr nach eil fallain
Ach lean thu eisimpleir dhiadhaidh nan naomh a thriall 's a chaidh dhachaigh
Is dhiùlt thu ionmhas na h-Eiphit, tha boladh breun nach eil ceart dheth.

Tha thu nis aig do dhachaigh, chuir thu seachad am fàsach
Is thàinig caochladh air d' ìomhaigh, a' chuid sin dhiot a bha bàsmhor
Ach d' anam theich mar air sgiathan, don bhaile-dhìon a tha sàbhailt
Is fhuair e fàilteachadh siorraidh, a-steach do chrìochan Chanaain.

An-aoibhinn dhuinne mar shluagh, bha le ar cluasan gad èisteachd
Ri cluinntinn d' earailean drùiteach, gun òg no aost ri toirt gèill dhut
Ach 's ann an cleachdadh na h-ùrnaigh, 's do shùil a' brùchdadh le deuraibh
A bha e soilleir don t-saoghal, gun robh an ùr-dhealt o nèamh ort.

Chan fhaic sinn tuilleadh do ghnùis, anns an robh an dùrachd ri leughadh
Cha chluinn sinn tuilleadh thu 'g ùrnaigh, 's thu cuid gu tùrsach às d' eugmhais
Tha an teang' a chleachd a bhith gnìomhach, ri luaidh mu Chriosd air a cheusadh
Na laighe balbh fo do ghiallaibh, 's am bas ga riaghladh le treun-neart.

Carson tha sinne gad ionndrainn, ged tha do ruim againn falamh
'S do ghuth, ged tuilleadh nach cluinn sinn, nach ann tha d' aoibhneas air teannadh
Co-chomann naomh agus ainglean, an-diugh gu saoibhir ga mhealtainn
'S tha òran-molaidh ga sheinn leat, nach sguir a chaoidh ach a mhaireas.

Ach chan eil mi airidh air m' òran, 's ann tha mi gòrach ga aithris
Ri labhairt briathran gun eòlas, tha 'n inntinn fheòlmhor cho carach
Ach shaoilinn na faighinn air m' òrdugh, gun gabhainn còta mo charaid
'S gu seasainn dìreach na bhrògan, cho fad 's bu bheò mi air thalamh.

Is bidh mi nis a' co-dhùnadh, cha chluinn thu dùrd de mo chòmhradh
Ach ged a chaidil an daonnachd, bidh àm do dhùsgaidh ro-ghlòrmhor
Bidh do shùil a tha duint' air a fuasgladh, bidh a' chluas tha fuar agus ceòl innt'
Is bidh an teang' tha balbh agus fuaim aic', air cliù an Uain a thug beò thu.

The original printing was done in Stornoway by Thomas Nicolson.

Appendix 5

Nicknames

In the following sketch, my father reflects on the Lewis custom of giving everybody a nickname, most of which were anything other than flattering in nature. Only after my visit to Lewis in 2012 did I learn my father's nickname. He was *Aonghas Rudair*.

No one ever bothered to go into elaborate research about how or when the crude Lewis custom of labeling one another with asinine nicknames in primitive abandon got its start. The Rev. Donald MacDonald, MA, Cross, was so constantly enraged at hearing noxious nicknames throughout the community that he spent a large portion of his long ministry in "quiet desperation" as Thoreau put it. Moreover, the dignified *Dòmhnallach* was too preoccupied and disgusted with its pagan origin.

It seems that the foul habit is as old as sin itself and equally obnoxious. Our Scottish Highlands are contaminated with this stupid syndrome, where hardly a home escapes the miserable misnomers—truly a blot of some hue or another in so-called Calvinistic culture. In Lewis, some families are plagued with as many as three loathsome sobriquets all in one household, baptized, as Mr. MacDonald contended, "solely by the devil."

By rare coincidence, an occasional nickname can have flattering overtones, but for an entire lifetime, a victim stigmatized with a negative epithet of shameless crudity is as stuck with the specter as he is with his shadow. Ninety-nine percent of Lewis nicknames are disgustingly derogatory, insulting, and full of abject humiliations, spewed from the gutter of ignorance and bad manners.

I once knew a woman who absolutely forbade the mere mention of a nickname within her household. Frequently this stricture proved very embarrassing when special guests and neighbors were promptly corrected. It mattered not one whit to this woman where the chips landed. Everybody stood corrected when any human, baptized in the name of the Lord, was so rudely belittled in her presence.

For shuddering statistics of this beastly behavior, let us consider our own compact street of a mere few paces long, comprising of seventeen homes in our day. Within these normally happy homes, sixteen decent residents were permanently debased with epithetical degradations. Getting closer to home, of the three males in our own family, my father and brother were known, and only known, by their nicknames every day of their lives.

Even within our own small village of forty-six homes, twenty full crofts and about 280 souls, couldn't be found a baker's dozen who had the remotest idea of who *Tarmod Dhòmhnaill Bhuidhe* and *Dòmhnall Tharmoid Dhòmhnaill Bhuidhe* were or whence their origin. Small wonder the dignified *Dòmhnallach* seldom set foot within our borders. It's quite possible that a scholar of his culture and refinement considered us borderline aggregates as just emerging from the jungle.

Appendix 6

Labor, Slavery, and Toil

Below is a list my father made of all the jobs he had ever had in his life, from the time he worked on the Tolsta Road to the time of his retirement. He entitled this list "Labor, Slavery, and Toil."

1. Skigersta-Tolsta Road. Late teens. Leverhulme. One year, three months.
2. Glasgow Shipyard, 1920. Stage hand. One year.
3. Local road repairs, on Leverhulme's disastrous departure. Seven months at South Dell. Walk ten miles a day.
4. Emigrated on SS *Marloch*, 1924. Toiled on lumber in Scotstown, Quebec, one year. Great Lakes, seven seasons (seven months a season). Idle for five winters.
5. New York City: first phase, five years; second phase, ten years—shoe trees. Dust, drudgery, and disaster.
6. Bigelow Sanford Carpet Co., San Francisco, four years. Designing and lock weaving patterns into rugs.
7. Cosmetic Co., NYC, Eighteenth and Seventh Avenue. Six years.
8. Casket Co., Long Island City, NY. Seven years.
9. House painting, NYC. One year. Foreman Angus MacRitchie.

10. Honolulu, Hawaii. Maintenance and security guard, ten years. Retired in May 1973, twelve years ago. Now living (1985) in Arlington, Texas, perhaps the most compassionate city toward the elderly and disadvantaged in all of America.

Appendix 7

Sermons for Himself

My father grew up in an environment in which the only acceptable reading material on the Sabbath was the Bible. In his case, this rule, far from being some kind of punishment, helped him to love the Bible. He stayed enamored of this text his entire life. He was fascinated by everything in the Bible: its heroic figures, its theological truths, its moral messages, its geography, its history, and its predictions in which a new world would be governed by a New Jerusalem. Since clearly he had no aspirations his biblical musings would ever be published, he wrote these lines for himself, for his own pleasure and edification. They were sermons for himself.

Joseph

One of the noblest personages of all time (Recollections, 1986)

How regrettable that Joseph's sepulcher containing his remains which were solemnly carried for forty years in the wilderness was not marked in Shechem where his noble bones repose to this day. The extent of his father's piece of ground bought for one hundred pieces of silver is not recorded. It is recorded, however, that he gave it to his son Joseph.

According to expert bible scholar, Henry Halley, Jacob's well—supposedly dug on Joseph's land—is ninety feet deep and is still there where the Lord sat and talked with the woman of "Sychar," a small town in Samaria.

Scripture records in Joshua 24:32 as follows: "And the bones of Joseph, which the children of Israel brought up out of Egypt, buried they in Shechem." Joseph, like Saul of Tarsus, was a chosen vessel destined for superb accomplishments affecting the whole destiny of mankind. Even as a mere child, the Lord revealed himself to Joseph in favorable, beautiful dreams and other blessings—sometimes arousing bad feelings in the family.

Even in prison as a very young lad in his late teens, he showed such leadership qualities that he was put in charge of lawbreaking, hardened criminals. Pharaoh took an instant liking to the man, and small wonder, because, besides his many other noble traits, Joseph was also somewhat akin to Absalom—"without spot or blemish."

His iron willpower against a scheming, young, beautiful woman of influence, wealth, and power shall be remembered from age to age as an example of a man who feared God and eschewed evil.

Ruth

It is impossible for worldlings to read and study the book of Ruth without wondering why an enormously wealthy and powerful figure like Boaz allegedly condoned the parting of his distressed cousin Elimelech and affectionate spouse Naomi to the land of Moab—Israel's perennial enemies.

Is it possible that Boaz, an upright, industrious man, became prominent during Naomi's ten-year exile? Is it also possible that this sacred book was written with the aim of revealing the background of the mighty David—perhaps the greatest monarch of all times, and prototype of Christ, beloved of God from his youth—and whose great grandmother was the lovely and lovable Ruth, whose love and loyalty shall be remembered by the redeemed forevermore.

David and Solomon

Famed ancient historian Josephus claims that King Solomon reigned eighty years and lived to be ninety-four years of age. This is not in harmony with sacred scriptures. It is quite possible that young Solomon was in his teens when his father David wrestled the crown from Solomon's half brother Adonijah, who actually did rule for perhaps a mere few hours.

This swift stratagem was the last mighty deed performed by the greatest monarch of all time—King David—sweet psalmist of Israel, ruler, warrior, giant killer, excellent musician, and inventor of musical instruments. Never as much as scratched in the numerous bloody battles in which he fought, hand to hand, like a bear bereft of her whelps.

The son of Jesse was handsome and powerfully built—destroyed a bear and a lion as a mere lad. He was much more upright and single-minded than any of his brothers. Was anointed with Holy Oil by the great Samuel—also as a mere lad. Wrought beautiful prophetic Psalms while under persecution, from caves to wilderness, chased like a partridge, in mortal danger from day to day, with only a few hundred malcontents and debt-ridden men doing their best as bodyguards.

Received the blueprints of Solomon's temple in a vision from God. Was prototype of the Savior of mankind. Was recognized by God as "my servant" more often than any patriarch in scripture. No other monarch in all of history can even come close to King David's stature.

Ancient Rivers of the Bible

I'd like to see the ancient river Kishon where the iron lady, judge, and mother in Israel—Deborah—along with Judge Barak, clobbered the Canaanites. Near the banks of this celebrated river the heroine Jael slew general Sisera under the most awful circumstances—gruesome to an uncommon degree.

The battle started at the foothills of beautiful cone-shaped Mount Tabor, 1,929 feet high, with Barak's ten thousand warriors who routed the enemy in such slaughter that their bodies rolled into the Kishon. It appears that the Kishon was flowing freely at the time, perhaps overflowing on its occasional westerly course toward the "Great Sea." What a fearful sight that must have been, a fast flowing river full of dead bodies.

I would like to follow the course of this battle on foot, and let the imagination work overtime visualizing what the brave Jael and the warrior Judge Deborah looked like. The ancient river Kishon falls into the "Great Sea" at the northern slopes of Mount Carmel, 1,791 feet high, where another warrior Elijah finished off Jezebel's prophets of Baal to a man. I like to think that I could find on the southern banks of ancient Kishon the very spot where this awful event occurred.

Late last night, a scholarly converted Jew appeared on my TV dial standing atop Mount Carmel, with the ancient Kishon snaking its way through the countryside in the background. It was the most pleasant surprise I've witnessed on TV since I bought my first one in the early fifties…Ancient Kishon—a river of triumph and beauty.

Valley of the Kings

I certainly remember my father speaking enthusiastically of the Valley of the Kings at our dinner table when I was a child. It was one of his favorite subjects. But the "Valley" that he had in mind was one where Israelite kings were buried such as King David and Solomon and Hezekiah and was situated in the promised land. This is not the Valley of the Kings recognized by archaeologists today, a valley on the west bank of the Nile, opposite Thebes, where, for a period of five hundred years from the sixteenth to the eleventh centuries BC, tombs were constructed for the Pharaohs. In modern times, the valley has become famous for the discovery of the tomb of Tutankhamun.

For many years, the Valley of the Kings in the City of David fascinated me and will be my first hallowed place to visit if I'll ever get to see the promised land. Without any doubt, the famed and fertile land of hills and valleys from Dan to Beersheba is the most prominent piece of landscape on the face of the globe. I often wondered if this famous valley was, or is, conspicuous as a valley per se. Was it, or is it long or short, wide or narrow, deep or hollow? The *Encyclopedia Britannica* alludes to the fact that no one knows now its exact location.

With all the fine pictures I have seen of Jerusalem, none showed the sacred Valley of the Kings where so many noted monarchs are buried—including David, Solomon, Jehoshaphat, and Hezekiah. One thing is certain: David's sepulcher was openly recognized when Peter preached on the day of Pentecost—over a thousand years after King David's burial. Herod the Great, who died four years before Christ was born, robbed David's tomb of much gold but could not locate the exact spot where the great monarch's bones repose—until the day dawns.

I once knew an English schoolteacher who calmly told me that she stood right in front of King David's tomb while visiting Jerusalem. Her utter lack of emotion or excitement crushed me. She did not seem to be overly impressed, and it bothered me no end.

If I'll ever be able to stand at David's sepulcher, fully convinced that the greatest monarch of all time is entombed right in front of my eyes, I fear that I'll be in too much of an emotional mess to enjoy it. He was my hero since childhood.

My next spot to visit will be Gibeon, where General Joshua ordered the sun to stand still, which it did for a whole day and thereon to the peaceful valley of Ajalon—where the moon also stayed.

Solomon's Temple

The magnificence and mystique surrounding King Solomon's golden temple shall never again be achieved by human ingenuity because its curious design was of God. Its plan and size were revealed to Solomon's father, King David, in a vision right down to the last detail, which in itself is also a great mystery.

Some biblical scholars estimated that billions worth of pound sterling was overlaid within its sacred confines along with exterior splendor. For example, sharp, needle-pointed golden spikes shooting out of its dome, so close and cunningly affixed that no fowl could alight, gives a glimpse of some exterior protection.

All the floors of the house were overlaid with gold within and without, and so were the cherubims, reaching from wall to wall in the holy of holies—each ten cubits high. The holy of holies was a square enclosure—twenty cubits each way.

The temple was a three-story edifice with winding stairs reaching onto the top compartments of indescribable beauty. All posts, including door posts, were square. So glorious looking was Solomon's temple that its exterior looked like a huge ball of fire in the morning sunshine.

We can understand why the elderly in Babylon who remembered, wept at the sight of the Second Temple. This wonderful holy house remained intact from the eleventh year of Solomon's reign until his son's fifth year on the throne; at which time it was made a shambles by Solomon's father-in-law, King of Egypt. What fiendish infamy?

Saint Paul: Man of Iron

The physical endurance of the apostle Paul boggles all scientific estimates concerning the toughness of the human anatomy, as clearly manifested in the person of Saul of Tarsus. Having been publicly flogged five times, enduring 195 stripes and survived, was, in itself, a sheer phenomenon. For example, in the British Navy of the sixteenth and seventeenth centuries, one flogging usually crippled an insubordinate sailor for life while some died.

These rods by which St. Paul was five times pummeled were wooden slats made of ash or bamboo expressly designed for the punishment of hardened criminals. Just a mere two or three whacks from such heavy instruments sufficed to numb any human body into death-like stupor.

Upon being stoned, he was given up for dead by his accusers, who cared less. The fact that he crawled up from under the huge pile of stones which were hurled at him and walked into the city is a clear testimony of the apostles' enormous resiliency and iron will.

Only one of the apostle's three shipwrecks, in which they fasted for fourteen days, taking nothing, is recorded in scripture. It is reasonable enough to assume that his night and day in the deep was preoccupied hanging onto flotsam and jetsam in order to survive.

He himself succinctly describes his ministry in Acts 20:23: "Save that the Holy Ghost witnesseth in every city, saying that bonds and affliction abide me." (This is more clearly stated in The New Oxford Annotated Bible Revised Standard Version, Acts 20:22–23: "And, now, behold, I am going to Jerusalem, bound in the Spirit, not knowing what shall befall me there; except that the Holy Spirit testifies to me in every city that imprisonment and afflictions await me.") Amidst all this anguish, there was always the fear of his own countrymen, whose zeal for the tradition of the fathers was such that they considered his murder a sacred service to God; and special honors to his assassins who frequently went under oath not to eat or drink until his murder was accomplished.

His nephew was instrumental in saving him from well-organized killers who had his death timed to the minute. Fear of robbers and vicious cutthroats roving and lurking in highways and byways all over every land of those days was ever present by every traveler of that lawless age. Paul kept on the move from place to place with the exception of his three years in Ephesus, two in Antioch and a year and a half in Corinth.

However, big cities were no protection to the apostle Paul, as we can read of two narrow escapes in Ephesus, a big metropolis of that generation. Neither were remote regions any security for the great apostle of the gentiles. It appears that he was in mortal danger nearly every day of his missionary message to the world.

Compounding his woes, sorrow upon sorrow, was the responsibility of all his newly converted Christians who were constantly attacked by heretics and false teachers. Bible expert Henry Halley thinks that St. Paul wrote many of his letters in tears. It is easy to assume that he wrote "Oh foolish Galatians" with a broken heart upon learning of their falling back to the dead works of circumcision.

Seven of Paul's letters were written in Rome by various brethren and helpers because of "the thorn in the flesh" which obviously affected both eyes. We are too ready to forget that St. Paul often went hungry and most assuredly in scanty attire, even though a skilled tentmaker, a craft in which he toiled hard to ease the burden of his converts. Here indeed was a man "of whom the world wasn't worthy" buffeted from all sides. His sterling character was as immovable as flint rock.

For example, the stern way he pointed out Peter's weakness and error clearly manifests the tremendous difference in the stature of the two great men. It must not be forgotten, however, that Peter was a member of the Lord's inner circle and greatly beloved by the "Son of Man." It is not on record that the apostle Paul deviated one inch from the Holy Mission assigned to him on the outskirts of Damascus.

In labors more abundant than any of his coworkers, suffering more than any saint, preacher, prophet, or patriarch in all of scripture from Enoch to the apostle John, he was presumably the last to die of the original twelve. Was more educated than any of the former saints and in all likelihood could speak and preach in several languages. Therefore, it should be a foregone conclusion and plausible assumption to all and sundry that the apostle Paul was the greatest man of ordinary generation that ever lived on this earth (Recollections, 1987).

Masada

The east face of Masada is 820 feet high and 600 feet high on the west. On the northwest, Roman commander Silva built the ramp almost clear up to the top of the fortress, which consists of twenty acres in size. Herod the Great conquered the fortress from his opponent Antigonus and immediately started to beautify the top of Masada into the most magnificent mountain top that ever was or shall be in this world again.

Three levels of terraces formed the north side of the mountain as if creation itself had proposed the construction of the fortress for something special. These three terraces were built into compartments, so costly with special polished stones and white marble that its labor, time, and expenses boggles the mind. Secret stairs joined the three terraces up to Herod's porch on the top overlooking the North and Northeast. A wall, supported by thirty-seven towers surrounded almost the entire top of the fortress.

The Romans conquered Masada after Herod died, but it was captured by Jewish Zealots in 66 AD in which nearly a thousand of them made a last stand against the Romans and perished in a most dreadful manner atop the mountain. Famed historian Josephus claims that seven women and some children survived.

> For the Lord will have mercy on Jacob, and will yet choose Israel, and set them in their own land: and the strangers shall be joined with them, and they shall cleave to the house of Jacob. And the people shall take them, and bring them to their place: and the house of Israel shall possess them in the land of the Lord for servants and handmaids: and they shall take them captives, whose captives they were; and they shall rule over their oppressors. (Isa. 14:1–2)

Isaiah 14:1–2 is only one of numerous scripture promises for the chosen people of God to ascend to world power and prestige in the near future. They are destined to become wiser, wealthier, and influential to a degree of achieving world domination, not in arrogance or tyranny but in the fear of the Lord. This blessed situation follows a repentance and bitterness for a two-thousand-year rejection of Him, as one that is in bitterness for his first born (Zech. 12:10).

This sudden and startling universal conversion of scattered and unbelieving Jews shall be as spectacular as a mass resurrection from the dead. Its impact on civilization shall be equated with the crucifixion and flood. Following these earth-shaking events, the Chosen's rightful kingdom, from the river Euphrates to the river of Egypt, as promised to Abraham, shall be their base and sphere of influence to rule the word—with Christ's blessings.

Their kingdom from the Euphrates to Egypt is going to resemble the original Garden of God—glorious to an uncommon degree. In this happy land, the lion will eat straw like an ox, and the tender babe shall sleep alongside the venomous cobra as secure as slumbering with a dime store toy—a blissful state for one thousand years.

Appendix 8

History as He Saw It

My father had no real interest in fiction, although he had some awareness of that world. He chose to read nonfiction almost exclusively: sermons, devotional literature, biographies, and historical treatments of themes that interested him. Above we have seen his interest in biblical history. Below we see his interest in Scottish history, European history, and American history.

Columba 521–597 AD

While growing up in Presbyterian Scotland in the early part of 1900, we found it hard to accept that the pious Irish missionary Columba brought us both the Gospel and civilization, which of course always go hand in hand. Columba had twelve apostles which he scattered all over Scotland almost a whole millennium prior to Luther's reformation. It is estimated that twenty-two kings are buried in the tiny, hallowed Isle of Iona where Columba laid his roots for the spreading of the Gospel. Historians claim that Columba was buried in Iona, reposing there for quite a spell, but was removed to Ireland. Then, in our young dilemma about an Irishman bringing us all these blessings, another historian came to our rescue by claiming that Saint Patrick was born in Scotland, even naming the village. This bit of electrifying news was received with glee because the fact that a famed

Irish saint was born in Scotland brought everything, as far as we were concerned, into its proper perspective. In our childish, biased minds, everything was now even-steven. Or was it? Art Linkletter, the well-known TV personality, put it all in three simple words: "People are funny." Prejudicial syndromes are not buried easily. We still haven't any great love for the Irish. And they of course reciprocate in kind.

John Knox and Mary, Queen of Scots

John Knox, a potent force in establishing the liberated principles of the Reformation in Scotland, was born in or near Haddington, where George Wishart and John Brown, two great Scottish beacons, preached the true Gospel, a divine doctrine considered sheer blasphemy by the cruel, reversed collared rogues of that dark and despicable age.

When the young and beautiful queen of France, dedicated, devoted, and arrogant, arrived in the person of Mary Stuart, backed by the mighty French army who stayed home, Knox met the challenge head on. This woman could be devastating. She looked like a queen, talked and walked like a true queen, and most important of all, acted like a queen. In propitious climate, at the right spot in the right time, she could have a veritable Scottish army trailing behind her.

All John Knox possessed was a little black Bible stashed into his long black coat, a shrewd, probing, analytical mind, sharp tongue, and the heart of a lion. It was no contest. The queen trembled like one seeing the supernatural—and in a sense, that's exactly what she saw.

The World of Sir William Wallace 1270–1305

Great Scottish patriot Sir William Wallace, cruelly abused in execution at thirty-five years of age by King Edward's savages, lived his brief span of life in one awful, gloomy period of time. These indeed were the worst of times. Even a famine, most dreaded of all plagues, prevailed during his last days on earth.

Dire tragedy struck early when, as a strapping youngster, on being insulted by an Englishman he struck back and slew his antagonist, thus becoming, as if overnight, an outlaw for life. Also, back in those days, there was a cowardly cluster of Scottish so-called nobles crawling like rats all over the Scottish lowlands at the close of the twelfth century and into the new, whose rottenness defies description, especially the reprobate Sir John Menteith, whose name shall live in infamy.

Their insatiable yen for money and mayhem, bribe and bounty sank them to the lowest degree of degradation, so much so that their warriors, patriots, mentors, and even friends were in constant danger from these grasping monsters from day to day.

At the snap of King Edward's finger, nearly all of these rich, cowardly rascals deserted the warrior Wallace in his darkest hour. Two of his closest fighting friends were killed in battle, driving him to near madness with rage.

Wallace was only twenty-seven years old when his canny stratagem was instrumental in the slaughter of the English army when crossing the Forth. Was made "guardian of the people" upon his return from devastating the north of England, all the way to New Castle.

In one of those cruel twists of fate, just when King Edward had ordered his army to return home to England, the position of Wallace's troops was handed to him, and pronto the old fire horse sniffed the smoke and immediately deployed for battle—hence the disaster at Falkirk. From thereon, Wallace's days were numbered.

King Robert the Bruce (1274–1329)

Robert Bruce, Scottish King, beat King Edward's army at the battle of Bannockburn with about ten thousand warriors against Edward's alleged twenty-two thousand. Following Bruce's army were a multitude of camp followers, men known as *Gillean* (*gille* in Gaelic means lad, boy, servant)—who followed the army in order to keep from starving, as common commodities were hard to come by back in those days. The brave *Gillean* swarmed downhill on the struggling Englishmen and slaughtered them right and left until the brook was filled with corpses.

Prior to this combat, an English nobleman, Henry de Bohun, wildly charged at the mounted Bruce, erroneously recorded as being without sword or spear, and was instantly slain by Bruce's battle axe. No English nobleman of that era would ever attack an armed King of Bruce's caliber unarmed. To report that De Bohun was unarmed is just another piece of encyclopedic balderdash.

Luckily for the Bruce, however, that Edward's father, King Edward I, wasn't facing him that day instead of his indolent son Edward II, who knew nothing about warfare, having been spoiled rotten by his warrior father. It is recorded that the brown boulder where the mighty Bruce stood in command and watched the carnage is still there on the slopes of Bannockburn.

Bruce humbly refused to become king of Ireland which a grateful people offered him following a brief, successful military campaign. Strange as it may seem, King Robert the Bruce, from which sprang the Stewart Dynasty, died at Cardross of leprosy. How, where, or when he picked up that ancient malady is obscure to historians.

Queen Mother of the Ages

Beauteous Elizabeth of York, eldest daughter of King Edward IV of England, was the sister of the murdered King Edward V of England and France, and lord of Ireland, besides the niece of the vicious King Richard III. Her marriage to King Henry VII of England virtually put an end to the longest war in history—the Hundred Years War.

As queen of England, she became the mother of two queens: Margaret, queen of Scotland, and Mary, queen of France. She also became mother-in-law to six English queens: Catherine of Aragon, Ann Boleyn, Jane Seymour, Ann of Cleves, Catherine Howard, and Catherine Paar. The most notorious monarch of all time, King Henry VIII was her only surviving son.

Queen Elizabeth I of England, daughter of Ann Boleyn, was named after her lovely looking grandmother but lacked her fine features or even a close facsimile thereof. It appears that Elizabeth of York's beauty could hardly be matched anywhere in Europe at that point of time.

The likeness of this gorgeous creature, Elizabeth of York, can be seen by all and sundry on playing cards since the fourteenth century when card playing was first invented. She is the queen of hearts to this day—meticulously sketched by an expert artist of that age for the express purpose of showing her lovely face to the whole world forevermore.

Can any visualize the trillions and trillions of times the image of that gorgeous creature has appeared to card players since the fourteenth century?

William Kiffin: An Interesting Figure in Murdina's Thesis

I loaned my father a copy of my D. Phil thesis, and he clearly read some of it. Whether he finished all four hundred pages, I do not know. He certainly made it to page 181, as he recorded his comments on William Kiffin, a Baptist minister who suffered much sorrow in those years of religious and political turmoil. I am touched that he was touched by this man's suffering.

William Kiffin (1616–1701) was a wealthy London merchant, minister of the Gospel and city official—coerced into that office by King James II, who for three years ruled with an iron hand. The Reverend Kiffin encountered personal tragedies, perhaps unsurpassed in the many sad episodes down through the ages.

Son William died at the age of twenty. Another son died in Venice—presumably poisoned. In 1682, his wife Hannah died, surpassing, as he said, all the other sorrows he had endured up until that time. Two grandsons were executed for their support of Monmouth's rebellion in 1685.

In his pitiful letter to King James, the crushed grandfather wrote as follows: "The death of my grandsons gave a wound to my heart, which is still bleeding, and never will close, but in the grave."

In 1698, his second wife was entangled in several scandalous misdeeds involving cash in which she falsely accused her upright husband of lying. Amidst all this terribleness, another son died. Both James II and Kiffin died the same year.

Napoleon and Wellington

While it is quite true that the famed Iron Duke, English great general, was a brave, intelligent, military man, he was nonetheless no match in military planning for his cunning counterpart, Napoleon Bonaparte. To pit these two war dogs against one another on the field of battle on equal terms would most assuredly spell disaster for the Duke.

If an intelligence quotient was made, it is possible that Napoleon would emerge with the highest IQ of all military men with the possible exception of the great American general Douglas MacArthur, whose academic learning greatly surpassed Bonaparte's know-how.

Uncharacteristic of the great Napoleon, it was personality quirks which were responsible for his disastrous defeat at Waterloo. For example, his peevish, childish rejection of King Murat's support—a cavalry expert and monarch of Naples cost the emperor dearly.

The king's cavalry warriors could have easily protected his eastern flank through which Marshall Blucher's army marched through—almost unmolested. We don't have to be military experts to reckon that without Marshall Blucher's assistance, Wellington would have been crushed badly simply because he was hopelessly outnumbered—both in infantry and cavalry.

Like all bitter losers, Napoleon blamed others in defeat. Key and Grouchy, both able generals, were bitterly blamed by Bonaparte for one of the greatest defeats in recorded warfare. To this day, many military experts are baffled as to how Napoleon managed to move an army of 360,000 men so swiftly from France to Belgium. Wellington's scouts didn't expect him for another full day, when, suddenly, he appeared within striking distance of Wellington's shoddy defenses. The element of surprise—Napoleon's most effective weapon—almost proved fatal for the Iron Duke.

Napoleon

Napoleon Bonaparte (1769–1821) was not only one of the greatest military geniuses of all time but also one of the greatest statesmen, with probably the highest intelligence quotient of any public figure in history. For example, the statements he made about Jesus Christ are masterpieces of wisdom, in which his keen knowledge of who He was is astounding.

Every public statement he made throughout his awesome career clearly signified that he was endowed with singular savvy denied most mortals. It can be truly said of Napoleon that he was one of a kind. His influence over current events and peoples were equally awesome, like the time he checked cold the steam-rolling European papacy of that unsettled era to a point where he set back that powerful body of dedicated Catholics for three hundred years—according to Henry Halley, Bible expert.

One of my favorite stories about Napoleon concerns the Scottish drummer boy who was taken prisoner in one of the emperor's European campaigns, as told by the great author, reporter, and world traveler, the late and lamented Lowell Thomas. Napoleon was fascinated by this youngster's vigor and enthusiasm for one so young. One day he asked the lad to play him a Scottish forward march, to which the boy complied with great gusto. "Now, play me a Scottish retreat," the emperor demanded. The youngster stiffened to attention and looked the terror of Europe straight in the eye and replied, "Sir, Scotland knows no retreat."

Two Geniuses: Two Tragedies

Robert Burns, Scottish bard genius (1759–1796), and Stephen Foster (1826–1864), American poet genius, shared much in common—

basic personality flaws, foolishness. Strange that two strong young men loaded with talents and gifts could not conquer one aggressive giant who constantly attacked them on life's highways and byways and who finally annihilated both in their late thirties.

Giant foolishness, well trained in personal combats, maintained masterly power over both all of their adult lives. It was said of Stephen Foster that he finally sank so low he actually sold what could have been a million-dollar song for a bottle of booze. All his songs project a serene, sensitive, and beautiful soul. His moving lyrics bring tears to the eyes of homesick American exiles to this day. Stephen lived a year longer than Robert Burns (i.e., died at thirty-eight to Burns's thirty-seven) and died in Belleview Hospital, NYC—wasted and spent as if picked from the nearby Bowery—the area of forgotten men.

It was said of Robert Burns that his folly was such he wouldn't remove his wet clothing in the cold Scottish winds until much too late, foolishly assuming that his heavy intake of local brew was ample protection. According to reports handed down to us by our elders, this was Robert's final undoing.

It is estimated by many literary experts that Robert Burns was the most directly inspired bard of all ages. It is quite possible that one of his most famous and poignant lines: "Would to God the gift to give us, to see ourselves as others see us" was composed in a mere flash of time. Tradition claims that he scribbled that line upon spotting a tiny, wormy parasite crawling along the back collar of a snobbish, local, unloved lady of those class-conscious days of long ago.

Thomas Paine (1737–1809): A Talented Tormented Soul

Patriot Thomas Paine, a tormented soul, was born in England in the tenth year of George II's reign, the year in which Queen Caroline died. Like all the miserable Georges, except the two noble George V and George VI., George II was haughty and arrogant in the typical German bossiness of his insufferable forbears. He paid no heed whatsoever to the plight of the poor, among which young Paine suffered much hardship as a common seaman on a few pennies a day and near starvation diet.

Since a mere boy, Thomas Paine loathed monarchy with a passion. Strange, is it not, that a man of this attitude would spend almost a year in a French jail for his compassion to the ill-fated monarch Louis XVI, when he publicly declared against the king's execution?

The fierce Robespierre promptly shoved him behind bars, suspecting that he, of all people, supported the aristocrats. He was released upon Robespierre's own execution, after spending about eleven months and eight days in prison. He just missed the dreaded guillotine by a mere short period of time.

Thomas Paine arrived in America on November of 1774 and published his first book *Common Sense* two years later, 1776—loaded with revolutionary ideas. The stuffy Burke, who seemed to assume that he was the literary Titan of his generation, couldn't stomach Paine's compassion toward the poor and downtrodden. The equally stuffy Pitt had Paine indicted for the exact same reason.

If we look close at Paine's writings, we can learn that he was the real father of the present Social Security system. No negative reflections on the great Franklin Roosevelt, who finished the job. Thomas Paine was a patriot, a brilliant author, a soldier, and an effective champion of the underdog—a truly great American.

Lord Kitchener (1850–1916)

While growing up in the Scottish Hebrides at the turn of the century and attending grammar school until fourteen, we heard much about Kitchener of Khartum from our stern schoolmaster George Milne, a scholarly individual. It was obvious that Mr. Milne considered Earl Kitchener one of the greatest military men of recorded history.

It was also obvious that Lord Kitchener's personal characteristics of few words, mighty deeds, greatly fascinated Mr. Milne. For example, his brief message, right out of scripture—"Fear God, honor the King"—to the British armed forces in August 1914 made Mr.

Milne exceptionally proud. Doesn't that just sound like Kitchener? Mr. Milne would mumble, smiling and shaking his head.

As the years rolled on in my adopted country, the good old USA, I couldn't help but recognize the close similarity between Kitchener and our own great military expert, General Douglas MacArthur who, like Kitchener, looked like a general, dressed like a general, walked like a general, talked like a general, and fought like a general—political pygmies notwithstanding.

Mr. Milne used to relate an amusing anecdote concerning Lord Kitchener, an incident which occurred in his famous drive through the Sudan, a campaign sometimes called the "River Wars." It seems that the vast possessions of a powerful African autocrat stretched directly across Kitchener's advancing army, which the general decreed to pass through in order to gain some strategic advantage.

On being officially notified of Kitchener's intentions, the big man, not used to being pushed around, hit the ceiling. He'd get up and bang his fist against desks, chairs and even walls, swearing on his aristocratic ancestors that no Britisher from Victoria down would ever dare trespass on his territory, on pain of death and disaster.

Personal confrontation was imperative as Kitchener walked stiffly toward the big Boer's long mahogany desk and stood there motionless as a marble statue, holding his white baton tightly tugged underneath his left arm. At the sight of him, the Boer rose with flailing arms and outpouring of objections, banging everything in sight as he paced back and fore. After an exhaustive spell, he sat down to stare at Kitchener, awaiting a response. It came in three crisp military words: "We shall proceed," briskly turning on his heels to walk triumphantly into the African sun.

Churchill (1874–1965)

Sir Winston Churchill, the greatest prime minister of the world's greatest empire, was also the wittiest by the same token that King Charles II was the wittiest of all British monarchs, according to historians. Sir Winston's verbal barbs against his opponents over the years were devastating and frequently hilarious. Probably the one concerning Prime Minister Atlee was the most comical.

When Clement Atlee became British prime minister, the average man on the streets of London was pondering out loud: "By Jove, what is this country coming to?" Poor Atlee took the heat from all corners, spearheaded by the razor tongued Sir Winston, and was barely surviving within the eye of the hurricane.

It got so bad that Mrs. Churchill, a compassionate woman who knew Mr. Atlee for many years, felt for the man and said so one morning from across the breakfast table, as her famed husband savored his tea and toast. "Winnie," she said softly, "I really think that all this attack on Mr. Atlee is unfair and entirely too much, because, after all, everybody knows that Clement always has been and is now a very humble man."

"Do you know of anybody that has more reasons to be?" growled the warrior who saved the world from the Nazi boot.

Our Father Is a King

When the present queen of England and her sister Margaret were roaming the Scottish landscape on their summer holidays in the long ago, they were happiest when the local folks accepted them as common, ordinary children enjoying their vacation.

At one time, while romping around having fun and freedom from crowds, an elderly gentleman, knowing who they were, appeared a mite overawed in their presence. In the course of conversation, Elizabeth, by way of putting the old gentleman at ease, said humbly, "Oh, we are nothing, but our father is a king."

Subsequently, the old worthy, obviously a Christian gentleman, reflected often on the child's effacing statement, comparing their status of the moment to the redeemed of God down through the ages, all of whom could say—no matter how mean their lot—"Our father is a king."

Meanwhile, it just so happened that the child's father, King George VI, was a king in more than a royal name and throne. He was a monarch of sterling character, unsurpassed, along with his father, George V, in all the history of the British monarchs, since William the Conqueror. These two decent, honorable Royal Georges made up for all their four predecessors of that name whose characters left much to be desired.

That comely and wholesome royal child, who loved the Scottish moors, is now a regal and beautiful queen of England for thirty-four years, greatly beloved and respected throughout the whole world, in the manner her own father was adored by his subjects.

Amazing Achievements of Immoral Men

It is rather puzzling to our finite understanding, the number of immoral men who created great beneficial blessings for disadvantaged fellow creatures. In the Scottish Hebrides of my young days, for example, multitudes of pitiful, unwanted elderly, suffering from the degrading status of no income, no production embarrassment were saved by David Lloyd George's old age pension.

To our age category, born at the turn of the century, Lloyd George was looked up to as a devoted man of God who worked long and hard, which he did, to alleviate the suffering of the elderly—who at times wished they were dead. Years later, we learned that the Honorable David, though honorable in many ways, often deviated from the straight and narrow.

Likewise, his fellow Englishman, Charles Dickens, who contributed so much to the literary world, strayed like the biblical prodigal into forbidden places. Lord Nelson, considered the greatest admiral of all time (who ruined Napoleon's prime plan of bringing England to heel since he first donned a uniform) cared not a whit about the seventh commandment.

All these great accomplishments pale somewhat in comparison to what the great and compassionate President Franklin D. Roosevelt secured for the safety and happiness of thirty-six million American elderly, including myself. This wonderful human being, perhaps the greatest of all the American presidents, occasionally broke the standard rule of conduct which most Americans adhere to and live by from day to day.

Contrasts: Mr. Roosevelt, born into wealth, had to fight tooth and nail against a pauperized clunk candidate who abhorred Social Security. This creature, who hasn't yet died of shame, was, when compared to Mr. Roosevelt's financial status, in fact a pauper. A lesson learned.

Appendix 9

On Celebrities

My father spent a lifetime in his room writing about things that mattered to him. Lewis, of course, was first in his mind, but he also wrote about biblical and historical figures, as we have seen, but also about people of the current day who interested him. He was like the early twentieth century international reporter, Lowell Thomas, who went all over the world to interview people, famously, of course, "Lawrence of Arabia." Angus never left his room—but he went everywhere in his imagination.

Nocturnal Jack Barrymore

In his young days, breaking in on the Broadway stage, the talented and handsome John Barrymore seldom enjoyed an hour of daylight pleasure. Nearly every day found the dashing Jack sleeping off the previous night's wild escapades—some making headlines. His father almost despaired of young Jack, often wondering if he'd ever get himself a normal job and live like other normal human beings.

The 1906 San Francisco earthquake found Jack in a stage play right in the heart of "Frisco." While soundly slumbering in the wee small hours, Jack was abruptly aroused by the National Guard to help the living and dead out of burning buildings, with nearly all of Frisco in shambles.

One can visualize Jack's large expressive eyes as he crawled out of bed, hoping to catch that unconscionable arsonist who ruined his sweet slumber at the obscene hour of 4:00 a.m. It is quite possible that Jack saved lives on this occasion, because he was physically powerful, young, and wiry as a cat at that point of time.

Sometime later, his father, back in New York, while hearing and reading details of the disaster and Jack's role in the matter, said pensively, "What do you know about that?" "It took an act of God to get him early out of bed—and the United States army to put him to work."

Jack Barrymore: One of a Kind

Famed thespian John Barrymore was forty-six years old when I arrived in New York City in 1928 at the age of twenty-five. I had no interest in theatrical personalities at that time, blindly and self-righteously considering them all, without exception, fallen creatures. With no TV in those days, we attended weekend Newsreels quite frequently, and this unusual-looking individual, often mentioned in press releases, and occasional headlines, weirdly strutting across the screen like a camel on the prowl, immediately arrested my attention.

His big, tall, shapely frame was different, the shape of his handsome head was different, his high prominent-looking forehead was different and likewise his perfect profile and finely balanced features, reminiscent of some mythical male idol god. His large, piercing eyes disapprovingly glaring out at me from the screen sliced through my soul like a pair of two-edged swords. "Ye gads," I said to myself, this individual is no ordinary mortal—and indeed he was not.

The great Jack Barrymore's disposition and mental makeup were just as different as was his physical appearance. He could hate intensely, was fiercely partial, and, as a perfectionist, so impatient with mediocrity that he could smell a phony all the way from the Bronx to the Battery.

It can be truly said of him what Margaret Mitchell wrote about the south: "look for his kind in books or dreams remembered" because the like of Jack Barrymore shall never again be neither seen nor heard among the children of men.

Dana Andrews: Movie Star and Gentleman

When I was young attending a movie now and then, Dana Andrews was our favorite Hollywood star. Something so sound and grand exuded from the handsome Dana that made him stand head and shoulders above the rest in our eyes. It was also quite obvious that the man was gifted, knew his craft, and did his homework—a splendid actor.

The following terrifying experience in Dana's career throws some light on the star's serene soul and tender compassion toward his suffering fellow creatures. It seems that Dana's folks were born in some Balkan country which subsequently and sadly came under the beastly boot of tyrannical communism—a pain next to death to Americans.

As a successful Hollywood star, Dana visited his parents' old birthplace from which they immigrated, obviously before Dana's arrival, as the official records show that this fine American first saw the light of day in the sovereign state of Mississippi.

During Dana's visit to his mother's home town, a young boy in the immediate neighborhood mentioned something negative that his parents guardedly discussed within the privacy of their own home to the dreaded police, bringing swift reprisal on two innocent people. In this case, it was either the disappearance of the father and mother without a trace—or execution.

It is now so long ago since I read about the incident that, regrettably, I can't recall which of those awful events put an end to the parents of that foolish boy. Either one was enough to make Dana sick to his stomach and his abhorrence of communism even sicker. To this day, that fine man sadly ponders that awful matter in horror and disgust and will probably nightmare about it for the rest of his life.

Frank Lloyd Wright (1869–1959)

Frank Lloyd Wright, classy American architect, received tremendous publicity mileage out of the many negative press releases regarding his superego and so-called immodesty. Mr. Wright was far too intelligent a man to be an egotist per se. Friends claimed that he fostered a robust sense of humor.

To Frank L. Wright, it was just a matter of laughing his head off all the way to the bank. One day sitting in his New York club among his affluent cronies, Mr. Wright, after completing a cross-country auto trip to the west coast related the following tale: "While passing through a one horse town in Midwest, a policeman dragged me to court for speeding." How else could a one grocery store, one cop, and one horse town survive?

When the judge inquired of the usual name and vocation, I looked him straight in the eye and said: "Your Honor, my name is Frank Lloyd Wright, the world's greatest architect." There was dead silence for a few seconds, when one of his club cronies spoke up and said, "Wait a minute, Frank, hold everything, you didn't really say that to the judge."

"Oh yes, I did," Frank retorted sharply. "After all, I was under oath."

Evangelist Moody (1837–1899)

When the famed American evangelist D. L. Moody and his hymn singing partner Sanky toured the Highlands many years ago, their combined efforts at spreading the Gospel were rejected by many Scottish Gaels. In some regions of strict Calvinistic climate, they were even ridiculed. Whether this was right or wrong must be left to wiser individuals to explain away, a praying people, who usually know the truth. And the truth makes them free.

In a sense, it seems regrettable, however, because these two pious men lived out their lives as scripture admonishes—unspotted from the world. Perhaps Mr. Moody was the wittiest preacher of his contemporary fellow ministers. He was never at a loss for a scathing rebuttal to his critics.

There was one about the time an acquaintance rushed up to him, obviously bent on mischief, to inform the popular preacher that one of his converts was seen downtown noisily drunk. Mr. Moody shook his head and said sadly, "Well, he sure sounds like one of mine."

Probably his masterpiece comeback was when a minister who wasn't too keen on Mr. Moody said to him on a chance meeting, "Mr. Moody, I've listened to your sermon as of last Sunday and remembered that you preached the exact same sermon three years ago." Mr. Moody again shook his head and said, pensively, "Well, that's rather strange, because I also remember a sermon that you preached three years ago, but can't recall a single word you said."

Billy's Somber Warning

Renowned American evangelist Billy Graham, of spotless Christian conduct for a whole generation, somberly warns all and sundry that one can be theologically correct and yet lose his own soul. This grave admonition from Billy is absolutely as scripturally sound as the Ten Commandments, which should be heeded by chronic hair-splitting dogmatic evil windbags in love with the sound of their own voices and so-called wisdom.

The great apostle Paul clearly declares and characterizes them in the singular: "He is proud, knowing nothing." He even alludes to the fact that such people, always anxious to get embroiled in dogmatic wranglings, are true servants of Satan, bent on their own destruction and that of others.

The matter does not end there, because it is clearly declared elsewhere in scripture that there's more hope for common fools than for such creatures. There is nothing more preposterous in this whole world than anyone, especially those of seamy behavior and still in their sins, getting overwrought about Divine matters away over their heads—it's blatant hypocrisy.

Robert Murray MacCheyne, a Scottish divine of other days used to call it "mass ignorance." In all honesty, the real motivation for this piece on my part stems from a guilty conscience. I was guilty of this revolting lifestyle for many, many years of a wasteful career: *mar mholl air fhuadachadh leis a' ghaoith* (like chaff blown by the wind).

Billy opened my eyes, a fact for which I should be eternally grateful to the man. I was also soundly clobbered by the prophet Zephaniah's line (Zeph 3:5), to wit: the unjust knoweth no shame: *chan eil eòlas aig an eucorach air nàire.*

Margaret Mitchell's Farewell to the Old South

"There was a land of cavaliers and cotton fields called the Old South. Here in this patrician world the age of chivalry took its last bow. Here was the last ever to be seen of knights and their ladies fair. Look for it only in books, for it is no more than a dream remembered—a civilization gone with the wind."

It is thought, but not verified, that Margaret Mitchell sold her movie rights of *Gone with the Wind* for fifty thousand dollars. The profits are now in billions, perhaps zillions.

I read that a man in Fort Worth, Texas, saw it twenty times when it first appeared in that city. Multitudes have seen it ten times. I saw it six times and long to see it again.

I have now lived in the Old South for eleven years and have discovered that while Margaret's civilization is no more, there is much chivalry, good manners, and compassion still in the Old South—enough to go around. And they are doing their level best to share their love with all and sundry.

About the Author

Murdina D. MacDonald was born in New York City, educated in Hawaii, Texas, and North Carolina before attending Oxford University and earning a doctorate in history (1983). She retired from the US Naval Reserve in 1997 as a chief petty officer and in 2009 from Craven Community College in New Bern where she served as a department chair and taught Spanish, religion, and history. On the death of her sister Christine in 2011, she inherited her father's ashes and his writings. This led her to Scotland where her father's ashes were scattered off the west coast of Skye and to the organization of his papers that form this book. Her brother Norman lives in Chicago. She lives with a very sociable, never-met-a-stranger black cat named Lewis in what she considers the most beautiful town in America—New Bern, North Carolina.